Managing Cash When You Haven't Got Any

Practical Cash Flow Strategies for Small Business

Volume 1: Dealing with Vendors
Volume 2: Managing Personnel
Volume 3: Managing Accounts
Receivable and Payroll

LORI L. SCHAFER

ISBN: 1942170459
ISBN-13: 978-1-942170-45-7

First Edition

CONTENTS

VOLUME 1: DEALING WITH VENDORS

INTRODUCTION

It's common knowledge among business owners and accountants that properly managing cash flow is key to running a successful business, and you will find plenty of resources that address topics such as budgeting, figuring out what to charge, managing debt, making the best use of excess funds, and ensuring that cash is available when your business needs it. These strategies are great for long-term financial planning and profitability, but rarely do they address THE PRACTICAL DAY-TO-DAY NEEDS OF BUSINESS OWNERS WHO ARE STRUGGLING IN THE SHORT TERM JUST TO SURVIVE.

Because unfortunately, most of the people who write books on cash flow don't live and work in the world in which you and I live and work. In our world, small businesses are barely making enough money to scrape by; they have no free cash, and often no ability to borrow more money. They cut paychecks with lumps in their throats, wondering if enough cash is going to come in in time to cover them; in our world companies wonder how many days they have until their suppliers cut them off all together, how long it will be before their contractors stop work because they have not been paid. For them every day is a struggle, every day is a fight to keep their business alive, yet they keep doing it because they know, they believe in their hearts that their company could be successful if only they could get through the cash crunch, if only they could somehow get through the rough times and on to the good.

There are businesses, of course, which are doomed to failure, for which improving cash flow management only postpones the inevitable. But for the rest of us, GOOD CASH MANAGEMENT IS THE DIFFERENCE BETWEEN SUCCESS AND FAILURE, AND OFTEN BETWEEN SURVIVAL AND DEATH. And if your business is teetering on the line between a slow, painful survival and a slow, painful death, this series of books is for you.

You'll find no abstract theory here, no conceptual finance; instead YOU WILL LEARN PRACTICAL, REAL-WORLD STRATEGIES FOR MANAGING CASH WHEN YOU HAVE NEXT-TO-NO-CASH TO MANAGE. I honed these strategies myself over ten years of handling the finances of multiple companies that were at serious risk of going under during the recession. The failing businesses survived, the borderline ones thrived, and the reason was clear to us all – it's because careful cash flow management really can turn around a desperate business, even when it isn't making enough money to pay its own bills and those of its owners.

In this first volume of the series, I will address the issue of DEALING WITH VENDORS. I'm not talking about setting up Notes Payable, or about figuring out how to borrow money at a low interest rate so that you can pay your suppliers, because if you're reading this guide, chances are good that your credit cards are already maxed out and you'll be able to wangle another bank loan when the dinosaurs come back to life. No, I'll tell you HOW TO TALK TO YOUR VENDORS, what they really want to hear to keep your account going, how to ensure that you pay them just enough to keep them from cutting you off. I'll tell you how to schedule outgoing payments so that they better fit your incoming cash, and how to compromise with your vendors so that your payment schedule meshes better with theirs. I'll explain the CRUCIAL IMPORTANCE OF HAVING A CASH MANAGEMENT PLAN and how having such a plan will ease the fears of your creditors even when you're unable to pay them in full or on time. Finally, I'll address how "BIG PICTURE" STRATEGIZING of your expenses and Accounts Payable can improve your cash flow, drastically reduce collection calls, and decrease strain on company personnel, making your business run more pleasantly as well as more successfully.

WHO THIS SERIES IS FOR

These books are primarily targeted at several types of businesses. First, those experiencing comparatively short-term cash crunches resulting from unexpected events, such as (hopefully) temporary changes in market conditions, unusual off-seasons, and unanticipated big-ticket expenses; for example, a lawsuit. These are typically businesses that were once self-sustaining but are now experiencing losses or sharp reductions in income which make meeting their ongoing financial obligations exceedingly difficult.

Second, these books will prove invaluable to businesses that experience recurring cycles of cash and no cash, such as companies whose service or product is seasonal and who therefore routinely have to cope with slow seasons in which not much money comes in, but plenty still has to go out. This also applies to businesses that are subject to market vagaries inside their industries or who are highly dependent on landing large projects for their survival. A residential contractor, for example, may flourish the year it lands the half-million-dollar job, and languish the year that it doesn't.

The third type of business that will benefit from this series is one that, on paper, seems to be making sufficient profits, but never seems to be able to raise enough cash to cover its bills. This is indicative of poor cash management and is often a problem that you can solve through various means of altering your payment and collection schedules so that they better fit one another.

This series may also prove beneficial to new companies, ones that are still becoming established and have had the sickening realization that they don't have enough capital to ride out the period of building a business. However, new businesses should be aware that many of the strategies I discuss in these volumes rely on successfully managing relationships with vendors and clients, and start-ups with few such relationships may have more difficulty in implementing them.

These books will help to guide you through short-term cash shortages, but more than that, they will teach you how to implement long-term strategies that will serve to protect your credit and your reputation when you run short on cash again in future, as you quite likely will. You will therefore note that I give attention to both immediate and longer-term fixes; if implemented properly, each should succeed in complementing the other.

What this series will NOT do is show you how to make your basic business more profitable, except through incidental reductions in expenses such as interest and late fees, and the benefits reaped from taking advantage of discounts. These savings can amount to thousands of dollars, and I have seen cases where businesses which were in the red were pushed into the black by these expense reductions alone. However, for most of you, while better cash management may carry you successfully through the tough times, it generally will not turn an unprofitable business into a profitable one.

While you're seeking to improve your cash flow, therefore, it's also important to consider the cause of your shortfalls. Do you mainly have timing issues, where money isn't coming in until long after you need it? Are you experiencing unexpected losses, or decreases in business, as has been so common during the recession? These issues can usually be addressed and do not necessarily reflect a substantial underlying flaw in the economic state of your business. However, if your business has never made money, or has been making insufficient profits for a number of years, then it may be time to address more essential problems with your operations, of which cash flow is only one part.

GLOSSARY

I have attempted to keep this guide as free of financial jargon as possible, but familiarity with a handful of commonly used terms is essential for your understanding.

Accounts Payable (A/P): Bills a company owes to a vendor or other creditor. An "A/P person" is an employee in charge of coding, entering, or paying these bills. Larger companies may have entire Accounts Payable departments. Don't get confused by context. Bills that you owe are Accounts Payable to you – they are Accounts Receivable to the company to whom you owe them.

Accounts Receivable (A/R): Money owed to a company by its customers. An "A/R person" is an employee in charge of creating or sending out bills and is also often in charge of collections. Larger companies may have entire Accounts Receivable departments. Don't get confused by context. Money that's owed to you are Accounts Receivable – they are Accounts Payable to the company that owes them.

Accounts Receivable-based Business vs. Cash-based Business: In this context, an A/R-based business is one whose income is primarily generated through Accounts Receivable – that is, purchases made on account, usually by other businesses. A cash-based business is one whose income derives primarily through cash payments made at the time of purchase, either by cash, check, or credit card. Strategies for projecting and improving cash inflows may vary greatly depending upon which style of business is involved.

Balance Sheet: Statement of the financial position of a business that states the assets, liabilities, and owners' equity at a specified point in time. Often overlooked by small businesses as a financial tool, the Balance Sheet can provide a wealth of useful information about the health of a business.

Bookkeeper: Technically, a person who records the accounts and transactions of a business. In practice, however, the bookkeeper in a small business may perform all of a firm's accounting functions, including A/P, A/R, payroll, month-end close, etc., and even those functions that in a larger firm might fall to a Controller. Such individuals are also often known as Full-Charge Bookkeepers.

Cash Inflows: Refers not to the income of a company, but to the pattern of receipt of actual cash. Understanding and controlling the timing differences between the generation of income and the receipt of cash is crucial to creating a viable cash flow plan.

Collections: The process of actively trying to collect on a debt, generally applied in the context of invoices or payments that are past due. Different firms have a wide variety of collections policies, and the strictness to which they adhere to them may depend greatly upon the ever-changing cash flow situation. In small firms, the intensity of collections activity is often dictated by the personality of the employee in the Accounts Receivable chair rather than by company policy.

Contractor vs. Independent Contractor: In common parlance, these two terms are often used interchangeably. In this context, however, I will draw a sharp distinction between the two. A "contractor" here is an individual or business who performs construction or remodeling work on either a residential or commercial basis. An "independent contractor" is the term for an individual or business who performs services of any type without being an employee. Your website designer, for example, may be an independent contractor. Some of you reading this are likely both contractors, meaning that you own a construction business, and independent contractors, meaning that you perform services for your clients without being their employees.

Controller: A financial person with a level of skill, expertise, and pay grade that falls below CFO and above Bookkeeper. A Controller should have the ability to create custom financial reports, select and maintain accounting software, perform all the functions of a bookkeeper or supervise staff performing those functions, and manage at least the basic cash flow needs of a business.

Financial Person: In this context I use this term to embrace all possible designations of the member of a company who handles its accounting functions, whether he or she be a Bookkeeper, Controller, Administrative Assistant, or Gal Who Works in the Office. In practice, small businesses are often unconcerned with the technical term for their one administrative employee, as all possible tasks related to accounting, human resources, etc., fall to him or her and the official title becomes somewhat irrelevant. In these types of businesses, it is quite possible for the Gal Who Works in the Office in one firm to have more power and responsibility than the Controller of another.

Human Resources (HR): Refers to issues related to the hiring, firing and maintenance of a company's personnel, and the person or department assigned to handle these issues. HR tasks may include everything from setting up and maintaining employee benefit programs, to ensuring that employment and compensation laws are obeyed, to writing and updating employee manuals and related documentation. A larger firm may have a person (or people) on staff who specialize in handling HR; in smaller firms these tasks often devolve to the bookkeeper or other administrative person by default, even though that person may have little to no experience or training in the field of human resources.

Owner's Draw: Withdrawals of a sole proprietorship's cash or other assets for the personal use of the owner. Contrary to popular belief, the owner's draw is *not* an expense and does not affect the income of the owner for tax purposes; however, it can have a massive impact on a company's cash flow.

Payroll Taxes: Refers to taxes withheld from employee paychecks and paid to the government by the employer as well as taxes paid by employers directly. Employee-paid taxes include Federal income tax withholding, state income tax withholding, FICA (Social Security and Medicare), and those applicable to some state Disability programs.

Employer-paid taxes include FICA (which matches the employee-paid amount), Federal Unemployment taxes or FUTA, and any relevant state taxes (in California these are the Unemployment and Employer Training taxes). This general description, however, doesn't convey why payroll taxes are such a big deal. In the payroll scenarios I've seen, payroll taxes often come close to half of the total net payroll – in other words, actual paychecks totaling $15,000 may have associated payroll taxes of $6,000 to $7,000. Since, for most people, tax payments are generally not due for several days (or in some cases, several weeks) after payday, deferring payment of these payroll taxes until the actual due date can have a substantial impact on cash flow.

Profit and Loss Statement (also P & L or Income Statement): Summarizes the revenues, costs, and expenses incurred during a specific period of time, usually a fiscal quarter or year. A P & L may accurately reflect a company's income; however, because it does not take into account debt payments and owner's draws – which are not expenses – it does *not* give a sufficient picture of a company's cash flow

Statement of Cash Flows: Financial statement providing aggregate data regarding the cash inflows a company receives from its ongoing operations and external investment sources, as well as the cash outflows during a given period.

Terms: The conditions under which a company's bill or invoice is due. Terms generally apply in any situation in which credit has been extended and will include due date, discount date, and any penalties for late payment.

Vendor: A person or company who provides you with a product or service. In this context, I use this as a generic term to indicate both suppliers and independent contractors.

Worker's Compensation: Employer-paid insurance covering employees in the case of on-the-job injuries. Rates are higher for firms in industries where serious injuries are more likely and for firms with poor safety records.

WHAT YOUR VENDORS WANT TO HEAR - AND HOW TO TELL IT TO THEM WITHOUT EVEN LYING

MAINTAINING GOOD RELATIONSHIPS WITH YOUR VENDORS IS KEY TO YOUR SURVIVAL!

If you've been struggling with your cash flow, then you may have already realized that your vendors are your last bastion of credit. You may already have borrowed as much as you can from your bank, and your line of credit, if you had one, may have been reduced or cancelled during the recession and its aftermath. If you're in the unfortunate position of having run up long-standing debts on your credit cards, these may be nearly impossible to pay down to the point where you have available credit again, and even if you do, it may not last long. Banks and credit card companies, too, are not only more likely to penalize you for any late payments, but they may also close or restrict your account without notice if they begin to suspect that you're a bad credit risk. Even if you have no late payments, your credit line may be reduced based on information reported to credit agencies.

Your vendors, however, especially if you have an established history with them, may be far less fussy about extending you credit, and it's because they need your business. Indeed, much of the A/P and A/R system is based on the concept that companies are more likely to give you their business if you give them more time to pay, and for many vendors the risk of default is worth the potential offsetting income.

If you're in a situation in which your cash flow has reached a critical mass, you may be more reliant than ever on your established suppliers, because they are most likely to allow you to borrow without checking and re-checking your credit or subjecting you to harsh terms, or, heaven forbid, cash and carry, which can spell doom for small

9

businesses that were already in trouble. If you want to have cash to manage, therefore, it's essential that you convince your vendors that even if you're not paying them in full or on time, that you *will* pay them.

TELL YOUR VENDORS WHAT THEY WANT TO HEAR

When most small business owners and financial managers receive calls from vendors looking for money, they instinctively want to respond in one way – with empty promises and vagueness:

1) "I'll send you a check, uh… sometime next week."

2) "I'll pay you when I get paid."

3) "Um… how much do we owe you again?"

4) "That depends… how much do I have to pay you to keep my account open?"

It's easy to see why small businesspeople make these kinds of answers. In fact, it can seem very logical:

1) I don't want to tell them I don't have the money, so let me try to put them off a week and hopefully some cash will come through before then.

2) My client is holding up payments – how am I supposed to pay my subs?

3) If I request a statement and maybe copies of invoices, that will give me more time and an excuse for not sending payment.

4) I need to know the bare minimum amount of cash that I need to send them.

These tactics might be effective once in a while. It's okay to equivocate for a week or two if you're not sure when you can send payment, it's okay to hold off paying your framing subcontractor if your client is out of town and can't cut you a check, it can even be okay to play dumb in regard to your accounting if you've had a change in staffing or employee absence. And sometimes you do have to come right out and ask your supplier how much you absolutely must pay them, and by when, to keep your account open. But employing these types of strategies on a regular basis is as good as telling your vendors that you have neither the ability nor the intention to pay them, and that can't lead your company anyplace good.

You have to remember that suppliers hear these types of excuses month after month and day after day from numerous other companies exactly like yours. They *know* that you're desperately trying to put them off, and it can be very irritating, especially if they can't pay bills of their own.

What kinds of signals do responses like these send to your vendors? They tell your vendors:

1) That you have no money with which to pay them and no real prospect of having it anytime soon.

2) That you are trying to avoid accepting responsibility for paying them what you owe them, and are passing it on to your clients.

3) That you have no handle on your financial situation.

4) That you don't respect them enough to try to pay them unless you absolutely have to in order to keep your account going.

Ultimately, these types of responses make your vendors question the stability of your business and the collectability of your account. A vendor who has no faith in you is far more likely to stop sending you product or doing the work that generates income for you. Worse, a supplier who is seriously concerned about your account may immediately step up demands for full payment.

UNDERSTANDING THIS IS THE KEY TO SUCCESSFULLY MANAGING CASH. Because only half of cash management is about cash; the other half is about management, and that means dealing with people.

Math matters, and it matters greatly, but ultimately you cannot make $5,000 turn into $10,000 no matter how you rearrange the figures. You can, however, make your $5,000 serve you nearly as well as $7,500, and that requires not mathematical, but psychological understanding.

Your vendors don't necessarily need for you to pay them in full, nor do they necessarily need you to pay them on time. As I mentioned above, one of the central premises of the A/P and A/R system is that businesses will spend more money with a vendor or supplier if they're extended credit and allowed to pay over time. In exchange, vendors accept the risk of companies defaulting, which is why they tend to get nervous if your balance gets too high or too aged.

You, as the business owner who's struggling, need to strike just the right balance between giving your vendor your business and giving your vendor your money. You want to minimize their risk and maximize their potential reward. No, let me rephrase that. You want to minimize *their perception* of their risk and maximize *their perception* of their potential reward. And this is why your responses to vendor inquiries are equally as vital as the money you send them.

WHAT DO YOUR VENDORS WANT TO HEAR?

They do not want to hear:

1) Excuses.

2) Protests.

3) Out-and-out lies.

4) Reminders about how you've always paid your bills before.

5) How bad business has been lately.

6) Your rant on how the government has screwed up the economy or how the damned IRS took all of your money.

But they also don't need to hear that you're going to get caught up with your balance, or that from now on you'll pay them on time, especially when they know as well as you do that these are promises you can't possibly keep.

This is what a vendor really wants to hear:

1) That you are going to pay them.

2) That you have a plan for paying them.

3) That you can tell them what that plan is.

This, in a nutshell, is what a vendor wants to know: that you will pay them eventually, and that you have a realistic, well-thought out plan for doing so.

Try to put yourself in the shoes of a vendor. When a customer tells you that they ought to be able to send you a check the following week, or that they'll pay you when their own customer coughs up some cash, this is essentially useless to you. I can't create a budget based on some vague promise of money I don't reasonably expect to collect. If I'm an A/R person, I can't tell my boss that "some money" should come in "any day now" on your account and expect not to get bawled out for not doing my job. Tell me instead that you're going to pay me a thousand dollars of what you owe me the following Friday, and the other thousand the week after that. At least I can work with that information, especially if I have confidence that you'll do what you say. And if you do do what you said you would? Then next time I'm going to trust you as well.

You don't have to pay your vendors in full, and you don't have to pay them on time, but you do have to give them confidence in your ability to manage your cash – even if you don't have any yourself.

CREATING A CASH FLOW PLAN

This is a subject unto itself, and I will discuss it in detail – complete with CASE STUDIES – in the forthcoming CREATING A PLAN volume of this series. For purposes of this discussion, however, it's essential to understand the rudiments of making a plan for managing cash, because this is the primary means by which you are going to be able to persuade your suppliers that yes, you will eventually pay them. And if you do it right and you do it well, then you may find, to your surprise, that you actually can pay them, and pay them as promised, because managing cash isn't nearly as difficult once you have a good plan.

The primary flaw in most small business' cash management strategies is failing to plan far enough ahead or to account for all of their forthcoming expenses. Many small businesses take one of the following approaches:

1) I'll wait and see how much money I have at the end of the week, and then pay bills based on what's left over.

2) I won't pay anything this week because we have our biweekly payroll, and I want to be sure I can cover it.

3) I'll pay what my accounting software says is due now.

4) We're broke, we're broke, we're broke, so I'm not going to pay anything unless I absolutely have to.

The problem with these approaches is that they're based on small-picture thinking. They tend to fail precisely because they represent flawed planning, and here are some reasons why:

1) If you spend all of the current week's money without knowing how much you'll be getting next week, then how will you cover your rent, insurance, payroll, etc. that's due the following week?

2) While it's often advisable to schedule outgoing payments in non-payroll weeks when you have the option, trying to bunch everything into alternate weeks may cause your non-payroll week cash outlays to be even higher than in weeks you have payroll! Ultimately that money is all coming from the same bucket, and an outright refusal to make any payments outside of payroll at all is a sure sign of poor planning.

3) Basing your payment plan on reports generated by your accounting software will cause you to overlook bills that haven't been received or haven't been entered into your

system, which may cause you to vastly underestimate your upcoming expenses.

4) Perhaps the most catastrophic strategy of all, the "We-can't-pay-anything approach" virtually ensures a self-perpetuating cycle of your accounts being shut off for lack of payment, often coupled with a demand from your supplier for full – not partial – payment before your ability to buy can be reinstated. This is how businesses find themselves operating cash-and-carry, which is doubly disastrous because not only do you then have to pay cash for your current supplies, you still have to make payments on the old balances to keep them out of collections! Unless you are quite literally on the verge of bankruptcy, don't fall into this trap. You will almost certainly pay more by not paying anything, and make yourself and your suppliers miserable in the process.

In short, these strategies are all reflective of poor planning, which is why they so often fail. But businesses struggling with cash often get sucked into them precisely because they are struggling so badly. How can I make a plan for paying my bills when I have no money?

Surprisingly, you can. Even if the end result seems like a terrible, lousy, utterly worthless plan, having a plan in place will make your financial life run so much more smoothly that you'll wonder how you ever got by without one.

That's not to say it's easy, though. The mechanics of projecting inflows and outflows can be complicated, especially as a business gets larger, which is why I decided to make the process of planning itself a separate volume. In the real world, I use an Excel spreadsheet of my own design that allows me easily to adjust my expected income and expenses as new money or information comes in – that way, it's flexible, so when there are changes, as there inevitably are, I can rework my figures quickly and easily. But if you're not comfortable using Excel, with a bit more manual addition and subtraction, you can get the same results on your lined yellow pad as long as you grasp the concept.

HERE'S AN EXAMPLE

Let's take a look at a highly simplified example. Pretend that we're projecting our cash flow over a four-week period, and that we have income and expenses as follows.

Income: $5,000 a week
Expenses:
Payroll plus payroll taxes, $4,000 in Week 1 and Week 3.
Rent: $3,000 in Week 4
Bills to suppliers: $9,000 over the course of the month

In this simplified scenario, it's pretty easy to see how this will have to go if I don't want to run out of money:

Week 1: Income of $5,000; Payments: Payroll of $4,000 plus $1,000 to suppliers
Week 2: Income of $5,000: Payments: $5,000 to suppliers
Week 3: Income of $5,000: Payments: Payroll of $4,000 plus $1,000 to suppliers
Week 4: Income of $5,000; Payments: Rent of $3,000 plus remaining $2,000 to suppliers

PERIOD	INCOME	MANDATORY		REMAINDER	
WEEK 1	$5,000	PAYROLL	$4,000	SUPPLIERS	$1,000
WEEK 2	$5,000			SUPPLIERS	$5,000
WEEK 3	$5,000	PAYROLL	$4,000	SUPPLIERS	$1,000
WEEK 4	$5,000	RENT	$3,000	SUPPLIERS	$2,000
TOTALS	$20,000		$11,000		$9,000

Of course, it worked out very neatly that I had just enough income to cover my outgoing expenses, didn't it? Yes, it did. But the results wouldn't change even if my bills due to suppliers were, say, $15,000. I can't not pay payroll, and I probably can't hold off too long on the rent, which means that my suppliers are largely going to bear the burden of financing me. They will only be getting $9,000 even if I owe them $15,000. In fact, when designing my plan, my primary goal is going to be to end up with a cash balance of no less than $0, even if that means I'm going to have to disregard bills totaling $6,000.

That's my original projection. Now let's suppose that we learn that our Week 2 customer payment may be delayed until the end of Week 3. Now I'd better change my plan and delay paying my Week 2 suppliers, or else I might not be able to cover my Week 3 payroll if that payment is late:

Week 1: Income of $5,000; Payments: Payroll of $4,000 plus $1,000 to suppliers
Week 2: Income of $0; Payments: $0
Week 3: Income of $10,000; Payments: Payroll of $4,000 plus $6,000 to suppliers
Week 4: Income of $5,000; Payments: Rent of $3,000 plus remaining $2,000 to suppliers

PERIOD	INCOME	MANDATORY		REMAINDER	
WEEK 1	$ 5,000	PAYROLL	$4,000	SUPPLIERS	$1,000
WEEK 2	$0			SUPPLIERS	$0
WEEK 3	$10,000	PAYROLL	$4,000	SUPPLIERS	$6,000
WEEK 4	$ 5,000	RENT	$3,000	SUPPLIERS	$2,000
TOTALS	$20,000		$11,000		$9,000

Conversely, let's suppose we finished a project ahead of schedule and have received our Week 2 payment in Week 1 – now maybe we can pay some people earlier if we're confident that our Week 3 payment is going to come in on schedule.

Week 1: Income of $10,000; Payments: Payroll of $4,000 plus $6,000 to suppliers
Week 2: Income of $0; Payments: $0
Week 3: Income of $5,000; Payments: Payroll of $4,000 plus $1,000 to suppliers
Week 4: Income of $5,000; Payments: Rent of $3,000 plus remaining $2,000 to suppliers

PERIOD	INCOME	MANDATORY		REMAINDER	
WEEK 1	$10,000	PAYROLL	$4,000	SUPPLIERS	$6,000
WEEK 2	$0			SUPPLIERS	$0
WEEK 3	$ 5,000	PAYROLL	$4,000	SUPPLIERS	$1,000
WEEK 4	$ 5,000	RENT	$3,000	SUPPLIERS	$2,000
TOTALS	$20,000		$11,000		$9,000

You can see even from this simple example why having a plan that extends beyond the current or immediately following week is so incredibly important. If I'm not planning at least four weeks ahead, then I'm likely to forget about the rent or the insurance and other monthly bills. I may be able to accommodate a change in the current week, but I could still be in trouble if I'm not looking forward to the next several weeks. What if my Week 4 customer is going to shortpay me by $3,000? Then I may need to *not* pay my suppliers in Week 3 OR Week 4 so that I can cover my rent.

In practice, the farther ahead you can plan, the better off you will be, and if the numbers are terrifying to look at, don't let that throw you. Every one of my cash flow plans has begun with negative numbers in the five digits, and had to be worked and reworked until they got up to $0. Strange as it sounds, it can be a very nice feeling to end up with nothing – when you started out with a lot less than nothing!

In addition, you will want the length of your plan to, in some way, reflect the income and expense cycle of your business. I personally always create an annual plan so that I can quickly plug in my recurring expenses, although in practice I'm generally only looking closely at about twelve weeks at a time. But if you're in construction, for example, you will probably want to project your income based on projects in progress, and that could mean plotting out your income several months in advance. (In fact, while it's tempting to frontload, it can be a good idea to design your client's payment schedule in a manner that ensures even cash flow, as I discuss in my forthcoming volume TIPS FOR CONTRACTORS.)

On the other hand, if your business is one that relies on an A/R cycle, then your income projections will need to reflect that, too. If your terms are Net 60, meaning that you expect clients to pay within 60 days (and your clients generally do), then you will want to have a plan that extends at least over two months. If your 60-day clients often stretch their payments out to 90 days, then you may need to look ahead farther. The same is true of your vendors – if the terms that they give you are Net 60 or Net 90, then you need to be planning for a minimum of eight or twelve weeks at a time.

So now I've designed my plan – what does it do for me?

The first thing it allows me to do, of course, is really analyze my situation. Am I going to have enough cash? What am I going to do with the cash I have? What changes will I make if there's an alteration in my expenses or income?

But in terms of your vendors, what having a plan does is ALLOW YOU TO TELL THEM WHAT THEY WANT TO HEAR. Now you can assure them:

1) That you are going to pay them.

2) That you have a plan for paying them.

3) That you can tell them what that plan is.

Again for simplicity, let's suppose that in the previous example I owed all of my money to one supplier. If I can tell that supplier that I expect to be able to send them $1,000 in Week 1, $5,000 in Week 2, $1,000 in Week 3, and $2,000 in Week 4, that is going to go over much better with them than if I tell them I'll try to get them the money – um, next week sometime. First of all, because I won't be able to do it and that will tick them off further, and secondly, because they still won't really have any idea when – or if – to expect my money. How are they supposed to plan?

But wait a minute, you may be thinking. That's fine if I only owe my vendor $9,000 – but what if I owe them $15,000?

And this is where we move away from the mathematics of planning and back to the psychological aspects of managing vendors. Because your goal here is to get your supplier to accept your $9,000 in place of $15,000 and be satisfied with that, at least temporarily. And you can accomplish this by minimizing their risk and perception of risk and maximizing their potential reward.

EXPECTATIONS MATTER!

When I was pursuing my Master's, I took an advanced course in Financial Accounting Theory. One of the topics was a study of how the stock market reacts to company financial reports. It's been shown that stock prices don't necessarily improve or decline based on a company's earnings. Rather, the market responds based on whether the earnings reports are as good *as expected* – whether they met investors' *expectations* of how the company was going to perform in a particular quarter. It's therefore possible for a company's stock price to drop even when it has positive earnings if those earnings were not as high as investors anticipated.

The same principle applies to managing vendors. You need to manage your cash, yes, but more importantly, you want to properly manage your suppliers' expectations regarding their payment. You need to shift them out of the position of being annoyed and frustrated with you because, in their eyes, you've overpromised and underdelivered. Instead you want to promise less and deliver more than they expected.

The businesses who supply your product and perform services for you on credit are, in a very real sense, investors in your company. They're giving you their goods and services in the hope of earning a return on their investment. And, like the stock market, their perceived value of their shares in your company will respond more strongly to whether you met the expectations they had of you than to whether you paid them in full or on time.

KEEP YOUR PROMISES!

When it comes to your vendors, the critical aspect of having a plan is following through on that plan, especially if you've shared it with them. Of course you are going to run into situations where this proves impossible, which is why it's so important to create a plan based on what you truly expect to happen with your finances, rather than on what you hope *might* happen. Because how long can I reasonably expect them to trust me if I continually don't follow through? If I can lay it out for my vendors, tell them how much money to expect, and then send it to them when I said I would, then they will be more willing to overlook my late payments because they have been reassured that they can rely on me and my plan.

Therefore, *do not* tell a vendor specifically that you'll send them a check at the end of the week if you're not really confident that you'll be able to do so. You may have some leeway depending on what type of company you're dealing with here – a large firm with a dedicated accounting department, for example, may be less likely to notice if your check is a couple of days later than they expected, because it will take time to work its way through their system. A subcontractor, however, may be anxiously waiting for your check to arrive so that he or she can timely cover a mortgage payment. In that case, you don't want to say that you'll mail a check out on Friday and then hold it until Monday, as that could be disastrous for them, and disastrous for your relationship with that subcontractor, too. Better to tell them you can't pay their bill until Monday and give them the opportunity to make other arrangements – they may still be angry, but at least they won't be disappointed.

Over the long term, you want to establish patterns with your vendors that will relieve you of the responsibility of having to advise them specifically of a check's mailing date. You want your subcontractor to know in advance that they can't necessarily count on your check arriving in time to cover their mortgage, so that they will automatically make other arrangements. You want your suppliers not to bother calling you seeking payment the first week of the month, because they know you always pay in the second week of the month and it isn't worth the bother of calling to them. Make it easy for your vendors to know what to expect from you and you'll have fewer hassles, fewer nasty surprises, and fewer moments of panic for both you and your vendors. (See USING PATTERNS TO YOUR ADVANTAGE, later).

HOW TO MAKE $5,000 LOOK LIKE $7,500 BY MAKING SMALLER BUT MORE FREQUENT PAYMENTS

I have found no more effective means of easing a supplier's reservations over whether you are going to pay them than sending them checks more often. With rare exceptions, this works incredibly well and is a terrific way to show your commitment to paying off your past-due balances, enticing vendors to keep approving your new purchases while simultaneously improving your cash flow.

Perhaps you're wondering why this works. Isn't it the same amount of cash, only spread out over more payments? Doesn't it create additional paperwork for me and my vendor, and what does it really accomplish for either of us?

Yes, it is the same amount of cash, but remember that our goal here is to make our $5,000 look like $7,500, even though it's not. A single check of $5,000 can only look like $5,000 – there's no other way to interpret it. But four checks of $1,250 looks like a heck of a lot more to them – and a heck of a lot less to you.

To illustrate, let's examine a sample scenario. Suppose you're a contractor and your lumber supplier has terms of Net 10th, meaning that the total of your month-end statement is due on the 10th of the following month. You know, however, from prior experience that they won't call looking for money until about the 30th, and you're never able to pay them before then, anyway.

Now suppose the bill averages $20,000. It's your biggest bill, and you always have a hard time coming up with enough cash to cover it. In addition, there never seems to be a good time to pay it, because your rent is due the first week of the month, and you have biweekly payroll – it's just almost impossible to come up with $20K all at once. As a consequence, you've fallen into a pattern of not paying the current bill until the middle of the following month, which results in numerous annoyed and impatient phone calls from your vendor seeking payment and the constant threat of you being cut off.

If this sounds familiar, it should. Many, many cash-poor businesses fall into this pattern, and it can be self-perpetuating – how can you possibly pay the current bill when you haven't paid the last one yet?

Now try an alternate scenario, in which you send your vendor weekly payments of $5,000. You send the first one out say, the third week of the month, not too long after the full payment was originally due. Your vendor might be confused for a moment, because you've broken your long-standing pattern of making full payment, but they'll be pleased, too, because having your $5,000 now is worth more to them than the $20,000 they hoped to get from you in a month. Remember the old saw about the bird in hand being worth two in the bush; the same principle applies. You've effectively reduced their risk and increased their reward.

The following week you send them another $5,000, then again the week after that. Now you're past the end of the month, and technically you're still way overdue. But your supplier probably isn't going to worry about that, because you've already paid three-quarters of what you owed them, and they trust that you'll pay the rest the following week because you've established a pattern of doing just that. They'll be happy, relieved, and ultimately, grateful. For once they didn't have to call and harass you for payment.

The end result is that you paid the $20,000 within the same exact extended timeframe, but without the threats and collection calls that make your life and the life of your vendor miserable. You've saved them a whole month of fear and anxiety, and improved their cash flow, too, which is undoubtedly worth a little additional paperwork and payment processing. More importantly, you've begun to establish a new pattern of expectations that will be far more flexible than your old method of paying your bill in full four weeks after its due date.

Think about it. If you're already stretching your vendor's limits by paying that $20,000 in the middle of the month after it was due, then you MUST pay that in full by then or risk being cut off. You can't simply decide to send them $15,000 four weeks late and expect to get by with that – they will throw a fit because you were already late and now you're shortpaying them. If, however, you've already sent them

$15,000 over the previous three weeks, and you find you can't cover that last $5,000 in the fourth, they're far more likely to let you slide – particularly if you send it the week after that. In other words, you've just bought yourself additional cash and additional time – and kept your vendor happy in the process.

Suppose now that I've been paying my lumber yard a little each week for a while now and I realize, thanks to my plan, that I'm going to be even shorter than usual in the upcoming month. Well, now maybe instead of sending them $5,000 a week, I send them $4,000. I'll still have my current bill paid off in five weeks, and although the amount of each check will be less, it will likely be close enough not to cause undue concern. And if your business is at all seasonal, as it is in construction, retail, automotive, etc., having this flexibility will save your butt during your slow times.

But wait a minute, you might be thinking. Doesn't this entail paying out more money sooner, not less? How can that possibly be better for my cash flow?

Mathematically, there is no logic in it. Psychologically, however, it's a lot easier to come up with four payments of $5,000 than one payment of $20,000, even over a brief, four-week period. Signing your name to a check for $20,000 is a much bigger commitment than signing a check for $5,000. Once you've sent that check out, you have no other options. A weekly payment you can delay by a few days if you run short. A weekly payment can be reduced if need be. But once you've made a single large payment, you have no choice but to let it ride, and that can be terrifying. And what if you've scrimped and scrimped and you still only have $19,000 available? Now you're holding up payment all together because you can't squeeze out another $1,000, which is going to tick off your vendor no end. This is exactly why we have credit. Otherwise we could all simply save our money for five years and pay cash for our new cars rather than paying interest on loan after loan.

DO NOT UNDERESTIMATE THE POWER OF THE FLOAT!

The second reason that sending more frequent small payments improves your cash flow is the old-fashioned float you achieve from checks being in transit. Even in the modern era in which checks clear faster than ever, the float of funds that results from sending out checks can still be highly significant. If I mail a check out on Friday to a local supplier, they won't receive it until Monday. They may not deposit it for a couple of days, and then it still has to clear my bank, which it likely won't do before the following Friday. In other words, I just bought myself a whole week of being on good terms with my vendor, and it didn't cost me a dime. And for a non-local supplier, that timeframe can easily be extended to two weeks or more.

Maybe this doesn't sound like such a big deal in an isolated instance, but believe me, if you apply this practice company-wide, it can make a huge difference. I once worked for a company that had a huge line of credit that had been reduced in the midst of the recession. The way it operated was that if there was a shortfall in the checking account, the bank would call and you could do a transfer from the LOC to cover the overdraft – in other words, there was no need to borrow money before the day it was actually needed. My typical A/P check run was $30,000 a week, and for over a year I ran the finances of this company with a bank ledger balance averaging *negative* $50,000 – without once having to borrow money on the line of credit. In other words, my checks in transit were substantially more than the amount of my weekly check run, buying me more than a week of additional time with the company's money. Not only did this save us literally thousands of dollars in interest, but when it came time to renew the loan, there was no question of the bank once again reducing the amount of the line of credit, because I hadn't even touched it. This is the power of the float.

Obviously I only got away with this because I had the funds to back me up if I needed them, but it can work in other scenarios, too. Consider the balances you've racked up on your credit card accounts. If you had $10,000 in float that you could apply to your credit cards, you could save yourself a substantial amount of interest with comparatively little risk, because if the float did catch up with you, you could always make new charges to cover your bills. It is a very, very nice feeling not to be throwing your money away on credit card interest, and the side benefit is that getting those balances paid down may improve your credit rating, too, which may, in turn, increase your ability to borrow more money.

And let's not forget that once my check has been mailed, I'm good with my vendor. Unless I have a history of lying to them about sending out checks, they will be placated as soon as I've sent it. There are few things in Accounts Payable management more satisfying than having a vendor call you and being able to tell them their check has already gone out.

WEEKLY PAYMENTS INCREASE CONFIDENCE AND DECREASE ANXIETY

Weekly payments can have an incredibly soothing effect on your vendors. No sooner have they finished processing your last check when you've sent them a new one, and the positive impression that makes can be profound. Okay, you're still past due, and you still owe them a bundle, but look at all of the checks they've gotten from you! Clearly you're making a sincere effort to pay them, and more importantly, they can reasonably expect that you'll continue to do so. No more waiting a whole month to see if you'll cough up the cash, by which time they've really extended themselves by continuing to supply you with product. You've increased their confidence and decreased their anxiety about your account, which is going to make them more likely to tolerate your late and shortpayments now, and also more likely to be willing to trust you in future.

This methodology can't keep you out of trouble with everybody. There are those who will initially react badly because you sent them less than the full amount due, and that will confuse them. But once they get on the program, I have yet to meet the vendor who wasn't far happier with my small and passably late weekly payments than they had been with the big and ridiculously late ones. Done right, it's an incredibly effective strategy for most and will go a long way towards restoring goodwill between you and your vendors.

HERE'S A REAL-WORLD EXAMPLE

I once designed a cash flow plan for a wholesaler with a recurring monthly bill from a supplier of about $40,000. When I started there, the firm was past due by nearly six months, which was a dire emergency because the vendor to whom the money was owed was the *only* supplier of that particular product, which, in turn, comprised about twenty percent of the company's sales.

Within a few weeks, I had gotten a handle on most of the company's other A/P, but I couldn't pay off even one of those past due bills. I simply could not come up with $40,000 all at once – there was no way to make that work, especially when the firm was overwhelmed with dozens of other unmet financial obligations. Finally the vendor wanted to schedule an in-person meeting – and you know you're in trouble when your supplier wants to fly out to see you. Naturally, they didn't want to give up such a huge volume of business, but of course they wanted to get paid, too.

I explained the situation to them. Apart from the firm's general shortage of cash, one of the reasons they hadn't been paid was because the size of their bills coupled with the vagaries of the firm's Accounts Receivable schedule made it extremely difficult ever to cut them a check for $40,000. In fact, their account comprised sixty percent of the company's total A/P, and this was undoubtedly a big reason why. I proposed paying them in weekly installments of $10,000 instead. They accepted the offer, and I began making payments the following week.

So what exactly did this accomplish? The positive effects were manifold, over both the short-term and long:

1) I reassured my vendor. By explaining to them the reason why the company had been unable to pay them, I persuaded them that the firm was not failing or at risk of defaulting, and although cash was indeed, short, a large part of this was due to cash management issues rather than deeper problems with the business itself. Furthermore, by making them the specific offer I did, I essentially told them that I had a plan, which persuaded them that I really knew what I was doing. It was confidence that cemented that deal, not cash.

2) I hardly cost the company anything. In fact, in the short term, I saved it a big chunk of money. Had I not made my proposal of weekly payments of $10,000, I undoubtedly would have had to come up with at least $40,000 to pay off one of the past due bills right away. This would have meant stiffing everyone else, which would have started the cycle with all of the other

vendors all over again. Instead, I only had to give them $10,000 upfront and I bought the firm a full week to raise it.

3) I was able to keep the account maxed out and past due – but with my vendor's blessing. They took my deal, right? As long as I kept sending them that weekly $10,000, they could no longer complain if we were six months behind and owed them in excess of two hundred grand. And they didn't complain, because not only were they getting paid far more regularly than they had been before, they believed that the company would continue to pay them, and that was worth risking the past due balance to them.

4) I was able to catch up on some of the past-due amounts – albeit very slowly. After 52 weeks, I had paid 13 of their monthly bills, which lowered our balance and improved the look of our financial statements as well. It took a few years before the account was up to a level of reasonable size and lateness, but in the meantime there were no phone calls and no demands for immediate payment, which dramatically reduced the stress in all of our lives.

5) It gave me some options. For the first year, I sent those checks out on Fridays without fail. But once we were settled into a pattern, I felt comfortable allowing myself a little wiggle room when needed, and if we had a bad month and I had to hold their check a few days before I could cover it, I did so without ever having a problem. And some years later, when we lost one of our biggest clients, I very quietly began spreading out those weekly payments so that I was paying $30,000 a month instead of $40,000, which bought me several additional months before the vendor finally called me, at which point we were nearly back on our feet and I could promise to step up my payments again.

This was a great method of handling an emergency cash situation, and I have applied it successfully with numerous vendors. If you've reached a tipping point with your supplier, I strongly suggest you give it a try. I will detail how to approach this mathematically in the forthcoming CREATING A PLAN volume of this series, but essentially you want to make an offer that will push the limits of their tolerance vis-à-vis your outstanding balance and lateness of payments, but without going past them. And you can generally figure out where this point is by examining the history of your account (also see UNDERSTANDING YOUR VENDORS' TERMS, later).

For example, if my vendor has been allowing me to carry a past due balance of $12,000, and my monthly purchases typically total $12,000, then I will likely be safe making an offer of $3,000 a week, which will keep me at the same level of being behind. Yes, of course, they may argue that this won't help me catch up, and they're right – except for those months that have five weeks instead of four, I won't really be sending them any more money. On the other hand, I won't be falling farther behind, and they'll still be getting my business. For most this is a risk worth taking, and the upshot for me is that I'll be paying no more than I was paying before. The only difference now is that I've made an informal commitment, so I had better try my hardest to stick to it.

WHAT IF MY VENDOR DOESN'T LIKE MY OFFER?

Do your best to be firm. It does neither of you any good to let them pressure you into paying them $5,000 if all you've got is $3,000. In truly dire circumstances, of course, you can agree to the $5,000 and hope for the best – the advantage being that if you're paying them weekly, you can miss or delay a payment if you absolutely need to. But it's far better to make them understand that you aren't making this offer willy-nilly; it's based on what you think is possible in terms of your cash management plan. You can say:

"I don't want to make promises I don't know I can keep. I know I can send you this much right now, and if I'm able to do more going forward, I will."

Or

"This is all I can do for right now. However, our busy season is coming up in a few months, and I should be able to send you more then."

Or

"Could we maybe give it a try for the next several weeks and talk again then? I do think I may be able to send you more, but at this point, I don't want to over-commit."

And it is definitely better to avoid over-committing. For example, I will frequently put my smaller and mid-sized vendors on a weekly schedule without even telling them – I simply start sending checks. This gives me all of the benefits of paying them weekly instead of monthly but without tying me down to a schedule, so that if I need to change it, I can.

DON'T OVERLOOK THE PRACTICAL ASPECTS

If you decide to go weekly, be sure to consider your vendor's accounting system when determining how to make payments. Virtually no vendor wants to receive payment for only part of an invoice, as it creates extra paperwork and complicates their accounting unnecessarily. Therefore, if you're trying to send a supplier weekly payments of $5,000, pick enough invoices to approximate that amount rather than trying to arrive at that figure exactly.

Also, most vendors will appreciate it if you pay their bills in order, as many types of accounting software will apply payments automatically, and it's a lot simpler for them if your check works that way, too. Remember, you want to MAKE IT AS EASY AS POSSIBLE FOR YOUR VENDORS, so that they don't have to call you to straighten things out. So pay them a little more one week, a little less the next, but try to keep your payments in order. The exception would be if there's an unusually large invoice somewhere in the middle of your outstanding pile. For instance, I once owed a $13,000 invoice to a vendor to whom I was sending $5,000 a week. In that case, I did pay the bills around it first to come up with my $5,000, then split the big one into two payments and paid it over a two-week period. You don't have to overextend yourself too far in the interest of making the accounting go smoothly, but your A/R contacts will appreciate it if you make an effort.

Likewise, you want to apply credits in the same way that they apply credits. If they apply credits to the invoices to which they apply, you want to follow the same practice, so that your outstanding balances match on individual invoices. If, instead, they apply credits to the oldest outstanding invoice, you do the same. Yes, of course, there should be no net cash difference, and you can always reconcile the two later, but that will most likely involve a phone call, and THE LAST THING YOU WANT TO DO IS GIVE THEM A REASON TO CALL YOU WHEN YOU OWE THEM MONEY. The exception here would be if you have enough credits to wipe out some of your old balances – for example, if applying credits to your old invoices, instead of to the invoices to which they apply, will get you out of the dreaded "Over 90" column (see UNDERSTANDING YOUR VENDORS' TERMS, later). In that case, feel free to apply credits in the manner which best benefits your account standing, and deal with the phone call if it comes.

Finally, consider the dollar amounts involved if you're going to send checks weekly. It does cost you money to send out a check – for the stamp, the envelope, and the check itself – and this may not be worthwhile if the payment is only a few hundred dollars. Personally, when I first walk into a new A/P crisis, I generally like to send out as many checks as I can to try to get back on good terms with vendors as quickly as possible. Once things have settled, I will then seriously reduce the number of small checks I send out, and will often pay invoices late so that I can combine two payments and save the cost of the additional postage and paperwork.

WHAT ABOUT INDEPENDENT CONTRACTORS? CAN YOU SEND THEM WEEKLY PAYMENTS, TOO?

My experience has been yes, you can do it, and do it successfully, but you will likely encounter more griping. Most independent contractors expect to be paid promptly, if not immediately upon job completion, and a vendor with whom you have no prior relationship is going to be less likely to be willing to bend their terms to yours. People with whom you've worked for a long time, especially those to whom you give a considerable volume of business, will be far more accommodating, but you're probably going to need to talk to them more; explain what you're doing and why you are doing it. This happened often during the recession, especially in the construction industry where contractors at all levels were suffering, and for the most part the subs I worked with were surprisingly understanding, and happy to have the work even if they didn't get paid right away.

My general experience, however, has been that you're less likely to have trouble with the guy who maintains your office machines or the lady who prints your brochures than you will with subcontractors, who, if you work in construction or similar fields, quite likely face the same types of cash flow problems you do. And the few hundred bucks you might owe for computer repair doesn't even compare to many subcontractor bills, which can be incredibly difficult to finance, even during good times. As you contractors know, you might receive a progress payment of $10,000 on installation of flooring and owe your flooring subcontractor $8,000 virtually the same day, which doesn't leave you much with which to pay your employees.

Handling such situations requires very careful planning, and if you know you're going to have a big bill of this sort coming up, it behooves you to try to work it into your projected payment schedule as far ahead of time as you can. In general, you should be prepared to prioritize payments to independent contractors over those to corporate suppliers. Very few are going to be willing to work for you again if you try to stretch their payments out 60 days, and even 30 days is borderline unacceptable for most. My recommendation in this instance would be to try to pay off the bill within two to four weeks, depending on your subcontractor's tolerance, but however you arrange it, to get the first payment out right away. Your sub is probably depending on that money as much as you are, and two grand in the first week is going to make him or her much more amenable to waiting on the rest. (See also the forthcoming TIPS FOR CONTRACTORS volume of this series for more advice on managing cash for construction.)

USING PATTERNS TO YOUR ADVANTAGE

I've talked a lot in this guide about establishing precedents and patterns of behavior that will ease your relationships with your vendors without requiring you to significantly alter your net output of cash. Let's look now at other ways of putting this into practice.

As I described, the psychology of vendors in receiving weekly payments from you is a powerful force. It will create a sense of your reliability and predictability, which will encourage vendors to let you slide in ways you might not have gotten away with before. However, in the long term, you want to avoid becoming too predictable, right? If you owe your vendor a ton of money, then it may behoove you to make sure they have a check in hand every Monday morning, if for no other reason than to keep them from freaking out. But if you've been paying them faithfully on a regular basis for some months, then you should, at some point, be able to take some liberties in remitting payments, even if you're still behind with them. And if you're a seasonal or cyclical business, you *need* that flexibility, because you won't get through the slow season without it. If done correctly, however, you can maintain good relationships with your vendors even during tough times. Here are some examples of how you can accomplish this without sacrificing your reputation for reliability.

CONTINUE TO MAKE WEEKLY PAYMENTS – SORT OF

As I discuss in the OTHER TIPS AND TRICKS segment of this volume, I have always told vendors that I cut checks on Fridays, but in reality I have consistently made a practice of sending some out on Friday, some on Saturday, possibly even Monday if the cash I was expecting hasn't come in. When times are particularly tough, you can stretch it a bit more – say, send one check out on Monday and the next on the Thursday of the following week, so that you're effectively skipping a week. This won't keep your account any more current, of course, but at least you'll still be sending regular payments, and from a vendor's viewpoint, that can be nearly as good.

SEND A LITTLE LESS THAN YOU HAVE BEEN

If you've been sending $3,000, try sending $2,700. Done as part of an overall program, these small shortpayments will help to carry you through a bad month or season without forcing you to stiff your vendor all together.

DON'T CHANGE YOUR PATTERN WHEN YOU HAVE A WINDFALL

It's always tempting to pay your bills extra-promptly on those rare occasions when you're flush with cash, but doing so will alter your vendors' long-term expectations and you should be very cautious about taking such an approach. If you want to cough up cash sooner when you can afford to do so, it may be best to reserve that privilege for those who will really appreciate the money and the effort, such as your independent contractors. The large corporation that supplies your light bulbs will appreciate your prompt payment, too, of course, but not nearly as much. If you have extra money to pay on your past due accounts, dole it out a little at a time and to a range of suppliers. This will help you to catch up with everybody without changing your pattern, and still leave you some flexibility if something goes wrong. A windfall can also be a great opportunity to pay off those nagging small bills that are just clogging your books and A/P reports, giving you less to keep track of and worry about. Of course, if you're confronting a dire emergency situation that only an outpouring of cash can resolve, then by all means, use the money for that if you've got it. But don't decide to get yourself current with a supplier who has been letting you slide if, in three weeks, you're going to need to fall behind all over again. By then they will have forgotten all about your big catch-up payment and will only remember that you are, once again, falling behind.

DON'T BE AFRAID TO PAY LATE

If a supplier doesn't charge a late fee and isn't too strict with terms, you can routinely send your check late and be fine. In my experience, most vendors will realize that this is your pattern and will eventually stop calling. For example, I had one vendor who always called seeking payment literally a single day after its due date. As it happened, I had sent out his check that morning and I told him so. The next month, he called again, and again I had already sent out the check. After that he stopped calling. Why? Because he figured my check was on its way, as it generally was. But later on, I could send my check a week or more late and still not get that phone call, even from someone who used to call after only one day. Why? Because he figured my check was on its way, and it wasn't worth the effort of calling me to confirm. I had established a pattern, and in the long run, it bought me more time. So be careful about paying bills too promptly if cash flow is an ongoing issue for you. If you delay payments slightly when you have money, as well as when you don't, then your vendor will come to expect it and will routinely allow you more time, which will help to protect your account when you most need it.

HOW TO COMMUNICATE AND NEGOTIATE
WITH VENDORS

Many people will tell you that successful management of past due Accounts Payable is dependent upon having good communication with vendors, but this is misleading. You want to have a good relationship with vendors, but you never actually want to have to talk to them. In fact, THE REAL HALLMARK OF GOOD A/P MANAGEMENT IS WHEN VENDORS *NEVER* HAVE TO CALL YOU.

That's it – you never want to have to call them, and you never want them to have to call you. You want to have established a pattern of regular payment that will make it less likely that your vendor is going to need to look too closely at your account – and the last thing you want is for them to look closely at your account. In fact, you want to be so reliable and so predictable that something has to go horribly, horribly wrong before a supplier picks up the phone and asks you what's up.

When you do get those calls, however, it's of crucial importance that you handle them properly. Remember that you want to tell your vendor what they most want to hear:

1) That you are going to pay them.

2) That you have a plan for paying them.

3) That you can tell them what that plan is.

Okay, so you've got your plan, you've got your cash flow budget prepared, you've got your payment schedule outlined. Let's run through some hypothetical scenarios of actually communicating with vendors.

Vendor: When are you going to pay this past due balance?
Wrong Answer: I'll catch up as soon as I can.
Right Answer: According to my current projections, I should be able to send you about $3,000 a week until we're caught up.
Why: "As soon as I can" tells your vendor that you have no plan for paying them, which gives them no faith in the stability of your account. If you can assign a dollar amount and schedule to your anticipated payments, it will reflect much better on you, even if it's less money and later than they expected.

Vendor: This order puts you $2,000 over your credit limit. I can't ship it until you get your account paid down.
Wrong Answer: Can I put that on my personal credit card?
Right Answer: I can send you $3,000 at the end of next week. Can you let us slide until then?
Why: Not only is covering business expenses with your personal funds a bad business idea, it establishes a dangerous precedent in the mind of your vendor, because it gives the impression that you could raise the cash if you really needed to, and are willing to go to some lengths to do so if your vendor demands it. The right answer tells them that you will have the cash shortly and will make the payment, and politely asks them to make a temporary concession instead. If you follow up on this and do what you said you would, the next time they'll be even more willing to trust you, and you won't be forced into such an awkward position.

Vendor: Is there a reason why this account hasn't been paid?
Wrong Answer: I'm sorry, but we just don't have the money right now.
Right Answer: Yes. One of our larger customers went bankrupt a few months ago, leaving their balance unpaid. I've had to re-work the budget accordingly. I'm projecting that it's going to take me another month or so to get back on track.
Why: Telling a vendor that you don't have the money right now with generic excuses like business has been bad, or expenses have been high, is a great way to get them to immediately want to close your account. If you have a financial problem that can reasonably be expected to be temporary, then fine – they know, as you do, that over the long term

that will probably work itself out. But why would they want to continue to extend you credit if your business is in trouble or failing? The risk may outweigh the potential reward for them.

Vendor: You have an overdue balance of $20,000 on your account. We're cutting you off until you pay it in full.
Wrong Answer: I won't pay anyone else, and I'll get it to you tomorrow.
Right Answer: I can't cover that right now. Can we work out some sort of payment arrangement? This is how much I can send you.
Why: Again, you're signaling to the vendor that if they push you hard enough, you'll get them the money even if you have to stiff everyone else to do it. This sets a bad precedent for the vendor in question and will likely get you into similar situations with your other vendors, creating a self-perpetuating cycle in which you have to pay your accounts in full in order to keep them operational. And what's the point in having an account if you have to pay it in full? Figure out what you can reasonably send them, and make them an offer. The worst they can do is say no.

Vendor: I appreciate the $3,000 a week you've been sending me, but I need to have $10,000 from you no later than Monday.
Wrong Answer: Okay, I'll get it to you somehow.
Right Answer: Let me look and see what I can juggle around. I'll get back to you later today.
Why: If you tell a vendor you'll send them the money they're asking for without even consulting your budget, you're indicating to them that you have the money whether you've got it or not. Instead, go back and re-work your payment schedule and make a reasonable offer based on what you can afford without completely destroying the rest of your plan. Of course you want to try to accommodate your vendors in special situations, especially if they've accommodated you, but you need to be reasonable about it, too. If your first proposal isn't acceptable, you can always go back to your cash management plan and re-work it again. And if meeting their needs simply isn't going to be possible without you stiffing or shortpaying somebody else to whom you've promised some cash, don't be afraid to tell the inquiring vendor that you need time to make phone calls before you can make an arrangement. Your other vendors have likely been in the same

situation, and will understand if, this one time, you need to make a change in your scheduled payment.

Vendor: I appreciate the $3,000 a week you've been sending me, but I need to have $10,000 from you no later than Monday.

Wrong Answer: Well, I can't raise ten grand that fast, so I guess you'll have to cut us off then.

Right Answer: Okay, I've gone over my budget and moved some stuff around. I can send you $5,000 on Friday and another $5,000 next Wednesday, so you should have it before the end of the week. Will that work for you?

Why: You almost never want to tell a vendor that you don't have the money or any reasonable expectation of getting it. There should always be some sort of negotiation, even if what you're offering is a really bad deal. Having a lousy plan is still about ten times better than having no plan at all.

Day 1:
Vendor: May I have your Accounts Payable, please?
Answer: She's not in right now; may I take a message?

Day 2:
Vendor: May I have your Accounts Payable, please?
Answer: Um, she's at lunch – can I take a message?

Day 3:
Vendor: May I have your Accounts Payable, please?
Answer: She's on another line. Can I have her call you back?

Day 4:
Vendor: Yes, can I have your Accounts Payable, please?
Answer: She's gone home for the day. Can I have her call you tomorrow?
Vendor: Well, this is the fourth time I've called her this week, and she still hasn't called me. Will you tell her, please, to call me tomorrow?

Day 5:
Vendor: I need to speak to your Accounts Payable person.
Answer: She isn't available right now. Would you like her voicemail?

Vendor: No, I think I need to speak to her supervisor.
Answer: Um…

What's right and wrong with this scenario:

There's nothing wrong with putting off talking to a vendor if you have a good reason for doing so. Maybe you're expecting a check in a couple of days and you're hoping you'll have good news for them. Maybe you said you'd send them a check but you didn't, and you haven't figured out what to tell them yet. Maybe the strain of taking collection calls has finally gotten to you and you just don't think you can handle it before you've had a long bath and an even longer cry.

But repeatedly refusing to talk to your vendors only serves to make them angrier and more likely to want to put restrictions on your account. Not only are you wasting their time day after day, you're not giving them answers, and in general they would rather have crappy ones than none at all.

The upside is, apart from actually paying them, there is absolutely nothing you can do to make your vendors have confidence in you than to pick up the phone when they call. Because if, unlike the dozens of other customers they may have tried to contact that day, you're willing to talk to them, then things can't be that bad.

And here's the thing to remember: your suppliers already know you have cash flow problems. It isn't a secret that you can keep from the people you're supposed to be paying. So most of the time it's okay to share with them where you're at – to a point. No, you never want to make it sound as though you're two steps from bankruptcy, even if you are. You never want to freak out on the phone and start ranting about how you don't have any money and can't pay your bills – and yes, I have heard people do that. It doesn't help anyone. But to a certain extent, you can tell them the truth, and quite often, they'll understand – after all, it's quite likely they've been there themselves.

Here are some good reasons to put off talking to a vendor for a few days, and some good ways of telling them why:

1) I will be updating my Cash Flow spreadsheet on Wednesday, can I call you back Thursday?

2) I'm just reviewing my Accounts Payable now; can I call you back later?

3) I haven't had a chance to reconcile your account; may I call you back towards the end of the week?

4) I didn't have you scheduled for anything until late next week, but now it looks like we might be getting a check on Friday and I may be able to send your payment sooner. Can I let you know then?

GET YOUR PAPERWORK IN ORDER

Nothing trips up a good cash management plan faster than discovering a giant bill that was processed incorrectly, or that you filed away accidentally without entering it. It happens more often than you would think, and the larger your volume of A/P, the more likely it is that someone will get into a groove and stamp a bill as "entered" without saving it into the system. It's also quite common for bills to be entered with the wrong date, or the wrong due date, so that they might not show up as being due for weeks after their actual due date. A bill may be entered with the wrong invoice number, or under the wrong vendor, so that it appears as the thirtieth invoice in the line of invoices due when it should be the tenth, or doesn't appear where it should be at all.

You absolutely must have procedures in place for preventing these types of errors, or for catching them when they inevitably occur. Why? Because, especially if you have a drawer full of A/P, you're unlikely to discover the error until the vendor calls seeking payment, at which point the bill may already be 60 or 90 days past due. An old outstanding invoice like that invites scrutiny of your account, which you likely don't want, and worse, as I explain later under UNDERSTANDING YOUR VENDORS' TERMS, many firms have policies in which cutting off your account is very nearly automatic when even a single invoice reaches a certain point in their aging schedule. Then you are virtually forced to pay off that old invoice right away, wrecking the rest of your planned payment schedule, and all because of some stupid paperwork error. DON'T LET THIS HAPPEN TO YOU.

RECONCILE YOUR VENDORS' STATEMENTS EACH MONTH

If there's a discrepancy between their records and yours, find out why. If you're missing invoices, call to request copies. Some vendors may take this as an opportunity to inquire about your past due balance, but in my experience, this happens rarely. Very often invoice requests are handled by clerks, or in some companies, even salespeople, so you may not even have to speak to the person who's truly in charge of your account to get a duplicate invoice. If you really need to be sure to avoid speaking to someone, fax or email your request, have someone else in the company handle it, or call and leave a message with your request for a faxed or emailed copy after they have gone home for the day, which works very well, especially if you're in different time zones. But if you do need to contact your A/R person directly, don't fret. Most will be happy that you're taking an active interest in properly maintaining your account and won't use that as an excuse to give you a hard time.

STORE BILLS IN ORDER

Many companies don't bother to do this, and there's no good reason why. They will have to be assembled in order eventually when you make payments, and if you put them in order when you put them away, you will be far more likely to realize it if something's missing. This is particularly important if you work in a company with more than one accounting person. Not everyone follows the finer rules of alphabetization, not everyone has the best eyesight, and invoice numbers, especially those with both alpha and numeric characters, or those that are too long to fit in your system, may be recorded differently by different people. In general, I prefer to organize invoices alphabetically by vendor, then chronologically by date, which will likely also correspond to the numerical order and the ascending due date. The most crucial aspect, however, is to make sure you store your bills in an order in which they will be easy to match what shows in your system or on your vendor's statements.

REVIEW YOUR PAPERWORK REGULARLY

In addition, I highly recommend taking your weekly check run as an opportunity to review the physical paperwork you have on hand. This may not be feasible in bigger companies or if you have large numbers of bills from one particular vendor, but for most of you, it should be possible physically to flip through the stack of bills as you're making payments. If you then match those to what shows up on your Accounts Payable aging, you will know at once if something is missing. Here is the procedure I use with my weekly check run to ensure that my A/P balance remains error-free:

1) Print a current Accounts Payable Aging in alphabetical order by vendor. (Your software may offer better report options, but this is a standard that everyone should have available. In Quickbooks, I prefer to use their Unpaid Bills Detail, but that is a matter of preference.)

2) Use that report to update my Cash Flow Plan with any new information.

3) Print out a copy of my Cash Flow spreadsheet for the current week, with the rough amounts I plan to pay to each vendor clearly visible to me.

4) Go to my A/P cabinet and, one by one, go through each alphabetical file, pulling bills that correspond to the dollar amounts I need as I go. Reviewing each file in full allows me to spot bills from vendors that aren't on my schedule – especially those one-offs I don't pay very often and which may be buried somewhere under "Miscellaneous" in one giant file. In addition, this will help to ensure that I find any outstanding credits, which, because of their numbering, sometimes show up in not-so-obvious ways in certain reports, and will also allow me to match them to the physical invoices to which they apply (see UNDERSTANDING YOUR VENDORS' TERMS, later).

5) Return to my desk with my pile and pay bills on my computer, making sure each bill matches the information contained in my software. Assuming I've stored my invoices in order, it should then be easy for me to see if I have a physical invoice and no corresponding entry, or, conversely, if I have a bill in my system with the wrong information or that's somehow gone missing.

6) Correct any errors and update my info accordingly.

Your procedures may vary based on your setup and software, but the concept will be the same, even if your office is entirely paperless. Make sure the records in your system match the records from your vendors, and your Accounts Payable system will run much more smoothly.

CONSIDER THE DETAILS BEHIND THE BIG PICTURE

I've written multiple times in this volume about the importance of having a plan, and understanding the big picture of your Accounts Payable is a large aspect of this. Too often companies get overwhelmed by the day-to-day management of overdue bills, and that's understandable, because they really can take over your life. And oftentimes, too, companies get so caught up in looking at the big picture that they can't see the details behind it.

"I have to save all of our money to cover our payroll."

"I'll pay this bill because it's more overdue than this one."

"I'm not going to pay this company because I can buy that product or service from someone else next time I need it."

"I can't pay the hardware store because I owe so much to the lumber yard."

These aren't unreasonable objections, but they can result in disaster, and here's why. Because it won't do you any good to be able to cover your payroll three weeks from now if you can't give your employees the supplies they need to get their work done.

When it comes to cash flow, dollar amounts do matter. Of course it's important to prioritize, to make sure that the more critical bills get paid before the less critical ones. But what good does it really do you not to pay the $200 you owe to the hardware store so that you have an extra $200 to pay on the $10,000 bill you owe to the lumber yard? I'll tell you what good it does – none. The lumber yard will be completely unimpressed by your two hundred bucks, and you'll piss off the hardware store and look pathetic for not paying such a small bill in the process. And don't kid yourself that your cash flow problems are your dirty little secret. Word gets around about who isn't paying their bills, and that can make both your current suppliers and potential new ones reluctant to extend credit to you.

I will be detailing my process for dissecting the big picture in the forthcoming CREATING A PLAN volume of this series, but for the moment, think of it this way – you want to tick off as few people as possible for the least amount of money. In practice, this usually means paying your small bills, and negotiating extended payment schedules on your big ones. Your hardware store doesn't want to futz around with you over the couple of hundred bucks you might spend with them in a month if they think they might not collect. But your lumber yard has a deeply vested interest in making sure you keep spending your monthly ten grand with them, and that is going to make them more willing to accommodate you – even when it means accepting extended and otherwise unacceptable terms.

And as for the argument that you can get away with not paying vendors you don't use anymore? Don't be so sure. Remember that every time a vendor calls you, it's costing you money you don't even have. It takes time for your employees to deal with those telephone calls, it takes time to deal with collections, and the end result is, you usually end up having to pay anyway, often with interest and penalties to boot. If it's a large balance, you can be relatively assured that it's going to go to collections, which may harm your credit and will still leave you in debt. Most of the time you'll be better off negotiating terms or a settlement. And if it's a small balance, then it may be more expensive for you to pay your employees *not* to pay it than it is simply to pay it. So don't simply ignore the $50 you owe to some office supplies company from which you ordered a specialized type of photo paper. If you pay your bookkeeper $30 an hour (which, with payroll taxes, worker's comp, and health insurance, probably costs you closer to $40) and he or she has to take a dozen different phone calls to avoid dealing with it, the bill could have paid for itself. In the long run, merely carrying that $50 on your books is going to cost you more than simply sending a check. And, as I discuss in the MANAGING PERSONNEL volume of this series, forcing your employees to take collection calls day after day is one of the surest ways to get them to leave you – which may cost you thousands of dollars in hiring and training new ones.

UNDERSTANDING YOUR VENDORS' TERMS

This is the most technical segment of this volume, and if you are unfamiliar with accounting software or how vendor terms work, you may find some of the details difficult to comprehend at first. If you're a very small company using mostly subcontractors and don't have a whole lot of formal A/P, terms might not be as relevant for you. However, if you're a mid-sized company with a decent volume of Accounts Payable, putting these concepts into practice has the potential to elevate your cash management from bad to good, good to great, or great to absolutely fantastic.

Have you ever wondered why your suppliers call when they do? Collection calls may be prompted by any number of factors, some of which are directly related to activity on your account:

1) Your latest order puts you over your credit limit.

2) They don't want to fulfill your latest order until you send payment.

3) They haven't received the check that you promised them.

4) They received your check but it was less than they expected.

5) Your subcontractor finished a job last week and will call every day until she gets paid.

Often, however, the calls you get are what you might call "routine" collection calls, and these are the phone calls your suppliers make on past due accounts in conformity with their personal habits or formal company procedures:

1) Your vendor always makes calls on Fridays.

2) Your vendor begins making calls on the previous month's outstanding invoices on the 15th of the month.

3) Your vendor calls once your invoice is more than 30 days past due.

4) Your vendor calls just before your new statement is about to go out.

5) Your vendor calls every three days on a past due invoice until you send payment.

These are terms in the very broadest sense, and understanding those terms and how they affect company policies will go a long way towards helping you maintain your credit with your vendors. Because as we will see, there's more to terms than what's stated on your bill – and understanding those nuances can make the difference between keeping your accounts and losing them.

For those of you who aren't terribly familiar with terms, here's an overview. In essence, "terms" define when your payment is due. If your rent is due on the 1st of the month, then its terms are "Due on the 1st." If your cable bill is due 30 days from the date of the bill, then its terms are "Net 30." In the business world, service providers – these would generally be your independent contractors – commonly have terms like Net 1, Net 10, or Due on Receipt, which means that payment is due in one day, ten days, or as soon as a bill is received. Product suppliers are more likely to have terms of Net 30, Net 60, or even Net 90 – the general principle being that it takes more time to sell and get paid for inventory so that you have the money with which to pay your supplier. In fact, companies with lengthy inventory turnover times sometimes use this as a bargaining chip in asking for extended terms, especially if they're placing a large order to take advantage of a bulk discount.

It is also worth noting that, with some variations, it is a fairly common practice in the industry for accounting personnel to interpret bills without stated terms as Net 10 for independent contractors or Net 30 for other suppliers, and you should feel free to point that out to vendors who come looking for money immediately when no terms were specified on their bill.

Other terms can be more complicated, particularly when dealing with suppliers who offer prompt payment discounts. A common discount term is 2% 10th, Net 11th, which means that if you pay by the tenth of the month following your statement, you get a 2% discount. If you don't pay by the tenth, your bill is due in full on the 11th. It's incredibly important to examine terms carefully, because subtle differences can vastly vary their meaning. A variation on the preceding example would be the term 2% 10, Net 11. This would mean that if you pay the bill within 10 days of its date you get a 2% discount; otherwise the balance is due in full 11 days from the date of the bill.

Terms can be awkward and very confusing. Most modern accounting software has the ability to allow you to pre-enter discount terms; however, because different companies have different policies on discounts, the automatically generated results are very often incorrect. For example, some companies will discount a straight 1% for prompt payment, whereas others may apply the discount only to the purchase price and not to the shipping, and still others will exclude sales tax when applicable. I highly recommend manually entering discount amounts on a bill-by-bill basis unless you're very confident that your software does it correctly for any particular vendor.

COMMON TERMS	MEANING
COD	Cash (or check) on delivery
Due on Receipt	Due on presentation of invoice
Net 1	Due 1 day after date of invoice
Net 10	Due 10 days after date of invoice
Net 30	Due 30 days after invoice date OR Due 30 days after statement date
2% 10, Net 11	2% discount if paid within 10 days, due in full 11 days after the date of the invoice or statement
2% 10th, Net 11th	2% discount if paid by the 10th of the following month, due in full on the eleventh

WHY NOT TAKING YOUR DISCOUNTS IS COSTING YOU OODLES OF MONEY

You may be wondering why I'm even talking about this, because if you're strapped for cash, you're hardly going to be taking advantage of early payment discounts, right? I mean, what do you care if you get a couple of bucks off of a $200 invoice?

Mathematically, you should care, because generally speaking, not taking a prompt payment discount is *very* expensive. Let's take the example of 2% 10th, Net 11th. If you don't pay that bill by the tenth, then borrowing the money for an extra day costs you 2% that you could have saved had you paid the bill on time. With 365 days in the year, 2% interest for one day equals an annual rate of 730% interest!

Of course, in real life, you're rarely going to be paying on the 11th if you've already missed the discount deadline. But let's suppose you still have to pay by the end of the month to keep your account in good standing. Now the 2% that you didn't save essentially bought you an additional 20 days in which to pay off your bill. You can calculate how much this is costing you pretty quickly. Since there are 365 days in a year, a year consists of roughly 18 20-day periods. 18 times 2% equals 36% – still higher than even the most exorbitant credit card rate.

As you begin to get a handle on your cash flow, it therefore stands to reason that one of your first steps will be to start taking advantage of discounts – honestly, you can't afford not to. If you do miss a discount deadline, it then behooves you to postpone paying the invoice as long as possible in order to minimize your loss on the discount, as this will reduce your hypothetical interest rate. The idea of paying a bill not only promptly, but early, may initially terrify you, and that is a common reaction. It can be tremendously difficult to wrench yourself out of the pattern of paying everything as late as you possibly can. But developing a habit of taking cash discounts can be a significant step in overhauling your overall cash management plan, and having a mathematically sound system will make it easier for you to prioritize payments to vendors who offer discounts – after all, that's why they have them. But don't be afraid to start small. Take the $4 off that $200 invoice and pay it on time, because even if your cash is a mess, you can probably afford to do that. See how good it feels to know you saved a few bucks and got that bill off of your Accounts Payable Aging, and pretty soon, you'll be ready to do more.

THE UNSTATED SIGNIFICANCE OF VENDOR TERMS

As I outlined above, many of the reasons vendors call you looking for payment aren't entirely related to activity on your account. More often they are related to company policy, and only in a loose, backhanded way, to your vendor's terms. Thus the A/R person who always calls you on Friday may have to prepare a report on expected incoming cash for every Monday. The one who calls when your bill is 30 days past due quite likely calls everybody once their bill is 30 days past due. The one who calls just before your new statement goes out may be trying to clean up your account before it hits the new month. These types of calls may have little to nothing to do with you – except for the fact that you haven't paid them.

Why does it matter? Because garnering an understanding of your vendor's procedures may give you the means of working around them – decreasing the frequency of those collection calls and scrutiny of your account. And a vendor who doesn't have to call you, or prepare reports that involve your account, is a happy vendor, one who will stay on your side.

To understand this, it's vital to know how most accounting departments function. A very small company may have only a bookkeeper who is in charge of both A/P and A/R, a mid-sized business may have separate individuals handling these functions, while a larger company may have different levels of personnel within departments, from an A/P clerk who codes and assembles bills, all the way up to a Controller, who will determine what gets paid when.

In addition, it's important to understand how companies determine who is past due. Most of the time, this information is garnered from Aging Reports, which essentially disclose how much money is owed and how long ago it should have been paid. Most accounting software generates reports breaking down balances into Current, Over 30 Days, Over 60 Days, and Over 90 Days – and if your company is in Over 90, that usually means trouble.

(Incidentally, although I cannot prove or quantify this, it has been my impression that larger, corporate-type businesses are granted more leeway for late payments than smaller sole proprietorships. Therefore, although I refer here to bills that may be 90 or even 120 days past due, you may personally find that your suppliers' tolerance runs very thin by the time you hit the 60-day mark, or, conversely, you may be allowed to lapse until 180 days without having a serious problem. There are ways to "ease" your suppliers into granting you more time over the long haul – see USING PATTERNS TO YOUR ADVANTAGE, above.)

In addition to variations in reporting and staffing, different companies may also have variations in the manner in which they apply and interpret their terms. For example, you may have a vendor whose stated terms are Net 30, which, for many vendors, means that the bill is due 30 days from its actual date. However, many other vendors interpret Net 30 as meaning bills are due 30 days from the *statement* date, so if they issue a statement at the end of the month, payment is due before the end of the following month. Understanding this difference this can make a huge difference in your cash flow, because if you place a $5,000 order on the first of the month under the first scenario, the bill has to be paid within 30 days. Under the second scenario, you have nearly 60 days in which to pay it before you're deemed late, because that bill won't appear on your statement until the last day of the first month. In the first case, you could place a large order on the last day of the month and it wouldn't make much difference in how soon you needed to pay it, because it would still be due in 30 days. In the second situation, however, you would want to avoid that if at all possible, because it would severely shorten the time you have to come up with the cash. If that invoice is included in your end-of-month statement, then it will be due in 30 days. Wait until the first of the following month to place that order, and you'll have a full 60 days before you need to pay for it.

What difference does it make? If you haven't paid the bill by the 61st day, who cares whether it shows up as Over 30 or Over 60?

Your suppliers do, that's who. Because in most companies there's a world of difference between those two columns, and it all has to do with Aging Reports and the people who are responsible for maintaining them.

YOUR A/R CONTACT CAN BE YOUR WORST ENEMY – OR YOUR BEST FRIEND

If you're working with an independent contractor or other individual who provides a product or service for you, then you may be dealing directly with that individual on matters of money without the "middleman" of an accounting department. But most suppliers – especially if they're handling inventory – will find it necessary to engage professional staff for billing and collecting, and that means that you'll be dealing with an individual whose job it is to manage your account and then report on its status to management. And if you're not in a position where they're going to have good things to report, then it behooves you to make sure that they at least have nothing bad to report. Because if you put your A/R contact in the uncomfortable situation, month after month, of having to explain to their boss why they haven't been able to collect on your account, then they will very quickly grow to despise you, and that does not bode well for your firm.

Again, the key point to absorb here is that one of the most effective ways of managing money is effectively to manage the people who handle that money. Remember that the continued survival of your open account doesn't depend on how much you owe or when it was due – it depends on your supplier's tolerance for what you owe and when it was due.

So once again put yourself, if you will, into the shoes of your supplier. Even if they're not like you, even if they don't really need the money, they have people working for them whose jobs hinge upon them meeting certain performance criteria – such as not having a huge balance in the "Over 90" column. These employees are generally expected to pursue collections of past due accounts vigorously – and it can get them in trouble if they don't deliver.

So what does this mean for you? Well, you may find that your vendors' A/R personnel may be quite lax with you if you keep your balances low enough and new enough to keep them out of trouble with their own bosses – and their stated terms won't necessarily tell you where that point is.

HOW TO DETERMINE WHEN YOUR BILL IS REALLY, REALLY DUE

What does all this mean for the unfortunate A/R person who's trying to collect money from you? It all depends on how their company operates. Their system may show that you're late on the 31st day following Net 30 and they may have to contact you right away. Or their system may not register that you're unacceptably late until after the end of the month in which you didn't pay. Even periods may be interpreted differently by different systems. Over 90, for example, doesn't necessarily mean that you're 90 days past due; it can also mean that the invoice is 90 days old. And the interpretation matters a great deal, because some vendors won't harass you until you're in their Over 90 column – however they translate that – and you can avoid a lot of problems if you know precisely when that is. Also, like the term Net 30, 90 days may mean 90 days, or it may mean the end of the month in which you became 90 days overdue.

Think about it. If I have a bill dated January 1st and I want to stay out of trouble with my vendor, this is a critical difference. My invoice will be 90 days old on April 1st. If it was due on February 10th, it won't be 90 days past due until May 10th. And if it was due February 10th, but won't "count" as 90 days past due until the end of the month, then I may really have until the end of May to get it paid.

These are huge, huge differences in when your bill is really, really due. You may have paid someone by April 1st because that's the date when your bill became 90 days old, when, in fact, you didn't really *need* to pay them until the end of May. Conversely, you may be in trouble because you paid your bill in May, when you really needed to pay it by April 1st.

Notice that this has nothing to do with the stated terms of the bill. The hypothetical bill was still technically due on February 10th; what I'm talking about here are the dates by which they truly need to be paid to keep you on good terms with your vendor.

And aging is only part of the story. Some companies care more about dollar thresholds than aging; I have seen situations where one vendor will aggressively try to collect a $200 bill that's only three days overdue, while another may disregard a $1000 bill until it's gone past 120 days, whereas the reverse may also be true. Other companies may not be too concerned if you're overdue as long as you're not bumping your credit limit, but they may cut you off even if you're current once you've hit your ceiling.

The point is, if you can glean an understanding of those unstated company policies, you may be able to prevent a large percentage of those collection calls – and nothing is going to make an A/R person more willing to accommodate your needs than if you make their job easier.

Suppose, for example, that one of your vendors has terms of Net 30. Now suppose you notice that their A/R person always calls you the last week of the month regarding your bills that were due the previous month. So if you had a bill dated April 15th that was due May 15th, they may not begin actively pursuing payment until the end of June. In this case, you can be fairly confident that their collections policy is based on customers whose bills have hit 60 days during the course of the month (which would have happened here on June 15th), meaning that the bill you incurred in Month 1 has not been paid although it is now the end of Month 3. (This initial contact, however, will often be a routine "touching base" type of collection call – it's when you get the same call in Month 4 that you're likely in trouble.)

So how can you use this information to your advantage? Well, suppose it's June, your bill is several weeks late, but you're finally ready to pay it. You want to make sure you send that check out so that the A/R person on the other end receives it before they make their end-of-month calls – probably about the third week of June. Then they won't have to call you, and instead of it looking like you sent payment only because they initiated the contact, you will have sent it voluntarily, which makes a much better impression with your vendor's staff.

Conversely, if it's only the first week of June and you're trying to decide whether to pay this vendor's bill or someone else's, you can use this information to help make your decision. Now you know that you don't *need* to send the check to this vendor until the third week – so maybe the other vendor should receive the earlier payment if theirs is more urgent.

In other words, you don't always have to be concerned with trying to pay your bill on time, because you weren't going to be able to do that, anyway. Instead, your goal can be to stay one small step ahead of your suppliers' collection schedule – and very often, that can be a very achievable goal.

The trick, of course, is that rarely do you simply want to ask your vendor, "Hey, how long do I really have to pay you before you cut me off?" Sure, you can say that to the telephone or electric company and not run into problems, but most of the time you want to avoid saying that to a supplier because:

1) It gives the impression that you don't know when or if you'll have the money.

2) It suggests that you want to take maximum advantage of their generosity in letting you slide.

They, in turn, are rarely going to want to tell you outright, "Hey, don't worry about it! I know our terms are Net 30, but as long as you pay us within 120 days, you'll be totally fine!"

There are exceptions, of course. If you really need to know the absolute last day you can pay someone, by all means, ask them. If they have a hard and fast deadline, very often they'll tell you.

But most of the time you will need to glean this information by listening and paying attention – and if you're already behind on cash, you should very quickly be able to gather the data you need. If you have too many suppliers to track in your head, then keep a list of dates on which your vendors contacted you and the invoices they were calling about. You can then look at the bill dates and due dates and relevant dollar amounts and piece together a good approximation of what their collection schedule might be. If you can't determine a pattern, don't worry – they may be following a schedule based on "when I get around to it," in which case they are likely not your most aggressive vendor when it comes to collections. And, of course, don't feel as though you have to track this data for every single vendor, although that could eventually prove useful. It's more important to gain an understanding of the company policies of those you use most often, as those larger accounts are the ones most likely to have past due balances and to require your most careful attention.

WHEN YOUR VENDORS ARE MOST LIKELY TO TRY TO COLLECT
As soon as your bill becomes past due
When your bill becomes 30, 60, or 90 days past due
Monthly, before they issue their monthly statements
During the same week every month
When your account exceeds or is approaching your credit limit
When they receive your check and it's less than they expected
Randomly, or when they need the money

DON'T LET INVOICE DISPUTES GET YOU IN TROUBLE

In the GET YOUR PAPERWORK IN ORDER section, above, I detailed the importance of making sure that your Accounts Payable records match your vendor's, because missing invoices and such can cause your account to be abruptly past due without you even being aware that there's a problem. The same thing can happen with invoice disputes, and even a $20 discrepancy can get you in big trouble pretty quickly.

Very often, especially in medium and larger-sized businesses, there are disputes over billed invoices. Perhaps the bill doesn't match the purchase order, the wrong amount has been charged, a duplicate item was sent, shipping was supposed to be free, the item has been returned, etc. These disputes may involve several levels of personnel, from accounting to purchasing and even to salespeople, and any acceptance or rejection of a disputed amount may require approval from management before a bill can be paid. As a consequence, these invoice disputes tend to drag on and on between companies, often taking months before being successfully resolved.

This is bad enough on its own, and a potentially big headache for accounting departments, which may have to send requested documentation back and forth multiple times in order to resolve a discrepancy of less than $100. Some companies, in fact, will simply shortpay a disputed invoice in the hope that the supplier will adjust it on their end, as they sometimes do. This is usually not a big deal if your account is otherwise current – but it can turn into a big red flag if you're not.

Depending on the company's policy, having a *single overdue invoice* in, say, the Over 120 Days column, can prompt a review of your entire account – which means that all those other nasty past-due balances will be subjected to scrutiny, too. You can be totally right in terms of the dispute, but now your account shows as seriously past due, and as a consequence you may even find yourself being forced to pay a disputed invoice just to keep your account open. All in all, it's bad news.

I have seen accounts cut off because an $11 shipping charge hadn't been paid. I have seen large accounts that were otherwise current put on hold because of one disputed invoice that got too old. I have seen accounts that were closed all together because a single bill or a part of a bill wasn't remitted. I have even seen credit denied ten years after an event because of one disputed invoice that wasn't paid – which can be a potentially serious problem if your product has limited suppliers.

Most of the time, you don't want to pay for disputed items just to prevent headaches with your account. But you do need to make darned sure you stay on top of them, because they can lead to far bigger problems than the often petty dollar amounts that are in dispute would suggest. Have procedures in place for promptly handling disputes, routinely review those that are in process, and get them off your account. If you absolutely cannot come to agreement, then seriously consider proposing a compromise settlement, or, if the error is egregious, no longer using that vendor.

OTHER TIPS AND TRICKS FOR MANAGING VENDORS

DON'T LET YOUR LOCAL VENDORS COME TO PICK UP THEIR CHECK

You don't want to let your vendors get into the habit of thinking that they can come by and pick up a check. You may think you're helping by getting them paid more quickly, and it's okay to break this rule on special occasions, but in general you will be setting a very bad precedent. If you let them do it once, they'll assume they can do it every time, and many independent contractors, especially, will use this as a means of applying pressure for payment. And it works, too. I can't tell you how many times I've gone into the office and been told that I need to cut a check for some subcontractor because he or she contacted the owner directly and was told, sure, you can come pick up a check – without regard to whether I could actually cover it. (This, incidentally, is why it's important to employ strict separation of duties in financial management, as I discuss in the MANAGING PERSONNEL volume of this series.) Many subs, too, will take that check down to your bank and immediately cash it – either because they need the money or because they're afraid it might bounce – which completely eliminates your float of those funds.

Use any reasonable excuse to avoid establishing this pattern. If you have a small firm and are in and out of the office, it may not be practical for a vendor physically to come by as there may be no one to meet him or her. Maybe the boss is out on a job and won't be around to sign checks. I don't even mind telling vendors that I'm sending their check so that they'll have it, but I might not actually have the funds available to cover that check before Monday, so there's no point in their wasting their time coming to get it on Friday. Make it tough for your vendors to come pick up a check, and eventually, they will stop asking. And the bottom line is, a mailed check is simply more professional for all parties concerned, and it eliminates some of the fear suppliers have of getting a bad check because they pressured you to cut it for them.

OPEN NEW VENDOR ACCOUNTS DURING YOUR FLUSH TIMES

Even when your credit stinks, it's frequently possible to acquire new open accounts with vendors who are anxious for business. Having a selection of suppliers can help make it possible for you to spread the wealth – or lack thereof – over multiple vendors, so that each account won't be quite as late or quite as over its limit. Don't overdo, it, though. Remember that the more money you routinely spend with a vendor, the more of a vested interest they will have in financing you, and you can't build those kinds of relationships if you simply take your business to someone else every time and then don't pay them, either. That being said, it doesn't hurt to create new accounts for new purchases when you know you can pay them, because, like making small on-time payments on your credit cards, this will help to establish your credit with a new business. And that can be vital to your survival when you find yourself needing a backup plan for maintaining your cash flow.

DO YOUR A/P CHECK RUN ONE DAY A WEEK

This is a common practice in the industry and won't raise many eyebrows among professional people. There are many small companies that will cut one or two checks a day, or when they have money, but this is highly inefficient as a process, and will also have the unfortunate side effect of leading your vendors to believe that you can and will cut them a check anytime.

If you only run checks one day a week, by contrast, it's a lot tougher for your suppliers to argue that you must pay them sooner without seeming completely unreasonable. Few vendors are going to demand a payment on Monday if you cut checks on Thursdays, which can buy you several precious days before you need to worry about making payments. If you're dealing with an independent contractor or other vendor with very short terms – say Net 1 or Net 10 (see UNDERSTANDING YOUR VENDORS' TERMS, above) – you will automatically buy yourself time in making payments if you restrict your check run to one day a week. If you don't receive their bill before you do your weekly check run, then naturally they aren't going to get paid before the following week, and sometimes those extra days can make all the difference. In addition, if they were slow in sending an invoice, it becomes their fault, not yours.

Personally, I like to tell people that I cut checks on Fridays, although realistically, I more often actually cut them on Wednesdays with a planned mail date of Friday. The weekend, with its no mail on Sundays, gives me a buffer if I need to hold a check until Saturday or Monday.

INSIST ON HAVING YOUR PAPERWORK IN PLACE

You don't want to get so nit-picky about this that it starts to look like you're making excuses for not paying your bills, but you should always have an invoice and any supporting documentation before making a payment. This applies to subcontractors, too, some of whom can be sloppy about submitting their paperwork, and then are unpleasantly surprised when you're not prepared to remit their progress payments. Get them in the habit of formally invoicing you, and you'll accomplish three things:

1) You'll force them to have to sit down to create a document for you, which will often delay their demand for payment.

2) You'll have fewer surprises, because instead of relying on your Project Manager to tell you when a payment is due, you'll already have the documentation.

3) You'll have a better paper trail and ultimately, better accounting.

DON'T BE AFRAID TO TALK LIKE AN ACCOUNTANT

Perhaps the most wonderful – and painful – aspect of proper bookkeeping lies in the many steps involved in the process, each of which can buy you time with your vendors. A larger company may have multiple layers of accounting personnel each bill has to go through before it's even eligible for payment, from the person who opens the mail, to the person who matches the receiver and purchase order, to the person who enters it into the system, to the person who actually decides what to pay when. And then someone still has to cut the checks and match them to the documentation, which may need to be verified yet again before they're given to the boss for signature, and then given to someone else to mail and to file. In a small company, one person may be responsible for all of these processes – but it's still a lot of processes, and you shouldn't hesitate to use that to your advantage.

There's nothing wrong with explaining to a vendor that their bill hasn't been coded or that the purchase order is missing or that the checks are sitting in a pile in the boss' office, but she's been too busy to sign them. Especially with vendors with very short terms, make them understand that you're a professional company, and regardless of what your business may have done in the past (e.g., writing checks on demand), you now have formal accounting procedures in place and it's simply unreasonable for them to expect their payment to be ready within two or three days. They may not like it at first, but once you've lowered their expectations, they will generally go along with the change.

DON'T CUT CHECKS AND THEN HOLD THEM UNTIL YOU HAVE THE MONEY

Many businesses seem to find satisfaction in having written checks to their suppliers, even if they're unable to send them. The problem with this practice is that it then becomes very difficult to determine 1) How much cash you really have on hand, and 2) How much you really owe your suppliers. The bank balance as well as the A/P balance in your accounting software will be affected by that check as soon as you write it, which means that you will then need to make manual adjustments in order to track the true amount in either account. I have seen numerous instances where bookkeepers will be sitting on a stack of checks in a drawer, some of them weeks or months old, and then they'll have to make a manual list of the checks that they're holding in order to be able to figure out how much money is actually available in their bank account.

This is a cumbersome and error-prone process, and it gives no comfort to a supplier when you tell them you've had their check in a drawer for six weeks. Don't get me wrong – I am highly in favor of sending checks out last minute, and there's no reason why, if you paid your phone bill with the previous week's check run, you can't hold that payment for a few days if it isn't actually due yet. But to make the long-term retention of cut checks a standard business practice will only confuse you, and will accomplish nothing in terms of your vendors.

AVOID REMITTING PAYMENTS ELECTRONICALLY

There are certain payments that you most definitely do want to schedule online, such as for your credit card bills. Any payment that absolutely must be remitted by a certain date or else it accrues penalties and late fees should be scheduled for that date, as this is actually safer and more beneficial for you than mailing a check, which you then have to send extra early to make sure it gets there on time. But when it comes to your vendors, in most situations you want to play it old school. As soon as you've mailed them a check, you can tell them that you've mailed a check, which is nearly as good as them having your payment in hand. But you'll still have a few days before they receive it, possibly a few more before they deposit it, and more after that before your bank clears it.

You lose all that with electronic payments, and if you think you're saving yourself the cost of a stamp and an envelope, don't be so sure. The cost of the labor involved for your accounting person in logging in to your account, entering the information and making the payment, then printing out the paperwork and matching it to invoices can be substantially greater than the cost of cutting a check, and is not necessarily any more green.

DON'T PAY THE LATE FEES

If you don't have a long history of making late payments, and you miss the deadline on a credit card bill, then by all means call in and request to have the late fee removed – frequently they will grant you a "courtesy waiver," saving you forty bucks in exchange for the few minutes you spent on the phone with them. This often works, too, with car payments and such, but only if you don't make it a habit. And frequently, even if you routinely pay late, it will also work with your vendors. They may never actually waive the late fees or interest they have applied to your account, and sometime down the road, you may get stuck paying them. But I have yet to see a vendor attempt to collect on an account based solely on outstanding late fees. Therefore, you can usually get away with not paying their interest or late fees as long as you continue to pay your regular bills. And oftentimes, if you do catch up, your vendor will eventually waive them as a mark of goodwill. Conversely, if the amounts are small and you want to get them off of your statement, you can offer to pay them as your own goodwill gesture, even if it's against your usual company policy. If it's only a few dollars, then you may be benefit more from coughing it up, and having no charges outstanding from a previous month, than you will from refusing to pay and carrying that balance forward.

PAY YOUR CREDIT CARDS IN FULL AND ON TIME

It sounds obvious, but many companies fail to do just that, to their great detriment. More and more vendors are accepting credit card payments, and it may behoove you to find out which ones will do so without charging a fee. Then you can take the money you were going to send to the vendor and use it to pay down your cards instead, which you can then use, in turn, to pay your vendors. Doing this will save you late fees and interest, improve your credit rating, and possibly get your company card up and running again if it's been so maxed out of late that no one can use it. And once you get on a cycle of making full payment, it can be far easier to maintain than you would have guessed.

Also, as a side note, if you sign up for one of those low APR deals, make sure you understand the terms of the offer. Most of the time, any payments you make on a card with both a promotional APR and a standard APR for different types of transactions will be applied disproportionately to the promotional APR charges. In other words, the payments you make will pay off the low-rate balances first, leaving you still paying interest on the higher-rate ones. If you're going to borrow money that way, max out the offer on the one card and then don't use it for anything else until the promotional period expires. And if in doubt, ask. Credit card companies will tell you how they apply payments, so you don't need to go into it blind.

DON'T BE AFRAID TO MAKE PAYMENTS

I referred to this strategy earlier as the "We're broke, we're broke, we're broke, so we're not going to pay anything" tactic, and most of the time, it will make your life miserable and needlessly screw up your A/P. Yet countless companies suffer from this very fear, and a paralyzing fear it can be. It can send you into a veritable panic, and it can be tough to persuade yourself to pay a supplier when you don't know if you're going to be able to cover payroll next week, which is why it's so crucial to have a good cash management plan. Because otherwise, it invariably ends in the same way – the firm pays nothing except on demand, and then they're stuck paying off much if not all of their balance, which ends up costing them more than if they'd just sent a smaller payment in the first place.

And don't think you can afford not to sweat the small stuff. I once saw a multi-million dollar company lose its Yellow Pages contract because it didn't pay the two hundred bucks a month to maintain it. That company could no longer advertise in the phone book. Over two hundred dollars a month that it didn't pay. I have a saying that I like to use when confronted with problems like these: "If I only paid bills we could afford to pay, I wouldn't pay anything." Pay them anyway.

HAVE FAITH IN YOUR PLAN

There's a great deal of confidence to be derived from having a solid cash management plan, even when it translates into shortpaying everybody. The mathematical certainty, the knowledge that, for the moment at least, your numbers add up, will make it possible for you to approach your vendors with the force of conviction, and that is just as important as having your columns of figures all end in black. If you believe in your plan, if you believe that you know what you're doing when it comes to your cash, then your vendors will, too. And that will give you a powerful edge in negotiating your way through the difficult times, and establish for you a reputation of paying your bills and getting back on your feet.

VOLUME 2: MANAGING PERSONNEL

INTRODUCTION

In Volume 2 of the *Managing Cash When You Haven't Got Any*
series, I discuss how to make the best use of your personnel in
maintaining good cash flow. I will tell you:

How employing strict separation of duties between management and
financial personnel will help to keep you out of trouble with your
vendors.

Why one person should act as the official contact person for matters
regarding your company's finances, and why it should not be the firm's
owner.

How financial personnel and management can cooperate in making
sound financial decisions.

How to bridge the gap between operational and financial personnel,
and how good communication between these departments is
absolutely vital for companies struggling with cash flow.

The pros and cons of telling your employees about your financial
situation.

The risks and costs of employee turnover: how to hold on to your
employees during bad times, and how to handle it when you can't.

The benefits of assembling a team with a variety of strengths and
weaknesses, and how to leverage these in managing your cash situation.

How to turn losing your bookkeeper or other Accounts Payable person to your advantage.

What to look for when hiring new employees for your cash-poor firm, and why the candidates who are best qualified on paper won't necessarily meet your company's needs.

Practical measures for protecting your company against the sudden departure of a difficult-to-replace employee.

HOW EMPLOYING STRICT SEPARATION OF DUTIES BETWEEN FINANCIAL AND NON-FINANCIAL PERSONNEL CAN IMPROVE BOTH YOUR CASH FLOW AND YOUR OPERATIONS

It's common in small and mid-sized companies for the lines delineating the job duties of various personnel to become blurred. Your Sales Manager doubles as your Office Manager, your Billing Clerk as your Administrative Assistant, or your Owner as your one-person clean-up crew. This happens more often in smaller firms because there simply aren't enough employees to assign to each individual job. As a result, employees tend to learn and even accept responsibility for multipl e aspects of the firm's operations, even when they are not required to do so. This is great, and even necessary in certain environments. If a restaurant stays open until midnight, but sends its dishwasher home at ten, then of course servers or cooks have to step in to run dishes. If a company has three people at work in its office and none of them is the receptionist, then naturally each of them has to be prepared to answer the phone. But when it comes to cash flow, allowing your non-financial personnel to deal with money issues, even tangentially, can harm your company in insidious ways and is a practice best to avoid.

It's rarely intentional. Few field or retail or service employees go out of their way to stick their noses into the financial side of the company, although sometimes this is unavoidable in the normal conduct of their business. It's quite natural in the course of writing or signing contracts that outside suppliers and service providers want to know when they will get paid, and equally natural, when the expected check doesn't arrive, for them to approach their primary contact with the company to find out why. And because your employees are accustomed to taking responsibility for functions that aren't necessarily theirs, they may not realize how attempting to handle these inquiries themselves can create problems for your firm. Indeed, they may even believe that they're helping you – the finance department is overworked, isn't it? Surely that's why those checks haven't gone out!

Your non-financial personnel don't know very much about your Accounts Payable system, and are unlikely to understand how it functions. They don't know how long it takes for an invoice to pass through your entire matching / approval / bill payment cycle, even when there's plenty of money with which to pay it. They sometimes seem to believe that bills go unpaid simply because the A/P person hasn't gotten around to printing the checks, and they may not realize that their paycheck was only good this week precisely because those bills did go unpaid. And because of this lack of understanding, they are far more likely to make promises to your vendors, either express or implied, which can derail the basis of your cash flow system and even wreck your carefully prepared cash flow plan.

I can't even count how many times this has happened to me. I come back from lunch and find an invoice on my desk for hundreds or even thousands of dollars with a note on it that says, "Please pay ASAP." Or "I told him I'd bring him a check on Friday." Or, worst of all, "He will be by to pick up a check this afternoon." I think the one that killed it for me was the cabinet bill for $15,000 that the Project Manager told the cabinetmaker would be paid the next day. The company had maybe $2,000 in the bank at the time. Never again!

These aren't willful errors on the part of your personnel. Perhaps your company has always done business in this carefree, haphazard manner, and if your cash flow issues are a comparatively new development, your employees may not realize that it is simply no longer possible for you to run your finances this way. Your non-finance people may never have had to work in an environment where money was chronically and critically short. All they see is a firm that's been in business a long time, that's busy, that looks successful… there must be plenty of money in the bank, right?

The fact is, they simply have no idea of the level of pain and suffering incurred by your owners and managers and financial people, the agonizing that goes into cutting those checks every week. And even if you don't want them to know about that (see SHOULD YOU TELL YOUR EMPLOYEES YOU'RE BROKE?, later), it still behooves you to ensure that their offhand remarks don't inadvertently make finance's job even more difficult – as they often do.

It's the nature of any business that people are more likely to want to deal with people they know – in fact, that's often the cornerstone of a successful small business. Those of you who have been in business a long time probably still have clients who insist on placing their orders directly with you – even if you now have a fleet of people working under you whose job it is to do just that. Your employees know this, too, and those whose positions revolve around these types of personal relationships work very hard at building and maintaining them. An independent contractor who has been treated well by your firm is far more likely to show up for an internet emergency than one who hasn't, just as another company's sales guy is more likely to cut a deal for your sales guy if your sales guy always buys from him directly, thus augmenting his commission. If your employee routinely refers potential clients to a firm with whom you do business, that firm is going to have a vested interest in making sure that employee continues to be happy with its work – leading it to maybe let your company slide on that questionable warranty item. In turn, if your sub or supplier finds that they're having difficulty getting a check out of your front or back office, they're quite likely to bypass your A/P department entirely and talk to the person they know – your employee. And if your employee consistently gets great deals and great service from that vendor, then naturally he or she will want to help them in turn – especially when that means ensuring that they get paid.

This isn't always inappropriate. Sometimes you do have to prioritize payments in the interest of maintaining good relationships between your employees and your vendors, and this may become necessary if, for example, your supplier is holding hostage a desperately needed shipment, or your sub decides to stop work pending payment. In such extreme situations, your employee may be able to offer invaluable input or even smooth things over with your supplier. But far more often than not, these types of situations devolve into cases of the squeakiest wheels getting the grease, and if you allow it to continue, the squeaky wheels will get even squeakier while the other wheels freeze up altogether because they're not getting oiled at all.

Your employee, however, does not have access to your full financial picture and won't see that side of it. They won't see that their valued vendor can only get paid if someone else's doesn't – they'll only see that their relationship is in jeopardy, and precisely because they're a good employee, they'll want to do their best to maintain it. It can be far too tempting, therefore, for your employee to try to act as a go-between for you and your vendor. Those of you who have been in the role of the employee may have used phrases such as these yourself when a vendor approached you regarding a past due payment:

1)   Let me see what I can do.

2)   I'll try to get you a check before the end of the week.

3)   Let me check with the front office and find out why there's a holdup.

And that right there is the heart of the problem: because of the personal nature of their working relationship, YOUR EMPLOYEE IS PERSUADED TO SPEAK AND ACT IN THE INTEREST OF THE VENDOR, NOT IN THE BEST INTEREST OF YOUR FIRM. Indeed, without even being aware of any wrongdoing, your employee has created a situation in which he or she is positioned as the good guy who defends your vendor from the evil greed of the penny-pinching finance department, and this is precisely the impression you do not want to give. Why? Because if you read the first volume in this series, DEALING WITH VENDORS, you'll realize that everything your employee is telling your vendors runs exactly counter to what you want them to hear – and you may not even know that they heard it.

Let's examine the impact of statements like the above from your vendors' perspective:

1)   The employee is my advocate – only through her intervention can I hope to get paid. In future I will be sure to approach her directly, and since she responded to my pressure so well on this occasion, next time I should start bugging her sooner.

2)   She's saying I should be able to pick up a check by Friday, so I will definitely get paid no later than early next week.

3)   If the employee is telling me that there's a holdup with my check, then this must be an unusually long delay in my

receiving my payment. In future I can probably expect to get paid far more quickly.

In essence, the vendor is very rapidly developing wildly optimistic expectations on when they'll receive payment, both now and in future, which ultimately can only lead to their anger, disappointment, and possibly even reluctance to continue to do business with your firm. And unfortunately, none of these things that your vendor is thinking have any relationship to the reality of what's going on in your office:

1) Your employee has – or should have – little control over whether a particular vendor gets paid. These decisions are – or should be – made on a company-wide basis as part of a strictly controlled cash management plan.

2) There's almost no chance that this vendor is going to get a check this week, and more likely not for two or three weeks. Now your finance department has to work damage control on the error and possibly even make your employee look bad for having misspoken. Her misguided attempt to maintain a good relationship with this vendor may ultimately end up making it worse.

3) By terming the delay in payment a "holdup," your employee has made it sound as though there's been an error in processing the past due invoice, or that your finance department has not been properly doing its job. Not only does this give a poor impression of your firm, but now you have to go back and gently persuade the vendor that the delay is perfectly normal and no cause for serious concern over whether they will eventually get paid.

In other words, your employee's good intentions have paved a rather unfortunate road – and now it's your job to yank your company away from the fire and brimstone before it gets burned.

The first step is re-education. Even if you wish to keep your employees in the dark (or at least in the twilight) about the true state of your financial affairs, they need to be instructed as to how such behaviors interfere with the proper operation of your finance department and may subvert the financial health of your company. As I discuss below, one of the most important aspects of proper cash flow management is BRIDING THE GAP BETWEEN FINANCE AND MANAGEMENT, so that your managers and clerks and salespeople are more keenly aware of the challenges faced by your financial people, and vice versa. And in practice, various members of your team will all contribute to making your cash management plan a success (see SUCCESSFUL CASH MANAGEMENT IS A COOPERATIVE ENDEAVOR, below). But as far as your vendors and other creditors are concerned, your financial people *are solely and fully in charge of making disbursements* – no matter what your employee might have implied or told them.

Insofar as it possible, therefore, you want to relieve your non-financial staff of any responsibility for managing money. If inquiries regarding outstanding invoices come their way, they should be politely referred to your accounting department. Your employees can be instructed to say "This is our new policy" or "I've been told to tell people to contact them directly" or "I don't handle that end of things; let me give you the direct line for accounting." Your employees should never be permitted to make promises of payment, or to authorize cash or COD payments that exceed a pre-determined dollar threshold without consulting your financial person or people. And except in highly unusual circumstances, they should *never* serve as the contact person for vendors seeking payment.

Why am I so adamant about this? There are several reasons:

1) It's inappropriate. You wouldn't let your accounting person make sales or manage your wholesale department – why would you permit your salespeople and department managers to handle your money? Don't let the boundary lines between jobs get trampled or blurred, not when it comes to your precious cash. If your bookkeeper only comes in once a week, you may feel awkward about telling your vendors that they have to wait until then for an answer regarding a payment. But if you've got a cash flow situation, this is exactly what you should be doing – *use* the fact that your bookkeeper only comes in once a week as a reason to postpone giving an answer. Don't be in a rush to respond because you feel that you have to – let your vendor wait until so-and-so comes in

to do payroll, ask him or her get back to them then, and be grateful that you have such a ready-made reason to create a delay. This will buy you some time while keeping your finances firmly under administrative control. Let your operational personnel focus on operations and your financial personnel handle the money, and your company will run much more smoothly.

2) Your non-financial people are more likely to try to give away the farm. First, because they don't know how many bills you have to manage, they don't know the details of your cash flow plan, and they therefore don't have the firm grounding of figures in front of them telling them that the company can't possibly pay some vendor's invoice within the next three days unless you discover a money tree growing in your backyard. And secondly – they have to work with these people. They're far more likely to encounter vendors at their place of business or at a job location, and when that vendor begins to ask about payment, your employee doesn't know what to say. Did a check actually go out last week or was it held until this week? What if your firm hasn't paid them at all? Oh, and now a customer has entered the store, the company truck is parked outside, and your employee really doesn't want to be talking about this anymore, so he tries to end this conversation as quickly as possible. "Um, yeah," he says, blushing, "I'm pretty sure a check went out for that." And then he crosses his fingers behind his back and hopes for the best. Don't let your employees get stuck in an awkward position that can ultimately be damaging to your reputation. Train them to redirect all inquiries to your office and your vendors will eventually learn to stop pouncing on your employees for information.

3) Your financial people are not only better mentally prepared for sudden inquiries and attacks by vendors, but owing to their position – which is often behind closed doors, or in a back office not readily accessible to your creditors – they're better physically prepared, too. Your office workers can check the Caller ID and decide not to pick up the phone if a vendor is

calling and they're not prepared to talk to him yet. Your financial personnel can take a moment to look at the status of a vendor account, make a final decision or consult with the owner on whether to pay this person or that one, or prepare a well-thought out response before returning a vendor's phone call. Your non-financial people rarely enjoy such luxuries when dealing with vendors. They are therefore far more likely to respond with the aim of pacifying the creditor at whatever cost to your company, particularly if the successful performance of their own job depends upon that vendor's compliance. Your financial people are generally removed from face-to-face interactions and are therefore able to detach themselves better from confrontations, permitting them to make planned, rational decisions rather than hasty, emotional ones.

4) They can't answer those questions, and that can be uncomfortable and embarrassing for them. One of my earliest accounting jobs was working under a Controller in a small firm. The Controller was the type who responded to vendor inquiries by never taking phone calls, and it was my job to tell vendors who inquired that I had no information for them regarding their payment. Needless to say, this was a sucky position to be in, as I was forced to take all of the abuse regarding payments about which I had absolutely no information and over which I had no control, and getting no answers never did much for the vendors, either. If your employees handle vendor inquiries, they're likely to end up in the exact same unfortunate position. They can't explain why the front office hasn't been able to cut a check for $200, nor can they guess when it might happen. Take away their responsibility for even trying and they'll be much happier, and so, ultimately, will your vendor.

5) It can harm your operations. If your vendors feel as though your employee is not doing enough to ensure that they get paid, they are far more likely to be resentful towards that employee, which can harm their working relationships. If resentment is unavoidable, it ought to be reserved for the

people who are in charge of the money – they're in a better position to take it, and it's far less likely to turn into a personal grudge.

6) If something goes horribly wrong on the financial end of things, the employee with whom your vendor has a good working relationship won't get blamed. Your financial people's relationships are generally with other financial people, not with other firms' salespeople and workers. Therefore, if the situation goes south, the only people likely to be affected are the financial personnel on both sides. If your employees have no relationship to finance, they won't get stuck in the middle of any ugliness or dispute. They'll generally be able to resume normal relations with their personal contacts, often before the financial issue is even resolved, leaving those important operational relationships virtually unharmed. (Incidentally, the reverse is also true. When management has a dispute over contracts or terms or invoices, the relationships between the financial personnel of the two companies concerned can usually escape ill effects, even when accounts become dangerously past due. In this situation, it's best to advise the vendor seeking payment that your department has been instructed not to pay owing to some management dispute and that they will need to check with the appropriate party on their end on how to proceed. You should be prepared, however, to play catch-up pretty quickly once the dispute is resolved and any unpaid invoices become, once again, your problem.)

WHY YOU NEED A DESIGNATED FINANCIAL MATTERS PERSON – AND WHY IT SHOULD NOT BE THE COMPANY'S OWNER

If you're a sole proprietor with no employees and a bookkeeper who only comes in once a month to tally your receipts, then of necessity you will also be in charge of your firm's financial matters and the following advice may not help you. But for everyone else, selecting someone to be at least nominally in charge of making disbursements will offer you a number of very practical advantages in managing your cash flow.

Note that I am making a distinction here between the people who effectively manage a company's finances and the person who operates as the official check-cutter or contact person. Owner(s) and other management personnel certainly should not be excluded from making financial decisions – in fact, as I discuss below under SUCCESSFUL CASH MANAGEMENT IS A COOPERATIVE ENDEAVOR, effective cash management requires input from a range of personnel and departments. But as far as your vendors are concerned, the boss should not be the person to contact when they're looking for money.

There's a surface logic in putting the owner in charge of the company's finances. In a small business, owners generally have their fingers in all of the pies that make up their company, and it's therefore reasonable for vendors to expect owners also to have a solid handle on receipts and disbursements. Owners who started small may also have been forced into performing the role of financial contact person because when their company began, it consisted of no more than two or three people, and the owner, as the only check-signer in the firm, naturally adopted the task of managing money. Subcontractors and suppliers with whom the company has done business likewise became accustomed to dealing directly with the boss regarding money matters and often continue to expect the same treatment.

The problem is that the owners of most small businesses suffer from the same disadvantages as non-financial employees when it comes to managing money. Even those who are adept at cash management will encounter difficulties being the "face" of cash management because of the pressures peculiar to their position. It's incredibly difficult for the owner of a company – who may have spent many years cultivating the relationships on which his or her business is based – to take a hard line when it comes to making payments. It can be humiliating for a long-time business owner to have to admit that he or she simply doesn't have the cash to cover a check to a supplier who may by now be his or her personal friend. Owners may therefore be more likely to acquiesce to vendor demands, even when doing so may be detrimental to the cash position of the company. Furthermore, it's a lot tougher for an owner to leave himself some "wiggle room" than it is for an employee. When vendors deal with financial people, they're well aware that the A/P person doesn't sign checks and that their promised payment will still have to be approved by the person who does. But in a small company, the boss is the check-signer; there's no higher level, and no way of delicately extricating oneself from a decision if the owner gets stuck in a corner during a high-pressure meeting or phone call.

Some business owners think it's degrading to have to defer a vendor inquiry to someone else. It's their business, after all – shouldn't they be able to answer questions regarding their finances and make payment decisions off the cuff if they like? Of course they should. But they'd better be darned sure they can do what they say. Because it is far *more* degrading to have to call a vendor back and tell them you're unable to remit a payment you promised them because now you've checked with your bookkeeper and you're three hundred bucks short of being able to cover their check. Your system worked fine when you had money. It doesn't work so well now that you don't.

The bottom line is that if the boss is in charge of making payments, then the boss will get blamed when those payments don't come. Of course, the boss is ultimately responsible no matter who is in charge, but by gently deflecting responsibility away from the company's owner and onto a designated financial person, you can help to preserve the working relationships the owner has developed at such time and cost. In other words, you're again creating a separation between finance and management, so that when your financial relationships suffer, your operational relationships don't have to fall apart, too.

Remember, too, that in a larger company, an owner would almost never be in charge of handling vendor demands for payment. Accounting and finance are generally not their areas of expertise, after all, nor are those usually the reasons they got into business. And there is nothing in the least bit demeaning about telling people that your company has gotten big enough where you have to have a person assigned to handle those routine financial matters – or that this simply isn't how the owner wants to spend time she could be spending meeting with clients and growing her business. Instead give the owner a financial role more suited to her position as the person in charge. Make it her job to act as a supervisor – the person in charge of approving invoices or payments, and of making tough decisions when no one else knows what to do; make her the person who smooths things over with vendors when the financial situation gets out of control. Vendors who always speak to the boss about money won't be impressed when he gets on the phone. But a vendor who only ever speaks to Accounts Payable will know that their concerns are being taken seriously when they're connected to him directly for once. Your financial person can handle the everyday stuff; let your owner act as Controller or CFO.

Now if the owner has a history of responding to vendor inquiries – especially if he's a soft touch – you may need to nudge your vendors into accepting a change in the system. Here are some delicate ways for the owner to extricate himself from the mechanical aspects of managing vendor payments without sounding as though he's evading responsibility:

1) I don't know the answer to that offhand. Let me have you talk to my bookkeeper; he keeps track of all that.

2) We'll be going over the Accounts Payable on Thursday; can I have my Controller get back to you then?

3) I don't really handle that kind of stuff anymore – from now on, could you contact my Office Manager directly?

4) I know we have you scheduled for a payment, but I don't recall precisely when it's going out – let me have someone in my accounting department get back to you with that information.

And if the idea of turning over the day-to-day management of your already shaky finances to someone else perturbs you, remember that there's a difference between giving up control and giving up *nominal* control. Owners can still have as much actual control over their company's cash as they like. But by surrendering nominal control, they will no longer have to deal with vendor inquiries and the potential hazards those may entail – such as not knowing exactly how much money is in their bank account on any given day. Instead, those inquiries can be referred to a designated Accounts Payable person who, whatever level of responsibility they bear for making financial decisions, can serve as the primary source and repository of information regarding your cash.

HOW MUCH RESPONSIBILITY TO GIVE TO YOUR FINANCIAL PERSON

Your financial person is not necessarily the person in your company who is best suited to deal with making decisions regarding the company's cash flow. Even if your firm can afford a Controller, his or her cash management skills may not suit your present-day needs, and in practice, those tough decisions on what to pay when may be better made by the company's owner or by upper management. You want to be wary, too, of granting too much power over your finances to one person because of potential fraud issues, although these risks are mitigated so long as the duties of approving payments and signing checks remain assigned to the owner. (Incidentally, you should *never* allow your bookkeeper to become a check signer on your account, and you ought to be wary of one who asks for this privilege. If your firm needs a second check-signer, give that responsibility to another owner or responsible key employee, one who has no relation to finance.)

However, the nature of the financial person's position will inevitably demand that your bookkeeper or accountant be heavily involved in the cash flow planning process. Your bookkeeper knows how to work your accounting software, your bookkeeper knows how much money is in your bank account, your bookkeeper knows when your credit card payment is due and how much your weekly payroll is. Your bookkeeper will likely be the employee who makes most or all of the calculations that relate to your cash flow, and who will perform the physical acts of processing payments and checks. He or she is generally in the best position to give answers to inquiries regarding your cash flow because he or she has the easiest access to that information, and to make management aware of big picture items such as upcoming expenses that may not necessarily be reflected on the reports that management sees. It is desirable, therefore, that financial people at least be included in the payment decision-making process, even if it is not their area of expertise, if for no other reason than because they know things that no one else in the company does.

How much responsibility you choose to give to your financial person in managing your cash will vary greatly depending upon their level of skill, experience, and knowledge of your operations and industry. Owners or managers may wish to receive weekly reports on outstanding bills and choose what payments to make all by themselves, or they may let their proven financial person make most of those decisions and only intervene if there's an objection or problem. Perhaps the best course is for owners to ask their financial people to use their intimate knowledge of the cash situation to prepare a detailed cash flow plan, which management will then review and either change, reject or approve. But however you decide to proceed, one principle is clear – if you want your cash flow to be manageable for all sides of your business, then personnel from all sides of your business must all work together in managing it.

BRIDGING THE GAP BETWEEN FINANCE AND MANAGEMENT

In firms where cash is not a huge issue, there's often little interaction between financial and management or sales personnel. Non-finance people simply presume that product can be obtained, that customers can purchase on credit, and that orders can be made and will be paid for in a timely fashion. This works fine as long as your company has plenty of cash – but it can be a disaster when it doesn't.

You financial people who are reading this know exactly what I'm talking about. You walk into your office on Monday morning and find a copy of a field check for $1100 on your desk, signed by a department manager. You don't know how you're covering your payroll that week, and somebody spent over a thousand dollars without even telling you. How are you supposed to do your job in that kind of environment?

You can't. And ultimately, neither can your managers or salespeople, because it is going to prove very embarrassing to them when you're unable to come up with the cash to cover that check – or those you have to write to your employees.

SUCCESSFUL CASH MANAGEMENT IS A COOPERATIVE ENDEAVOR, OR THE IMPORTANCE OF EAVESDROPPING

Although your bookkeeper or other financial person may be completely in charge of the logistical aspects of your cash flow, and may also assume responsibility for many of the decisions that relate to it, this does not mean that maintaining cash flow is solely your financial person's responsibility. To work well, it should be a company-wide endeavor, with everyone from your lowest-paid delivery driver to your

CEO an active participant in making sure that cash flows smoothly.

In many firms, however, there tends to be very little direct communication between members of your financial team and other members of your staff. Any consultation that happens is likely to consist solely of inquiries regarding the approval or status of an invoice or check. In a medium-sized firm the bookkeeper may not even know about a new employee until he or she is requested to provide new hire paperwork, or about the impending bankruptcy of a big client until he or she sees the name vanish from the detail of open A/R. There can be a very firm distinction between what are considered management matters and what are considered financial matters, with neither being the concern of the other department.

This attitude, however, does not serve to foster good cash management, and the more cash-poor you are, the worse it will be. No, management may not technically have a responsibility to seek approval from the company bookkeeper to hire a new person who's sorely needed, but they should do it anyway because that bookkeeper needs to plan for a bigger payroll that won't initially be compensated for by higher productivity. Some people think that the loss of a client is a problem mainly for the sales department, but if finance doesn't know about it as well, then A/R projections could be way off and the firm's cash flow management will suffer accordingly.

And it works both ways. A Project Manager who's putting together a large order for the lumber yard may not know that your credit line is nearly maxed out with them. To your financial person this might be a routine blip that happens every month between payments and is not even worth mentioning. But if the Project Manager needs $10,000 worth of materials to start a project that's going to bring in $30,000 in the first week, then it behooves you all to make sure finance diverts a big chunk of the customer deposit to the lumber yard so that you can get that new project going. And the only way this can happen is if you communicate.

Yet it's tough to get people to do this, even when they want to, because Sales doesn't know what Accounting needs to hear or to know any more than Accounting knows what matters to Sales. There's a huge disconnect there, and it's caused not by a reluctance to share information, but by ignorance over what information even needs to be shared. It isn't that the right hand doesn't know what the left hand is doing – neither hand really knows what the other one does.

From a financial perspective, the absolute best remedy I have found for this information gap between departments is eavesdropping. Constant, shameless eavesdropping. Not of private or confidential conversations, of course – no, I'm talking about the kind of listening in you can do when you work in a shared office and are therefore privy to the conversations and telephone calls of the people around you. It's simply amazing what you can pick up that you need to know that no one thought they needed to tell you. Maybe your CEO just cut a major deal for discount on product that will go into effect in two months, or maybe that dispute with one of your vendors is turning into a lawsuit. Maybe one of your major suppliers got bought out and they're changing their terms or their personnel, which could mean that the A/R contact with whom you've built such a solid foundation is going away. Maybe one of the women in your warehouse is pregnant or one of the guys in your corporate office ran off and got married. This is not idle gossip; there will be new expenses for health insurance and maybe time off, or your firm may need to hire new employees to pick up the slack. This is all information that affects your finances and ultimately, your cash flow, and if your financial person is sitting quietly by herself in the back office doing her work, there's a good chance that she may not hear it until it's too late to make a new plan.

As time goes on, and the people in your company become more and more familiar with the type of information that needs to pass between sales, finance, and management, the more automatic, and ultimately, more useful, such information-sharing will be. Eventually your personnel won't consider hiring a new person or placing a large order without running it past your finance department first, and your finance department will routinely update management on the ongoing status of vendor accounts. But if your financial person is missing out on information he needs to hear, it might be time to consider a more direct approach to information-sharing, one that goes beyond merely eavesdropping.

WHEN EAVESDROPPING ISN'T ENOUGH – HAVE A MEETING

If you're a small to mid-sized company, then you should be able to set aside an hour or two once a week for a meeting of all of your key personnel. In a construction company, this might consist of your owner, project managers, and bookkeeper; in a wholesale environment you might include upper management and salespeople. You may already be holding regular meetings of this nature to review work in progress, any problems which may have arisen in the previous week and their solutions, how close your salespeople are to reaching their quotas, etc. What I am recommending here is that you make use of such meetings to introduce a more explicit financial component, and that means bringing in your bookkeeper or other financial person.

In certain fields this is not even optional if you want to have manageable cash flow. Any type of project-based company – residential construction, for example – can experience wild and sometimes unpredictable weekly variations in cash flow because of the nature of the inflows and outflows. If you have payments due on Start of Project and Completion of Demolition, you may be receiving large checks from your client literally within a few days of each other. On the flip side, if you have cabinets and tile being installed back to back, your budget may require huge cash outflows to the subcontractors doing the installations.

Your financial person, however, may not be aware of this. After all, he likely works mainly in the office and not in the field, and may not know that your countertop gal takes three weeks from templating to delivery and that she will expect a check on delivery. Even if he is generally familiar with the construction process, he is probably not going to automatically understand why one project may be ready for rough inspection in one week and another in six. And if historically, you've simply taken the tactic of dropping the bill on the bookkeeper's desk and expected it to get paid, you can no longer expect it to work that way once cash is an issue. Your company's cash flow plan has to be worked out weeks, if not months, in advance, and that means keeping your financial people up to date on aspects of your company that may have been largely irrelevant to them in the past. In turn, your financial people should make other key people in your firm familiar with their end of the process. After all, it doesn't help anybody if your Project Manager knows that you're going to owe the cabinet guy $15,000 next week and your financial person doesn't know it.

But even firms that don't experience these types of inflows and outflows can obtain tangible results from holding weekly meetings, for the following reasons:

1) Even the most fabulous cash flow manager can benefit from the knowledge, experience and input of the company's other key personnel – in fact, a willingness to learn from one's coworkers is part of what makes for great cash flow management.

2) It promotes the exchange of information. Without regular meetings it can be far too easy for your key personnel to forget to tell your bookkeeper not to pay such-and-such a vendor because there's a dispute, or for your bookkeeper to neglect to alert management that unemployment taxes totaling $10,000 are due the following month and that the company will need additional cash to cover them.

3) It forces regular examination of a company's financial status. When your firm is experiencing a cash crunch, you simply can't afford to wait for the quarterly Profit and Loss to come out before addressing any financial issues that may have arisen.

4) A regular meeting creates an opportunity for group decision-making, and important cash flow decisions should not be made in isolation.

Cash flow concerns can usually be addressed by merely expanding the scope of the routine meetings you may already be having to discuss operations. This works especially well in a project-based environment like construction because the current status of the project is inextricably tied – and often timed – to the income and expenses associated with it (see the forthcoming TIPS FOR CONTRACTORS volume of this series for an example of a customized meeting format designed for contractors). Generally, however, the cash flow portion of company meetings in any industry should contain the following elements:

1) A review of recent and upcoming income. If the company failed to meet projections over the last month or few weeks, key personnel should be made aware of this fact, as well as the consequences for the company's cash flow situation. By

contrast, if the firm has received large numbers of orders that can reasonably be expected to be fulfilled within the next few weeks or months, everyone needs to know this, too, because that means additional money coming in to your firm. Don't ever assume that your financial person has no interest in hearing about some aspect of your business because it has to do with operations and not cash. Operations are EXACTLY what your financial person needs to hear about because he or she will have no other source for that information.

2) A review of significant recent and upcoming expenses. This is a good time for the financial person to inquire whether there's an installation date yet on that expensive software upgrade your computers require, or to alert everyone to a vendor's meltdown regarding an unpaid invoice the previous week. The sharing of such information can help to ensure that all of your key personnel are aware of potential financial problems in the offing.

3) A review of your account statuses. If you're operating in a cash-poor environment, you know that one of the most commonly asked questions inside your office is "How are we with such-and-such a vendor?" This is a good time to report on any major changes to your usual answer to that question. Maybe the new A/R contact at one of your main suppliers is a real hardass and won't process any more orders until the account is under 30 days – is there another supplier you can use for that product instead? The retail store has to have a new printer right away – do you want to dust off the old Dell account, put it on the credit card if there's room, or finance it some other way? Is your sheetrock installer no longer returning management's calls? Maybe he's had it with your slow and late payments. This is an opportunity to discuss your alternatives and options.

4) A review of the current, past and future state of the firm. Are you in better shape overall than you were last week or last month? Are you in worse shape, but the projections for the next couple of months look really good? If your condition

took a serious nose-dive over the past several weeks, discuss why.

5) Periodic presentation of financial reports, to the extent feasible in accordance with the owner's desire for privacy (see SHOULD YOU TELL YOUR EMPLOYEES YOU'RE BROKE?, below). Financial reports are not merely created for accounting or tax purposes; they're chock full of gems that can give you an abundance of information about your company and clue you in on needed changes in your operations. As I will discuss in detail in the forthcoming CREATING A PLAN volume of this series, they can also tell you where your cash went – and you might be surprised to learn that it wasn't just burning a hole in your pocket.

Here are some examples of ways in which an open exchange of ideas and information between management (M) and finance (F) can help to improve your company's cash flow. All of these are based on real-world conversations I've had in the course of my career, all of which proved to be tremendously useful.

F: It's the third week of November, and so far our sales are way down for the month, which is going to make our A/R really short in December. Is there anything we can do to beef up our income before the end of the month?

M: How about if we run a promotion for the week after Thanksgiving? Twenty percent off on product sold by the 30th.

Or

M: I'll offer our salespeople a bonus incentive for product sold before the end of the month – an extra 5% in commissions on our profit margin.

Or

M: I don't think there is much we can do on short notice. I contacted our regular buyers last week and they've all used up their budgets for the month already. I do have a ton of orders lined up for December, though – will that help?

F: Well, it won't help me pay bills in December, but if I know I've got a bunch of money coming in in January, I can ask people to be patient with some shortpayments for a few weeks. They'll probably go along with that as long as they know in advance that the money is coming.

M: We could also try offering a cash discount, just this once. Customers who pay cash instead of running our invoice through their A/R get one or two percent off. That way some of them will pay us in December instead of in January.

F: Let's consider that. I'll estimate how much that's likely to cost us on one end versus how much trouble it will save us on the other.

***

F: I hear we just landed a big new client. Congratulations!

M: Thanks! The only trick is, I've given them extended terms – no payments for 120 days.

F: Oh. That's going to mess us up in the short term, then. Most of our inventory suppliers have terms of Net 60.

M: I'll call up my contacts and see if I can get us extended terms on invoices for this client in turn. The orders will be large – I'm pretty sure I can get them to agree.

F: Perfect. That will help out a lot.

***

M: One of our vendors is offering me a substantial discount if I order $20,000 worth of product before the end of the month. Can we manage it? The invoice would be due in 30 days.

F: Is this product we would need to order anyway?

M: We'll probably use most of it in the next couple of months.

F: Does it all have to be in one order, or can we split it up?

M: I'm not sure. I can check.

F: See if we can do that instead. It would be nice to take the discount, and if it's on product we're going to use in the short term, it sounds worth it to me. But it will work out much better on my end if we can break it up into smaller invoices that I can pay one at a time instead of all at once.

***

M1: Have you found someone to do the granite on that project yet?

M2: Well, I got two bids – one from our usual guy, and another from a new guy that was 10% less. The quality of work looks to be about the same.

F: What are the new guy's terms?

M2: He wants a 50% deposit before he starts work.

F: Hmm… well, what do you guys think? Our regular guy will let us slide a lot longer on payment, both on the front and back end. Are we still happy with him?

M1: Yeah, but he's pretty booked up for the summer, and remember how we had to wait to get him to do our last job?

M2: Yeah, I got the feeling he didn't want to do our project until he had a hole in his schedule. Not that I blame him. Prompt paying customers come first.

F: Right. Well, if this new guy's cheaper... Do we have other projects we might use him on?

M1: I've got one coming up that might work.

F: Well, if we think we might want to use him in future, maybe this is a good time to give him a shot. What do you guys think?

M2: Sounds good to me. But can we cover the deposit?

F: Not until next week.

M2: I'll tell him to send us an invoice. He's eager for the work; that should be good enough to get him started.

***

F: I need $15,000 by next Thursday to cover payroll, and since that couple bailed on that one big event, I only show $5,000 coming in next week. What can we do?

M1: I have a new event scheduled for next Thursday. That'll bring in $5,000.

F: Yeah, but we probably won't get the final payment before Monday or Tuesday, though, right?

M1: It's no problem. I'll let her know that I need to get a check from her no later than Friday, and that I'll come pick it up if necessary. If we get it in the bank right away, it should be fine, right?

F: Yeah, we should be okay. You're sure that won't be a problem?

M1: I'll make it happen.

F: Okay, cool. What else have we got in the works?

M2: I'm almost ready with the bid for that anniversary party. That will bring in a $3,000 deposit. They've basically approved it – the problem is, I can't finalize it because they haven't made up their minds on the centerpieces.

F: Hmm… any way we can hurry them along?

M2: Well, I do need to get their stuff on order pretty soon – I guess I can tell them I need a decision by Monday. But then we'll have to actually place the orders, and that will cost money, too.

F: Who are we buying from? One of our regular vendors?

M2: That depends. I got a lower bid from a newer company, but we don't have an account with them, so we'd have to do a check or credit card.

F: Let me have their contact info – I'll see if we can set up terms with them. That would make sense if we might want to use them again, anyway.

M2: Will do.

F: Okay, but we still need at least $2,000 more.

M3: I have a change order in the works that might cover that.

F: Really?

M3: Yeah. I don't know if they're going to go for it, though, and with so much other stuff going on there, I haven't had time to work out the numbers.

M1: Well, what if the three of us sit down and bang it out after the meeting? We should be able to put together an estimate pretty quickly if we do it together.

M2: Works for me.

M3: Okay, good. I'm meeting with them tomorrow afternoon to go over some details, so if I can have it ready by then, I'll present it to them and hopefully get a check.

F: Cool. Please call and let me know how it goes. If it doesn't work out, we'll have to come up with something else.

You can see from the preceding examples how vitally important it is for all of your personnel to contribute to maintaining adequate cash flow. Every person in your company plays a different role in its functioning; each has a different arena of knowledge and expertise. The more effectively you can bring together your various people and departments, the more effectively you will be able to manage your cash flow situation. What owners and high-level managers have to decide now is how much information they want to impart to their employees concerning their cash crunch, and whether they're willing to risk the consequences if they do.

SHOULD YOU TELL YOUR EMPLOYEES YOU'RE BROKE?

Perhaps one of the toughest questions any cash-strapped business owner has to face is that of how much to share with employees regarding a dire financial situation, and when to start sharing it. Many owners will say nothing to anyone until pay cuts and reductions in benefits become necessary; others may share this information immediately, but only with key employees; while still others believe that even their lowest-level employees ought promptly to be made aware of circumstances that will ultimately affect them. Unfortunately, there is no one-size-fits-all answer to this question that will satisfy everyone, and owners must ultimately weigh the risks of letting employees in on their dirty little secret against the potential rewards.

The risks are serious, and may include the following:

1) Increased employee turnover. Employees who fear for their job security are far more likely to seek employment elsewhere. Those who do may find that they can make more money at a new firm than they can at their old one, and where before your downturn, they might not even have considered abandoning you for an extra forty or eighty bucks a week, now the idea may have sufficient appeal to tempt them away. Even those who don't choose to actively seek other positions may begin the process of "keeping their eyes open" which can end in the same result, especially if time drags on and your situation worsens or does not improve. These employees may even end up following after ones who departed successfully for new firms at better terms, further conflating your woes. And not

96

only may you lose your most reliable and valuable workers, but now you may have to part with big chunks of your precious cash in order to replace them (see THE COST OF EMPLOYEE TURNOVER, below).

2) Growing employee demands for compensation and other benefits. Your increasing belt-tightening may ultimately have the same effect on your employees as it does on your vendors – your inability to cough up cash may prompt them to ask for even more. This may stem from multiple causes – a desire by employees to make sure they "get theirs" while it can still be gotten, a desire to acquire a larger piece of an ever-decreasing pie before anyone else can take a big bite, fear that their job may go away and a corresponding desire to build up their financial reserves, even a wish to bump up their current compensation package in an effort to obtain greater leverage with potential future employers. In short, precisely at the moment when you want to give away less, you may find your workers asking for more than ever before.

3) Word may spread that your business is failing. Work is one of the main topics of conversation both in the home and at social occasions, and no matter how well-intentioned they are, it's inevitable that your employees will either reveal or let something slip to their spouses or friends regarding your situation. If you live or work in a community where such things may become generally known – and even those of you who operate in large metro areas know how small such circles can be – this can pose a real threat to your business, even on top of the troubles you already have. Customers may be reluctant to start projects with companies that may not be able to complete them owing to financial woes, or they may fear that their money may go to pay off some debt instead of producing their product. Neither of these are irrational fears, and if word gets around and you lose potential clients because of it, they can be self-fulfilling.

By comparison, the potential rewards may seem smaller and more elusive:

1) Sharing your troubles with your employees may foster a spirit of camaraderie among your personnel and ultimately strengthen the bond between you and your workers. This is particularly true in very small companies with only a handful of employees and an abundance of "family" feeling. There is nothing like facing adversity to prompt members of a group to work together in the interest of defeating a common enemy, even when that enemy is economic forces at large. In fact, in these situations, *not* telling your employees your troubles can recast the owner in the position of "enemy," as your silence can create a wall with the penny-pinching boss placed firmly on one side and the hapless workers placed on the other.

2) Telling employees directly may stave off rumors that make the reality appear even worse than it is. No matter how hush-hush you try to keep your cash flow problems, there are certain things your employees simply can't fail to notice. Like vendors calling seeking payment, or holding up orders. Layoffs or reduced hours or employees who have quit that you haven't bothered to replace. The fact that you haven't yet fixed the glass in that broken window, or that a company car has been in the shop for three weeks because you can't afford to pay for the repair to get it out. Broaching the subject with your employees before their fears run away with them – especially if you have a solid plan in place for dealing with your cash flow issues – can go a long way towards restoring employee confidence in your firm and preventing employee turnover and the other problems I've outlined above.

3) Your employees can do a better job of assisting you with cash flow problems the more they know about them. As I discuss under BRIDGING THE GAP BETWEEN FINANCE AND MANAGEMENT, above, non-financial personnel rarely have a good grasp on your financial situation because it's usually outside of their active arena. The owner sighing and silently gritting his teeth in exasperation because a salesperson still hasn't closed that five-figure deal is not going to be nearly as effective as him saying to her directly, "I need

the first payment by Monday, okay?" There's a certain freedom that comes with having no secrets, both a freedom of speech and a freedom of action, and sometimes the benefits of those freedoms can outweigh the downsides of confessing those secrets.

4) You no longer have to carry the burden alone. Especially if you're a sole proprietor or the sole employee in charge of finance, when your company is having cash flow problems, it can feel as though the weight of the world has been firmly placed on your poor broken shoulders. It can be quite a relief to be able to offload some of that burden, not only emotionally, but in a practical sense as well. If you can delegate tasks such as completing sales, collecting payments, and working with vendors, you will be able to share the responsibility for keeping your company going with employees who may have nearly as much vested interest in it as you do.

Whether you're willing to run the risks in order to maybe reap the rewards will depend heavily on the nature of your business and the types of relationships you have with your employees. Can your employees take it? Do they deserve an explanation for your recent cutbacks? Will they find out anyway, so there's no point in keeping it from them?

When making your decision, keep a clear eye on your goal: protecting your business. Will your purpose be better served by enlisting the aid of your employees, or by keeping your secret? Will revealing the truth cause you to lose employees, or encourage them to stick it out and stay? Only you can guess the answer to this, just as only you can calculate the full cost of your workers leaving.

THE COST OF EMPLOYEE TURNOVER

We all know what it's like to lose a trusted employee, especially in a small firm. Apart from the hassle of having to find, hire and train a replacement, the departure may be physically felt at all levels of your business, giving your remaining personnel the odd sensation that something is missing. It's particularly painful to lose someone you liked because you were unable to provide them with the compensation or benefits you felt they deserved – especially when you add up the expense of bringing a brand new person on board.

A few years ago I had the opportunity to do just that, and to do it quite accurately, as I was integrally involved with every step of the process. That's because the person who was being replaced was me! Just before I became a full-time writer, I had, in addition to my private clients, two part-time jobs as the Bookkeeper/Controller for two different firms, working twenty to twenty-five hours a week at each. One was a fairly standard bookkeeping job, but with a number of specialized and customized elements, while the other was an incredibly difficult position that was more suited to a CPA or accounting person with an equivalent level of knowledge (but at a bookkeeper's pay rate). I had to be replaced at each of these positions, and here is what it cost each of the companies involved.

For the first job:

Primary employment advertising venue: Craigslist (Cost: $75)

Number of resumes received: 100

Resumes initially rejected: 80

Resumes of potentially acceptable employees sent by me to management for further screening: 20

Resumes sent to key employees for review and telephone interviews conducted: 10

In-person interviews conducted by me, the company owner, and two key employees: 6

This was merely the pre-screening process, and you can easily see how much company time it ate up. By the time I wrote the advertisement, reviewed the resumes, sorted out the potential candidates, printed copies of the most suitable resumes and then reviewed the positive and negative points of the leading contenders with key personnel and management, I already had ten hours into the process. Add in five hours for the telephone interviews and another five for the in-person interviews, and I'm up to twenty hours. Figure in another six hours each for the two key employees to review resumes and conduct interviews, and another eight for the owner to pre-screen as well, and we as a company had already invested about forty hours of labor in hiring this one person.

Not too bad so far – until you add in the training. I personally contributed the equivalent of three weeks of full-time training, with additional nominal training provided by other office employees and the owner in my absence. Then figure in the administrative time for doing new hire paperwork, adding the new person to the health and 401(k) plan, the cost of ordering and printing business cards, creating a new web profile and email address, and the inevitable learning curve a new employee experiences, and we racked up probably another 150 hours of labor in addition to the labor of the person we hired. In other words, in the first month, the new employee cost close to 200 labor-hours. Depending on the pay scale in your area and the amount of your labor burden (expenses on top of an employee's straight pay, such as payroll taxes, health care, etc.), this could easily translate into a cost of six to eight thousand dollars – and you didn't have any money to begin with.

Now what I haven't told you is that this was the expense associated with the *last* employee we hired – there were two others who came before her. One quit as soon as she found a job where she wouldn't have to work so hard at maintaining the cash situation, and the other proved incapable of managing cash effectively and had to be let go. The one who quit so quickly received hardly any training, but between the two who were hired and trained, the company still spent over 400 hours of paid labor in acquiring one employee – who, I recently heard, had to be replaced again two years later.

Because of the difficulty of the position, the situation at the other job turned out even worse. Rather than running the gamut of endless interviews and resumes, the company elected to use an employment agency, which cost $9,000 but included a warranty should our selection prove unsuitable. And well that it did, because all in all, we had to hire eight people before we found one that was capable of doing the work – eight separate people, to each of whom I had to devote several weeks of training before they gave up or I did. Over a period of more than a year, I probably spent thirty full-time weeks training people to do a job I could do in twenty hours a week. In other words, during that year the company had to cough up eighty hours of pay for every twenty hours of actual work. Depressing? You said it!

LABOR COST OF ACQUIRING A NEW EMPLOYEE – LOW END (@$30/HOUR)	LABOR HOURS	COST
ADVERTISING	1	$30
EVALUATING POTENTIAL CANDIDATES	1	$30
CONDUCTING INTERVIEWS	1	$30
NEW HIRE PAPERWORK & PROCEDURES	1	$30
TRAINING	16	$480
TOTAL	20	$600

LABOR COST OF ACQUIRING A NEW EMPLOYEE – HIGH END (@$30/HOUR)	LABOR HOURS	COST
ADVERTISING	8	$240
EVALUATING POTENTIAL CANDIDATES	24	$720
CONDUCTING INTERVIEWS	60	$1800
NEW HIRE PAPERWORK & PROCEDURES	8	$240
TRAINING	160	$4800
TOTAL	260	$7800

Not all of your employees are going to be so expensive to replace, of course. Not every position is going to require so much hands-on training, or so many members of your staff to interview and assess. But as this example makes clear, the expense can still be daunting, and the expense can be the least of your problems. What if I had been unable to stay on to train new employees before we found one who worked? What if I had simply given the customary two weeks' notice before I moved on to a new job and was entirely unavailable to do any interviewing or training at all? What then? Now imagine losing your foreman or your one salesperson and think about the immediate and potentially devastating effect this might have on your productivity or income, and at a time when there is no room in your budget for slippage or error, and you'll have the true picture of the cost of employee turnover.

On the plus side, smaller companies do have a certain advantage when it comes to employee retention. Employees often have a more personal relationship with the owner in a small company than they do in a large one, and may bond with their co-workers on a deeper level as well. Such employees may be willing to sacrifice a fair amount of compensation and fringe benefits in order to keep their place in a firm in which they, quite literally, feel at home. Those employees who stick with you may accustom themselves to the vagaries of your circumstances because they're happy in other respects. However, you may find it extremely difficult to replace those who do choose to move on, because your new hires simply won't have the level of loyalty that your old employees retain. Your new hires may not even stick around long enough to develop the fellow-feeling on which a lot of small companies depend, and this can worsen an already desperate financial situation. Your new hires, too, are far more likely to notice and be perturbed by conditions your current employees may have come to accept – and some of these are only indirectly related to your cash situation.

YOUR COMPANY IS NOT PLEASANT TO WORK FOR

Prior to your financial downturn, your company may have had the most cheerful, reasonable, and genial staff in the world. It does not anymore. The more readily you accept this, the easier it will be for you to combat the problem, and it is a very big problem. Why? Because it's incredibly stressful being constantly short on cash, and no one really wants to work in an unpleasant environment.

Everyone handles this type of strain differently. A boss who's a yeller by nature may yell more. A manager who internalizes may lie awake nights or sneak off to her office to cry. But it isn't only them, of course – every person in your company is affected, from the sales force which has to meet ever-increasing quotas to keep you afloat, to the workers who are expected to do the same amount of work in fewer hours for less pay, to your middle management people, who are responsible for ensuring that all of this is done on time and on budget. Even your most dedicated, loyal employees – the ones you know will never voluntarily leave – will suffer under the strain of worrying about whether the company might close. And the aura that emanates from the owner – especially in a small company, where he or she is likely to have personal contact with all or most of the employees on a regular basis – has a profound effect on the working environment, and that, in turn, is going to affect both your operations and your employee retention.

An employer of mine told me something once that's given me a great deal of food for thought. "You're good at all aspects of this job," he said, "But what's really made the difference for me in having you here is that even though we still don't have any money, I just don't have to worry about it anymore, because I know you're taking care of it. The stress was killing me."

And when I thought back on it, I realized just how right he was. The man had a congenial and rather cheerful personality, but when I had first come on board, he had been constantly irritated, worried and on edge. One potential office worker had even refused employment because, as she told the employment agency, "There was a lot of yelling" – which, as I had already learned, was the same reason my predecessor had left. Two years later, when the cash flow situation was firmly under control, my boss was his old self again – upbeat, charming, and a real pleasure to work for.

I'm not saying this to glorify my own accomplishment, although I'll admit it does give me a warm, fuzzy feeling inside to have had that kind of impact on a person's life. But it does poignantly illustrate what a difference having an effective cash management plan in place can make, because even if the company isn't making any more money, it's a far better place for everyone to work, employees and owners included. And a pleasant working environment means greater employee satisfaction, better employee retention, and a greater willingness on the part of your employees to stick it out through their tough times because they really like working for you.

It is not the point of this book to tell you how best to handle the strain of your financial worries on a day-to-day basis. Everyone is different, and for you the solution may involve hot baths, heavy metal, or a half-marathon run. The best solution I've found, however, is to take a proactive approach and really try to get a handle on your financial failures and on your cash flow. Nothing builds satisfaction and confidence faster than knowing you're tackling a tough problem – and that goes for how you handle your employees as well as your cash.

HOW CAN I AVOID LOSING MY EMPLOYEES?

Retaining your financial personnel under conditions of great strain poses its own special challenges and warrants separate discussion (see I'VE LOST MY BOOKKEEPER – WHAT NOW?, below). But given the expense associated with employee turnover and the fact that a cash-poor firm is at increased risk of losing its employees, an employer may find it desirable to expend additional effort to try to keep the employees it has. The catch, of course, is that while most firms use compensation and benefits to attract and retain their valued employees, yours lacks the cash to successfully implement such time-tested strategies. It may behoove you, therefore, to think outside the proverbial cash-box and come up with alternate ways of keeping your employees satisfied with their positions even when you're unable to pay them what you (and they) think they deserve.

GET CREATIVE

In Volume 1 of this series, DEALING WITH VENDORS, I detailed the three things your vendors most want to hear:

1) That you are going to pay them.

2) That you have a plan for paying them.

3) That you can tell them what that plan is.

In many ways, your employees are just like your vendors. They understand that businesses have good years and bad, and they understand that industries and economies have ups and downs. Most of them are not going to abandon you because one year you didn't give them an annual raise, any more than your vendors would cut you off because you once made a late payment. But, like your vendors, if your business never again becomes as successful as it once was and your cash situation becomes chronic, then they, too, may begin to feel cheated. They, too, may begin to worry that you will never catch up with the raises you promised them and that you will continue to reduce their already scant benefits. And just like those vendors who wonder if their unpaid bills will eventually get thrown out in bankruptcy, your employees also may wonder if ultimately, after sticking through all that with you, your firm will go under and they'll lose their job, anyway.

But your employees, too, can be reassured, and in much the same way as your vendors. They want to know that you have a plan; that you aren't merely keeping your fingers crossed while you hope for the best, but that you're *doing* something to address this cash situation. And like your vendors, they may be satisfied just knowing that you're making an effort, even if this means they have to wait on more money.

So get creative. If you've had to cut pay or benefits or you haven't been able to raise wages in three years, come up with some alternative, cash-conscious means of showing your employees you haven't forgotten them. Following are some great examples of how you can restructure your compensation or benefits packages without incurring additional cash expenditures or making your employees feel as though you're denying them everything.

OFFER ADDITIONAL VACATION TIME IN EXCHANGE FOR REDUCED WAGES

If most of your employees are full-timers working 40 hours a week, then taking this approach won't cost you any additional cash, but will have the effect of increasing your employees' pay rate on an hours-worked basis. Employees are far less likely to grumble over pay cuts when they receive something in return, and giving them extra days off – especially when your workload is lighter than usual, anyway – can be an excellent way to achieve this.

EXPLORE ALTERNATIVE HEALTH CARE OPTIONS

Many employers with generous health plans are reluctant to switch to cheaper plans with lower premiums and higher out-of-pocket costs out of fear that their employees will react badly. This is indeed a significant risk, especially if your workforce is older or experiencing serious health problems. However, in my experience, employees handle these types of changes better than one would expect, particularly if they're paying a portion of the premium and changing plans means that more money winds up in their paychecks. Therefore, when you receive your health insurance renewal packet, carefully examine the available options and calculate the actual differential between the various plans, as these may vary considerably depending on the age and marital and family status of the people in your firm. You may be surprised by the results. I performed this type of analysis for one company whose total premium under a Gold level plan was literally half of what it would be if they continued their Platinum level plan. Out of fifteen employees on the plan, all except one had a substantial reduction in their annual premiums (the employees paid half), for a total combined annual savings to them of over $10,000. Instead of being angry that the employer was reducing their benefits, nearly all of them were thrilled with the change. Yes, their copays would be higher, but only those employees with significant ongoing medical conditions or prescriptions were likely to incur enough additional expense to offset the level of savings.

Some of your employees may also benefit from leaving your plan altogether and moving to an exchange under the Affordable Health Care Act. The nuances of the Act are beyond the scope of this book, but for lower-wage employees and those with family incomes under a certain amount, the benefits available in the form of premium tax credits can actually be greater than the benefits you're providing. For example, I know of one employee, a man in his middle fifties with a wife of the same age who did not work. Under the company-sponsored plan (a Gold Level plan), his premium was $700 a month, of which he paid half. Through the exchange he was able to get the same plan for $170 a month. Now a company is not permitted to reimburse an employee for health insurance obtained through the exchange – that's a big no-no – but in this case, the savings were such that it still benefitted the employee to come off the company plan altogether, which saved both the company *and* the employee a fair amount of money. There may be other compensating factors – if your firm is eligible for the Small Business Premium Tax Credit, for example, that may help to offset some of your costs – but the point is that you can't know without doing the math. And in this case, it was definitely worth doing the math.

And math, incidentally, was the key to demonstrating to the employees in both these situations that this was not an attempt by the company to pull wool over their eyes – these were real dollars we were placing squarely back in these employees' pockets, and I was able to prove it to them. In the plan change circumstance, we held a meeting for everyone who was on the company health plan and explained the situation to them exactly as I described it above. On top of that, I issued to each employee a half-sheet of paper showing what their total premium was under each plan type, what their half would be, and the net savings to them on a monthly and annual basis. Therefore, we didn't merely say to them, "Hey, we need to save some money, so here's what we're doing," and then expect them to accept it without question. Instead I quantified the results for each of them – even the one unfortunate fellow whose rate went up by $3 – and that lent a lot of legitimacy to the switch. In the second circumstance, I went onto Covered California, which is the online marketplace in my state, and looked up potential rates for the employees based on what I knew or guessed about their personal situations. I didn't feel it would be appropriate to directly approach employees whom I thought might benefit, as this sounded like an invasion of privacy, but what I did instead was to issue a memo with a series of illustrative examples showing under what types of circumstances and income levels an employee might be better off on the exchange. In other words, although I did encourage people to come to me with any questions, I also gave them the tools with which to do the research themselves, and that made it sound way less like baloney the company was making up to get employees off of its health plan.

REIMBURSE EMPLOYEE-INCURRED EXPENSES

This may sound like a no-brainer, since most employers do reimburse employees for expenses incurred on their behalf, but many firms overlook one very big and entirely tax-free benefit: mileage. Yes, if you have employees who drive their own personal vehicles in the course of their work for you, you can reimburse them *tax-free* for the miles they drove at the federal standard mileage rate, which has been fifty-some-odd cents a mile for the last several years (you can find the current mileage rate – which does occasionally change mid-year as well as at the end of the year – on IRS.gov). Your employee will have to keep a log documenting those miles – you absolutely must stress to them how important having written documentation is – but a timesheet, spiral notebook or cell phone makes it easy enough to keep track of where they went and why, and once you explain the benefits available if they do this, I can almost guarantee that they'll be on board. Once again, you have to show them the math.

Suppose you have salespeople who drive their personal vehicles 200 miles a week in the course of working for you. If they log their miles properly and submit them to you, you can then reimburse them at 56.5 cents a mile (or whatever the current rate is), meaning that you give them a check for $113. Now suppose they're in the 25% federal tax bracket and a 5% state tax bracket, for a total of 30% (presuming your state also allows tax-free reimbursement of mileage). That means that because you reimbursed them for an expense rather than paying them additional wages, they've saved 30% of $113, or $34 a week, nearly $1800 a year. In addition, both the company and the employee save an additional 7.65% or $450 because mileage reimbursement, when properly documented, is also not subject to FICA – Social Security and Medicare. By taking this into account when making salary arrangements, you could save your company and your employee a combined total of $2700 a year at a net cost to you of only a modicum of paperwork.

You can reimburse mileage for any employee who drives his or her own vehicle while on the job – employees who have to visit multiple jobsites, or your assistant who drives to the post office and bank, for example – but you *cannot* reimburse employees for miles they spend commuting. The commute to your premises or their first job of the day if they go there directly from home is considered a personal expense, not an employee expense, and thus is not eligible for tax-free reimbursement.

RECONSIDER WHETHER YOU WANT TO MAINTAIN YOUR 401(K) PLAN

Employees love 401(k) plans, and owners often do, too. Indeed, because they have such high contribution limits, small business 401(k) plans offer a ton of benefits for owners who are seeking to sock away more money than is possible with an IRA. However, if your business is struggling and you're no longer making those contributions, you may want to ask yourself whether it's really worth the expense of maintaining it, which can be substantial. As far as retirement plans go, 401(k) plans in particular are highly regulated and the penalties for violating their terms can make you cower in terror. This understandably leads many business owners to turn to expensive full-service administrators to ensure that they don't run afoul of the law. However, firms may not realize when they sign up for one of these plans that the associated expenses go far beyond the cost of preparing the original plan document and paying a quarterly fee. There may also be fees for adding employees, processing contributions, and making loans and distributions, not to mention the annual tax return preparation and any amendments needed to keep your plan document in compliance with the constantly changing tax law, which occur more often than you would think. All of these factors can make a 401(k) far pricier than a SEP or SIMPLE IRA, and if you and your employees are not truly taking advantage of all of the benefits a 401(k) has to offer, you may wish to rethink whether it's worth the money you're spending on it.

If you really want to keep your 401(k) but it's costing you a fortune, consider shopping around the administration. I was working for one firm that was paying $6,000 to $8,000 a year to maintain a 401(k) plan for 10 to 12 employees when I began working for another that was only paying $3,000 for 25 to 30 employees. The administrator at the second firm was an individual QPA (Qualified Pension Administrator) rather than a corporation, and while the arrangement with her required more hands-on participation on the part of the company's office personnel, the cost of the extra labor was more than offset by the money we saved versus the cost of full-service administration. When I switched the first firm over to her office, the annual fees dropped down to about $1200, which was far more reasonable, and only resulted in a cost of maybe five minutes of additional labor per payroll plus two hours annually. I've since run into other remote administrators who will perform most of the daunting legal functions of pension plan maintenance for a base fee as low as $50 a month for a small firm, so it's definitely worth looking into. If you have relationships with other small business owners or HR people, ask around. Nowadays almost everything can be done remotely, so you are no longer restricted by the entries in your local yellow pages and can search a fairly wide field for the best deal.

INVESTIGATE STATE-RUN PROGRAMS

Everyone knows about unemployment, but in California the Unemployment department also runs a lesser-known program called Work Sharing which I have found tremendously useful in retaining employees during slow times. The essence of California's Work Sharing program is that instead of individual employees being laid off entirely, a number of workers take reduced hours and, in turn, receive unemployment on a pro-rated basis for the hours they missed. Financially, this can be highly beneficial to the employees concerned because, unlike regular unemployment, in which any wages earned over $100 offset the potential benefits at the rate of seventy-five cents on the dollar, the wages earned on work-sharing aren't counted against the employee's work sharing benefits. For example, suppose you have five employees making $25/hour, 40 hours a week, and you lay off one of them entirely so that he or she goes on full unemployment. Based on this income level, he or she will qualify for California's maximum benefit of $450 a week. If, by contrast, you put all 5 employees on a work sharing program and have them work 32 hours a week each rather than 40, they will all qualify for the equivalent of 1 day's worth of unemployment benefits, or $90. In addition, they can still collect full wages for the other 4 days worked, bringing earnings for the week up to $890, which is pretty close to the $1000 they were earning before, and certainly a huge improvement for the one employee who was going to be laid off. Without work sharing, your 4 remaining employees will earn $4,000 and your 1 laid off employee $450 for a total of $4,450. With work sharing, your five employees earn $890 * 5 or $4550, $100 more, and at no additional cost to you. Perhaps most beneficial from an employee's perspective is that in this scenario, they will all continue to qualify as full-time employees for health insurance purposes, and in my experience, that is a *very* big selling point. No one gets laid off, no one loses their insurance, and your company saves money – it's win-win-win.

It isn't my intention here to review all of the parameters of California's work sharing program, which has its own rules and pieces of paperwork that can be annoying until you figure them all out. But if you're a California employer and you're considering reducing your employees' work hours – and the 4 days a week I use here is only an example; in reality the program is quite flexible on the number of weekly hours you're allowed to reduce work, which can be as little as 4 for a full-time employee – then I would certainly encourage you to look into it. Residents of other states can contact their state's own employment department to see whether they have a similar program in place. You will save money, you will retain your employees, and perhaps most importantly, you will demonstrate to your employees that you care enough about them to try to find alternative solutions to simply letting go of the lowest man on the totem pole every time you run low on work.

CAREFULLY ORCHESTRATE OPPORTUNITIES TO GET EMPLOYEES OFF YOUR PAYROLL WHEN YOU DON'T REALLY NEED THEM

Ideally, you want to arrange this so that your workers won't be harmed by the unintended vacation. Got a guy with a new baby who hasn't taken his state-sponsored Paid Family Leave yet? Encourage him to take the time off during your upcoming slow season – that way he still gets paid, and you don't have to feel guilty for not having enough work to keep him employed. Is your company dead between Christmas and New Year's, or on the day after Thanksiving? Offer unpaid days off to employees who wish to extend their long holiday weekends.

CONSIDER ALTERNATIVE PAY STRUCTURES

There are limits on what you can do when it comes to compensation – many employers, for example, are tempted by piece-meal or questionable salary arrangements, which can easily run afoul of minimum wage and overtime laws and should be approached with extreme caution. But in certain situations, coming up with creative ways to compensate or to reduce compensation for your people may substantially contribute to the improvement of your cash situation. The trick here is that employees are naturally going to be suspicious of any changes to their wages, so ideally, you want to structure any decreases in pay so that they get some benefit in return, even if it isn't in cash. For instance, if you needed to cut the pay of your office assistant, you could offer her the option of working from home two days a week. Less money for you, and less commuting and more time with the family for her. Or suppose she's currently working thirty-five hours a week, seven hours a day – perhaps you offer her four eight-hour days and a three-day weekend instead.

Alternative pay structures can sometimes be used to further the goals of the business as well. Suppose your salesperson who brings in $300,000 a year is currently earning a fixed salary and no commission on sales. Maybe you want to consider reducing her salary amount and offering her a bonus based on her sales volume instead. The added advantage of such an arrangement would be that, if structured properly, it would give your employee an incentive to bring in the additional business you need. Make sure you make the new goal achievable, though. If your salesperson suddenly has to bring in $400,000 in sales (a 25% increase) to achieve the same level of pay, then she will probably feel – to put it politely – screwed by the new arrangement and will be unlikely to even try to meet such a daunting goal. Therefore, you need to make the target more reasonable – maybe she needs to bring in $320,000 to keep her pay rate the same as it is now. If she brings in $350,000, her bonus will be higher; or perhaps it will operate on a sliding scale, so that if she does make it to $400,000, she'll receive an even greater percentage. Again, you will want to illustrate potential scenarios to your employee with cold, hard math so that she knows exactly how each would compare to what she is currently earning. This will permit her to see, in black and white, the worst-case scenario as well as how she might ultimately benefit from the change.

HIRE TEMPORARY RATHER THAN PERMANENT EMPLOYEES

Some business owners take the idea of employee retention too far, and get so attached to their employees that they have difficulty letting them go, even during their slow seasons. Don't let yourself get trapped into paying to keep someone on staff all year when you only need them for six months, especially for your lower-level positions that don't require much training. Inform your potential new hire up front that the position is temporary and you'll be less likely to be tempted to permanently add one more mouth you don't have the money to feed. If you are in a position where temporary employees can work well for your firm, make sure to adjust your employee policy manual so that fringe benefits are deferred for a long enough period where you won't be required to begin accruing holiday pay or vacation time for an employee who may only be with you for a short time. It can be very annoying to hire someone to help out for two weeks in September and then discover that you have to pay them for Labor Day.

LIBERATE YOUR EMPLOYEES FROM THE FORTY-HOUR WORK WEEK

Don't keep your employees standing around for an hour at the end of the day with nothing to do just so they can get their eight hours in. Send them home early, and let them beat the rush hour commute for once – it won't be the end of the world. Better yet, plan ahead. If you won't have enough work for everybody the next day, ask someone to take the day off. The occasional unpaid day is unlikely to ruin anyone, and it's a heck of a lot better to tell someone in advance to stay home than to force them to come in for two hours before you admit you don't really have a full day's work for them. Give them a day off, let them sleep in and run errands and enjoy time with their hobbies or families, and everyone will be happier because of it. If your employees are paid hourly and your work situation permits it, you can encourage your employees to be flexible with their schedule, too, and ask for unpaid days or hours off whenever they want them. Finally, here's a chance for your employee to go see his son's school play, or his wife's piano recital. Finally, your employees can have the opportunity to have a life outside of work, and that, to many, is well worth the occasional paycheck that's a few hours short.

ASK YOUR EMPLOYEES FOR THEIR OPINION

Nothing will make your employees feel that you care about their happiness and well-being more than including them in decisions that affect them, rather than making those decisions unilaterally and without their input. And sometimes you just can't know how a company decision is going to affect an individual. For example, in one company I worked for, I proposed switching everyone over to a high-deductible health plan (an HSA). The figures worked out such that, with the premium savings, the employer could contribute a rather large amount of money to each employee's HSA to help cover out-of-pocket expenses, and still save everyone concerned a substantial sum of cash. We held a meeting to discuss the change, explained the potential concerns – the biggest one being that higher out-of-pocket expenses could create cash flow issues for employees who were not prepared to deal with them – and advised everyone to carefully examine the terms of coverage to see if they might be seriously adversely affected by the changes. And one employee did in fact approach me a few days later. He didn't have serious health concerns, really, all he had was one prescription – a brand-name only prescription that would have cost him $800 a month under the HSA plan! Well, clearly this was unacceptable. Under our health insurance, we were permitted to offer more than one plan, so I sat down with him and reviewed his actual needs until we were able to come up with a suitable alternative – a plan with a fairly high co-pay for doctor's visits and other services but a low co-pay for prescriptions, even brand-name ones. The premium was higher, but without the employer's HSA contribution, it cost the company about the same as the HSA plan would have, and saved the employee a sum of cash that would have seriously negatively affected his well-being and lifestyle. Yet had we not invited employee input, and simply implemented the change, this poor guy might have really gotten screwed on this one prescription, and for no real reason other than we never bothered to ask.

So if you are considering making a change to your employees' benefits, think about asking them what's important to them. You don't have to give them everything, but you can certainly ask for their input on what they really want. Would they rather have health insurance or a 401(k)? Would they prefer layoffs and unemployment or a reduction in work hours across the board? Give your employees the power to help you decide and not only will you relieve yourself of part of the burden of making those painful decisions, but you will make your employees feel even more invested in the firm that you've all built together.

WHEN DO I LET SOMEONE GO?

This is a tough decision for any employer, particularly when it's made owing to a downturn in business. Many small employers think of their employees like their extended family, and the notion of letting someone go, even temporarily, feels very personal. And as I detailed under THE COST OF EMPLOYEE TURNOVER, above, layoffs owing to temporary reductions in workload can be quite costly for the firm as well as for the employee, if you have to turn around and hire someone new three months later.

Before you make the decision to let someone go, therefore, you need to evaluate whether this is truly to be a temporary measure, or whether it represents a permanent reduction in staff. Companies become accustomed to having a certain number of managers or assistant managers, or a certain number of sales reps working the floor, and it can become difficult for them to recognize that a change is needed, or, in fact, that it has already occurred. But as expensive as it is to hire new people, it can be even more expensive to "make work" long-term for an employee whose labor is no longer required, particularly when benefits such as health care are involved on top of their pay rate. And if your cash flow shortage is the result of a long-lasting downturn in business, then perhaps you don't really need six employees full-time anymore, when five would serve you just fine.

It's fairly easy to evaluate this for workers whose jobs involve providing a service or producing a product. If your current staff is able to complete the work that's available and still have standing around time, then you may have too many people on the clock. If, on the contrary, you're losing out on business because your current staff isn't able to get through as much work as you'd like, then you may have too few. Where many companies – especially those with seasonal needs –

falter is when they're straddling the line between having too much and not enough. Then those companies have to make decisions on whether to try to engage employees part-time or consider making use of the dreaded "O" word – overtime.

Having part-time employees you can turn to when your workload increases and that you can send home when it decreases can be highly advantageous to firms whose needs are constantly in flux. It works particularly well in industries that aren't necessarily built around the eight-hour day, as in restaurants, and in professions where full-time employment isn't always expected, as in bookkeeping. However, while part-time work may work great for students, artists, or those seeking "mothers' hours," it rarely provides a sufficient living for your average worker. And unless your employee is able to successfully schedule and coordinate more than one part-time job, he or she is unlikely to be satisfied with part-time work indefinitely, which can create turnover problems for you. If you're in an industry where you can hire and replace employees with little training, maybe this is not a big deal. But if part-time employees don't work well for your firm, or are simply not available for the type of position you're offering, you still have another option short of hiring another full-time employee, and that's to pay overtime.

Overtime – yes, at one-and-a-half times an employee's usual pay rate, it's daunting to employers and particularly horrifying to those who are already experiencing cash flow problems. Yet, surprisingly, it's not always as dreadfully draining on the budget as it initially seems.

Suppose you have four full-time employees who are paid on an hourly basis. During your slow season 160 hours a week of paid labor is just right, but during your busy season, you really need 180 hours to keep up with the work.

What are your options here? Well, if you can hire a 20-hour-a-week person to fill in the gap when you're busy and then let them go when you're not, great. If, by contrast, you tried to hire another full-time person year round, you wouldn't have enough work for everybody even during the busy season, and would end up either paying your employees not to work or cutting their hours, which is going to lead to widespread dissatisfaction. So what will it cost you if you decide to pay overtime instead? If each employee makes $20 an hour, then the overtime hours will cost you $30 an hour (plus applicable payroll taxes, which, for simplicity, we're disregarding here) for a total of an additional $600 a week. Each of your four employees will make an additional $150 a week for the extra five hours of work, for a net average pay rate of about $21/hour ($950 total earnings divided by 45 hours) and a percentage increase in total pay of about 19%.

Most of the time, this is going to make your employees very happy – and particularly if you've recently cut their pay, handing out some overtime hours can go a long way towards restoring their goodwill towards your firm. If you hire another full-time person instead, the extra pay is going to go to the newbie, who will be extraneous once the slow season rolls around again anyway. And unless owners and managers are extraordinarily diligent about sending workers home early when the work runs out – which many are not – you'll likely wind up paying the new person to work full-time even though you only actually need him for 20 hours. In short, this may cost you a full $800 a week rather than $600, and do nothing to increase job satisfaction among your current employees.

There was a time when I would have passionately argued against overtime as an expense to be avoided at almost all costs. But once you do the math it becomes clear that in a cash-poor environment, paying your current employees occasional overtime pay is often a better solution than hiring new ones. You incur no expenses for hiring and training, avoid the costs associated with fringe benefits, and the heart-wrenching decision of when to give up and finally let that new person go.

This won't work in every company, of course. In businesses where employee fatigue or safety is a concern, or permissible working hours are limited by daylight or official regulations, it's probably best not to rely on overtime hours. Similarly, if you have other long-range goals – such as replacing an aging work force that's nearing retirement – then acquiring new and permanent help may ultimately prove cheaper for you. And if the amount of weekly overtime needed is greater than the cost of hiring a whole new employee, then the math simply might not work out. But if you estimate your weekly overtime needs at 26 hours or less (26 hours at time-and-a-half equals 39 hours of regular pay), this may be the better option for you and is worth considering. When in doubt, you can always ask your employees what they'd rather do. They will appreciate the chance to offer input, and you'll find out if overtime is a viable or desirable option for them.

Other types of employees may pose different challenges, and here I would caution you to be aware of how your situation has changed, because your employees will rarely tell you straight out that their job has become obsolete. It's up to you, therefore to decide whether you still need an Office Manager as well as an Administrative Assistant. Maybe your Supervisor is no longer being kept busy enough with supervision and can relieve your overworked Warehouse Manager of a part of his duties. There's no special trick for evaluating the necessity of these types of employees, and you have to use your own judgment. However, this is not always true for one other class of employee, and that is your salespeople.

Please note that I am using "salespeople" in the broadest sense possible here. If yours is a firm in which you have Project Managers who both sell and manage jobs, then they will be salespeople in this sense just as much as the lady who literally travels door to door with your product. Salespeople are a separate animal when it comes to compensation, because they may be salaried, paid on commission, or commonly, some combination of both. Those who are paid solely on commission are less likely to pose a problem because they will only earn a percentage on what they sell or what business they bring in, such that your company won't have a fixed overhead-type of expense associated with their pay. But those who also earn a flat rate of pay of necessity require a separate calculation when you're trying to determine when to hire or fire, because at a minimum they *must* be able to sell enough to cover their own pay.

This often poses a special problem for firms who hover between needing one to two salespeople or perhaps two to three. On the one hand, if your one or two salespeople are unable to take maximum advantage of the business available within your market, then taking on another person will mean more work for the firm. On the other hand, if the *additional* sales an extra person is able to bring in are insufficient to cover his or her salary, then the advantage of expanding your sales team is lost.

Note how this differs from the employment issues involving some of your other employees. Your CEO, your bookkeeper, your retail Store Manager – these may be fixed expenses, too, but they are not optional, and you will have to pay them even if your firm has no income at all. But a salesperson is only worth the money he brings in, or the business he handles.

To illustrate, suppose your current revenues are $1 million, and, based on market conditions, you estimate that having another salesperson would permit you to bring in an additional $500,000. If your gross margin on sales were 10%, then you could compensate a new salesperson a total of $50,000 ($500,000 times 10%) and not lose money. If your gross margin is less – or your gross margin on the additional sales is less, which often happens – then the salesperson is not paying her freight. Suppose instead that the new person brings in an extra $1 million, giving you a net profit of $50,000 on those sales after deducting her compensation. Fabulous, right? Well, maybe. Because if your sales volume suddenly doubles, then it's quite likely that your overhead will have to go up, too. Maybe you now have to hire a second accounting person, or another foreman for your growing line of workers, or you have to lease additional equipment or warehouse space. If these new expenses total $50,000 or more, your profits are gone.

For small businesses, therefore, it's vital to consider the actual benefits of making that jump from small to medium-sized. In the above example, the firm might do very well if it was able to handle say $700,000 in additional business without incurring additional overhead expenditures. Then it would net $20,000 on its new salesperson. But at $1 million more the firm might be back to square one, and unless this type of expansion is part of an overall business growth strategy, the increase in revenue is probably not worth the added pressure on the company's cash flow situation. Because of course the big problem with those overhead expenses is that they *do* have to be paid whether you have income or not – and if your volume or margin drops off after you've already got yourself set up to be a $2 million a year firm, you will be in trouble.

The same logic applies to downsizing. Will making your firm smaller allow you to move to a cheaper location, or not really? Will getting rid of a salesperson and doing less business cause you to lose bulk discounts you're currently enjoying? Or would reducing your sales force decrease your market presence to a point where your revenues might be reduced disproportionately?

Size does matter when it comes to the health of a firm, but don't fall into the trap of assuming you can solve your financial problems by either growing or shrinking. What works for one firm may not work for another, and remember that what really counts is not how much money you take in, but how much money you *make*. Proceed with caution, therefore, when hiring people who may make you bigger, but not necessarily better.

HIRING IS A WHOLE NEW BALLGAME

Back in the days when you were flush with cash (or at least comparatively so), you hired employees based on a certain set of criteria, most of which probably involved how well-qualified they were to do your job. You wanted guys in your shop with the most knowledge or experience, maybe those who were punctual and eager to work as much as they could. You wanted salespeople who would turn over the greatest profits or make large sales to new clients, and office people who could process vast volumes of paperwork with accuracy and efficiency.

All of these qualifications are still important to you, but now that you're in cash crisis, they may no longer be as vital as you once thought. The needs of your business have changed, and the nature of your decision-making needs to change, too.

Flexibility, for example, becomes highly desirable when you're short on cash. All other things being equal, which would you prefer, an employee who insists on working exactly forty hours per week, or one who's happy to work thirty or thirty-five? Do you want to hire someone who's leaving their current job in search of more pay, or someone who stayed at their last job until the shop closed? If your shop has down time that could be used for training, then maybe this is a good time for you to take a chance on an inexpensive young person with little experience but a desire to learn. Or conversely, if you don't have quite enough work for another full-time person, maybe it's worth paying an elevated rate to a semi-retiree with lots of experience and a flexible schedule, one who may bring his former customers to your shop to boot.

In other words, it's no longer just about skills and experience. It's about trying to build a lasting relationship with a competent person who will work well within your cash-poor firm. And if conditions at your firm are going to make your employee unhappy, then chances are pretty good that you'll end up unhappy, too.

When you are in the process of building or rebuilding your team, you want to consider the mix of employees as well – how their various strengths and skill sets may serve to augment your cash situation. Pretend you're interviewing the following two salespeople:

Option 1: Specializes in large, long-term projects with high volume but low profit margins.

Option 2: Specializes in small jobs with high profit margins and quick turnaround times.

Salesperson #1 seems to offer something your company needs – a large volume of work that may not have much money in it, but will provide a steady and ongoing stream of cash. But there are clear advantages here in selecting Salesperson #2 as well, because this person will be able to provide you with profits from jobs that can be turned over quickly, making you money fast when you need it most. I had a guy like this on my staff once. I could go to him on Friday and say I had to have $6,000 by Thursday and he would go out and sell a job and get me the money. If you find someone like that, I say grab him. No, this person is probably not going to provide your company with its bread and butter – you still need Salesperson #1 for that – but it can ease your fears considerably knowing that you have someone on staff who can rake in some dough on short notice.

The ideal solution? To have one of each. If you already have a #1 on staff, seek a #2, and vice versa. The point is to evaluate each candidate not as an individual alone, but on the basis of how he or she will work with your team with an eye to conserving and maximizing your cash. And don't be afraid to offer incentives to encourage one of your people to be more like the other when the situation warrants it. Say you operate a retail store and your salespeople work on a sliding scale of commissions, so that their percentage goes up as their profit margin on product increases. You may have one woman on the floor who takes longer to make sales because she marks up the price higher, and another who generates greater volume by settling for less. In this situation, if you need cash fast, the second lady is probably going to be better at getting it for you. And if you really need cash fast, perhaps a good strategy to would be to offer an incentive to the first lady to turn product over more quickly.

OH NO! I'VE LOST MY BOOKKEEPER!

Perhaps one of the most devastating potential personnel losses – particularly in companies already struggling with cash flow – is the unexpected departure of a bookkeeper or other financial person. Those of you whose businesses engage only one financial person are quite likely painfully aware that he or she may be the only man or woman in your firm whose position cannot be covered by any one of your remaining employees. Even worse, most firms cannot avoid or postpone replacing a bookkeeper the way they might avoid or postpone replacing a laborer when work is slow, because then who will cut checks? Who will run payroll? Who else knows how to use that stupid software your CPA told you to buy?

And if your firm is struggling to make ends come anywhere close to meeting, then your bookkeeper is often the person most likely to leave you. Why? Because the job really stinks.

Next to the owner, the Bookkeeper or Controller of a small business suffers the most from a firm's cash flow problems, and this can make work extremely unpleasant for them. Think about the issues they have to face:

1) They handle the majority of collection calls. Even in working environments where this responsibility is shared or not really theirs, it's inevitable that they be heavily involved in speaking with vendors, because they're the people who know where the paperwork is and how to look up when the last check went out. This means that they get to experience the joy of having to explain to creditors over and over again why they aren't getting paid while simultaneously trying to keep your company's accounts up and running or out of collections.

Consequently, they usually have to deal with far more personal abuse in their day-to-day lives, especially from those vendors who believe that screaming obscenities and threats over the phone will help them get paid. It's an unpleasant position for anyone to be in, and can burn out your bookkeeper in a very short space of time.

2) They get the blame even when they don't have the power. Again, because the Bookkeeper or Controller at a minimum handles the physical aspects of bill payments and checks, he or she is often held responsible when the company runs short on cash, not just by vendors, but often by owners and employees as well. Undoubtedly this sometimes is the fault of the financial person or of a flawed cash management system, but in general the bookkeeper is not to blame for the decrease in sales or the downturn in the local economy that brought a company to crisis. Yet the bookkeeper may bear the brunt of responsibility for the everyday management of less and less money, and that can be a heavy burden indeed. Even worse, financial people are frequently put in the position of having to defend decisions they didn't make, such as when they were unable to pay the vendor they thought should be paid because the boss insisted that that money go to someone else. Situations such as these, inevitable as they may be, can only generate dissatisfaction and conflict.

3) Your cash flow problems may harm their reputation. This is particularly true of those with high levels of responsibility, like a Controller, and can be a huge concern for your financial people, who, like the rest of your employees, are wondering what they're going to do if their job goes away. Unlike most of your employees, however, who will likely escape blame if your company does fail, your Controller may be keenly aware of the poor impression it will give on a resume going forward if your business goes under while he or she was at its financial helm. Indeed, this factor alone has prompted many financial people to jump a sputtering ship long before it was in serious danger of sinking, the unfortunate consequence being that their departure may actually hasten its descent to the bottom.

If you adore your financial person, or simply don't want to waste the time and money involved in finding a new one if yours leaves you, then you will want to do your best to address the specific problems your bookkeeper faces.

1) Recognize your financial person's limitations – and those of your other personnel, too. If your financial person is also your Office Manager and is great at working under stress and with people, then he or she may be perfectly suited to handling phone calls from vendors and inquiries from employees who haven't had a raise in three years. However, if your bookkeeper is a more traditional "numbers" person who likes to sit quietly at her computer solving accounting problems, she may not be so adept at handling people. On the flip side, the gregarious Office Manager who always paid your bills on time when you had money may simply be incapable of allocating funds where they're needed most now that you don't. By contrast, your quiet numbers person may see this as merely another complex accounting problem and may even excel at solving it. Whatever your people's personalities, it's unreasonable to expect that they will be fabulous at every aspect of your now incredibly tough job, and that is ultimately going to do harm to your company as well as to them personally. So pay attention. If your Controller bursts into tears every time her phone rings, while your A/R person handles collection calls calmly and firmly, then maybe it's time to consider changing up some of their job responsibilities. Maybe the extroverted sales guy who works out of your home office is actually better at talking to vendors than your bookkeeper is; perhaps it's time to make an exception to company policy and permit the two to work together in handling inquiries. Or maybe after avoiding financial management all his life, it turns out that the owner's got quite a knack for designing payment schedules, and maybe he should be in charge of figuring out what to spend when.

2) Recognize that the job has changed. You may have hired your financial person with merely an eye towards having someone to help out with the paperwork and to be ready for tax time.

Your needs are completely different now, and your bookkeeper, who was once completely competent to fulfill your needs, may no longer possess the skills you require. That doesn't mean you should run right out and replace him or her, because, as I discuss below, this may prove far more difficult and disappointing than you would think. However, you will want to make an effort to ensure that your bookkeeper has the support he needs to do the job as well as he can, the knowledge to provide you with the information you desire, and the incentive not to stagnate in his constantly evolving position. In the past, your financial person may only have given you one report a month – a Profit and Loss. Now maybe you want a weekly report on unpaid bills, outstanding receivables, or projected sales; maybe you want a daily report on your available bank balance. These are easy enough to generate in most accounting software programs; it simply may not have occurred to your bookkeeper that you might want to see them. Want a cash flow projection for the next month? Ask for one! If you want or need something from your financial person that he or she does not know how to accommodate, then consider additional training in the form of free webinars or inexpensive books such as this one. You may be surprised at how well your bookkeeper steps up once he or she realizes that a change is needed.

3) Be sure that your financial person has the opportunity to take real time off. And that means no email, no phone calls – no contact from the office whatsoever. It can be draining enough to have to face that environment day after day, but a bookkeeper who reads her email or checks her voicemail after hours only to find yet another message from a vendor looking for money will never get an opportunity to refresh or rejuvenate. It's nearly impossible to get rid of that kind of strain anyway, and if you carry work home with you, too, it may never go away. I don't want to tell you how many times I've half-woken up in the middle of the night and found myself trying to hash out some complex financial problem in my sleep. And I'm sorry, but dreams should *never* be in Excel format, and when they are, the columns never add up anyway.

> Give your bookkeeper a break, and while you're at it, give
> yourself one, too – you need it even more badly than they do.

In spite of your best efforts, you may still lose your bookkeeper and have no choice but to seek someone else. If this happens, however, don't fret. As I discuss under I'VE GOT A NEW FINANCIAL PERSON – WHAT NOW?, below, the benefit of having a new financial person is that it can provide you with a wealth of golden opportunities for buying you time with your vendors, and may even help to press the re-set button on your relationship with them. As you might imagine, these both can be steps in very positive directions.

FINDING A SUITABLE REPLACEMENT

If you've ever searched for a bookkeeper or other financial person on Craigslist or through an employment agency such as Robert Half, you'll be abundantly familiar with how overwhelming the responses can be. Here in the Bay Area, a simple Craigslist ad will garner well over a hundred responses within a couple of days, which sounds great until you actually start sifting through resumes and realize that they're basically all the same.

Yes, that's an oversimplification, because of course certain individuals will have more experience, or perhaps more knowledge of your industry, or more formal education. But the bottom line is, almost all of them will indicate that the applicant has knowledge of A/P, A/R, bank accounts reconciliation, journal entries, etc., and unless you're a financial person yourself – and often even if you are – you're unlikely to be able to tell from the lines on the resume whether this person will work for your company or no.

This can be a problem anytime you're seeking to hire someone, but it's especially unsettling if your firm is in financial trouble because of the risks involved – the risk of them hating the job and leaving, the risk of them being unable to handle your cash situation, even the risk of them making it worse. You simply can't afford to hire the wrong person – especially not someone whose performance is so vital to the survival or ongoing health of your firm.

Perhaps the most irksome aspect of hiring a bookkeeper in a small business is that there may only be one person in your company who's qualified to evaluate potential candidates, and that's your outgoing bookkeeper. If your departing employee has already given two weeks' notice and said his farewells, you may be stuck trying to figure it out for yourself, and that can be daunting indeed if this isn't your field. Here are some tricks, therefore, that can help you and your team to sift through the pile of candidates and weed out those who are least likely to suit you.

BIG RED FLAGS

Here are my top seven "big red flags" when it comes to evaluating potential replacements for your financial person:

CANDIDATES WHO LOOK TOO GOOD TO BE TRUE USUALLY ARE

I'm not even talking here about the all-too-common phenomenon of resume padding, but about candidates who seem obviously overqualified for your position. It's tempting to think that maybe you've finally gotten lucky and are going to land a really awesome person who just happens to be available right when you need them. But unless your firm is seeking a highly qualified accounting person, I would caution you to be skeptical of applicants with too-impressive job histories. If I'm hiring a Full-Charge Bookkeeper at $30 an hour, and I get a resume from a Controller who made $120,000 a year at his or her last job, my Spidey-sense ought to be tingling. Yes, there may be good reasons why a person with a fancy title and job history might want a bookkeeper's job. Perhaps they had to work a lot of overtime and now they want a less stressful position or to spend more time with family. But it's more likely that:

1) They've lost their job and are applying for anything they can possibly get. They'll take your position and keep it only until they can find something better.

2) They were fired or politely asked to leave their last job, and now they're forced to accept a lower-level position.

3) Their last company went out of business. This may not have been a result of their own job performance, but it certainly ought to raise another "big red flag," as I describe below.

Remember also, when you see titles like "Controller" or "CFO," to consider the source. Any company can have a Controller, but it may not mean very much in a firm with low revenues or three employees. If you see someone advertising themselves as a Controller or CFO and they weren't making much money or supervising any employees, ask yourself whether they may have been given the title as a nicety and whether it therefore has any real significance.

Unless your job actually is a CPA-level position, I would also be wary of applicants who are CPAs. A CPA is a highly qualified accountant – if a person with that level of qualification really wants to work for you for the money you want to pay them, your books will likely be well-kept. But CPAs are not bookkeepers. They were not trained to perform the everyday aspects of managing the financial end of a business – and to start with, they may not even possess the *practical* know-how of your billing clerk. Did your applicant really spend two years doing auditing and six months studying for a very tough exam so they could match and assemble invoices, file paperwork, and stuff checks into envelopes? Don't get me wrong – being a bookkeeper is great, and we accountant-types are naturally inclined to derive satisfaction from processing paperwork and filing it neatly away. But this is not why people become CPAs, and you owe it to yourself to question why one wants to work for you.

And this caution applies throughout the whole spectrum of accounting positions. A Full-Charge Bookkeeper will rarely be sincerely seeking a job as a $12 an hour Accounts Payable data entry clerk and probably won't be happy in the position long. If you're unfamiliar with the different types of accounting personnel and how they rank in terms of skills and experience, Robert Half publishes an annual salary guide that may help you; you can find the current one on their website here: https://www.roberthalf.com/workplace-research/salary-guides. Not only will this apprise you of the going rates for financial people (although these can vary vastly by region), it will also give you a good idea of how to perceive candidates in terms of the positions they've held and the position you're offering. As I said, you don't necessarily want to reject a candidate on this basis, because it is entirely possible that there's a legitimate reason why they're seeking a lower-level position – but you do want to be sure you find out why before you consider making them an offer.

A CANDIDATE WHO LIVES FAR AWAY

Here in the San Francisco Bay Area, even a comparatively short distance can turn into an interminable commute. Why is this person willing to drive over an hour each way to get to your job? How long will it be before they've had enough and start looking for a position closer to home?

If you suspect that this may become a problem, there are a couple of ways you can find out sooner rather than later. First, examine the shortest-term positions on their resume and ask them why they left. This is a good question to ask anyway, but I've been surprised by how often the answer has been "the commute." Second, ask them to come for their interview during rush hour, then question them about how long it took them to get there. It should be apparent if they were seriously unhappy with the commute, and some candidates will even withdraw their application, realizing that the twice-daily drive is going to turn into a serious drag.

THEY CAN'T HANDLE STRESS

Many, many candidates will tell you outright that they left (or are leaving) their last job because it's too stressful. No matter how wonderful they otherwise are, those candidates simply will not work for your cash-poor firm. But don't merely ask them how they perform under stress, as most will come back with some variation of "Very well, thank you." Instead, ask them:

What stresses you out? What do you do to combat it?

What's the most stressful position you've ever been in? How did you handle it?

THEY'RE JUMPING A SHIP THAT'S ABOUT TO GO UNDER

When asked why they're leaving their last job, these potential hires may say things like, "Business has been down lately" or "The company has cut my hours" or even "Our financial situation is really bad." You can't blame someone for protecting his or her own interests, and it's perfectly understandable why an employee who is not making enough money will begin seeking other employment. But there is simply no point in bringing that person in to your company, where they will be in the exact same situation and just as ready to jump ship – possibly even before their training is over.

THEIR LAST COMPANY WENT BANKRUPT WHILE THIS PERSON WAS IN CHARGE OF ITS FINANCES

No, a failed small business is not necessarily the fault of the financial person, who often only manages figures and has no real control or even input over operations. But this type of situation does call for additional questioning, and you may find that your candidate's answers will prove highly instructive:

Why do you think the company failed?

What, if anything, could have been done to prevent the company's failure?

What measures did you personally take to try to avoid the company's failure, and what were the results?

If you had been the firm's owner, what would you have done differently?

Questions such as these will help you to differentiate between the financial person who didn't really have a clue how to manage a company's finances, and one who has good ideas for solving financial problems but whose hands were tied in their last position.

THEY WANT TO WORK ALONE

Successful accounting for small business requires a special type of personality not often found in other professions. It tends to be a rather solitary position, and therefore does not work well for employees who long for more social companionship; these types of employees who do wind up in accounting are often less productive because they will unconsciously seek excuses to leave their desks, make conversations, etc. Bookkeepers who are too solitary, however, may do fine with accounting but are less likely to do well when it comes to managing cash flow, because cash flow management is, of necessity, a cooperative endeavor that cannot be accomplished by one person and a spreadsheet alone.

A closed door can be highly imposing. The very act of knocking on someone's door can feel like an imposition or an invasion of privacy, and many people simply will not do it unless the need is sufficiently great. Instead, they will wait for the door to open, and if they have not yet forgotten what they wanted to say or to ask, then perhaps they will take this opportunity to address the door's owner. More often, however, that opportunity is lost forever because the closed door signals that the person behind it does not wish to be bothered, or is not interested in interacting with the rest of your office. It sets up a barrier that's tough to surmount, and that can have highly detrimental effects on your ability to manage your cash flow.

In general, you will not be hiring a bookkeeper or other accounting person based primarily on his or her personality. This is not a sales or customer service position in which a pleasant demeanor plays an integral part of successful job performance, and as long as your employee is not downright nasty, certain flaws in personality can be overlooked provided the work is done as it should be. In cash-poor firms, however, the role of bookkeepers inevitably changes. They don't have to be "nice," but they must be approachable, not only to vendors, but to employees, who may have questions regarding changes in their benefits or their compensation, and to your other staff members, who may frequently need to inquire about payment status in the course of their ongoing work with suppliers and subcontractors. Allowing your financial person to shut himself away behind a closed door ensures that many of those questions will never be answered because they will never be asked.

This can present problems for some financial people, many of whom need absolute silence in which to work and a minimum of interruptions. What makes the problem worse is that accounting jobs can range from laughably easy – you can do them while watching TV – to mind-bendingly difficult – you practically need a Ph.D. There may be variety of mathematical calculations, complicated spreadsheet design and setup, and research into HR (human resources) law or problems, which in a small company normally land on the bookkeeper's desk because there's no one else to solve them. Some people are able to multi-task, and some people are able to tune out their physical environments and concentrate in spite of background noise, but some cannot do either, and this will make it difficult for them to interact with your other personnel and also perform their primary job functions.

This is not to say that your accounting person should not have a private office. Indeed, depending on how your office space is designed, there may be no other option, just as you may have no choice but to give them a corner in a cramped open room with three other employees. But you should make an attempt during your interview to determine what their preferred working environment is, because that will help you to assess the type of working personality they will bring to your firm. A person with a private office whose door is literally always open can convey a greater level of approachability than one who hunches over a desk in a central location, scowling with eyes steadfastly fixed on her computer. Both types of people may be equally effective when it comes to recording your transactions, balancing your books, and maintaining your accounting system. But the approachable person will be more likely to take advantage of opportunities to better understand the big picture of your operations, and that can only help her to effectively manage your cash flow.

THEY CAN'T HANDLE CASH – OR THE ABSENCE OF CASH

In all of the many hundreds of resumes from financial people that I have seen in my career, I can't recall a single one in which a candidate listed "cash flow" or "cash flow management" among his or her skills. There are several potential reasons for this. First, because in smaller firms, financial people often have no real control over expenses and are relegated to managing only small bills, such as the phone and the office newspaper subscriptions. Second, because cash flow management is not always recognized as a relevant skill, at least not in the way "general ledger maintenance" and "month-end close" are. But whatever the cause, your odds of finding an adept, experienced, and affordable cash flow manager when you're seeking to hire are incredibly slim. Instead, you may be trying to evaluate candidates on the basis of what you (or they) think they *might* be good at. Even then, it's a wild card, because in my experience, most candidates, when asked how they are at managing cash, will answer "Fine – I guess," or something of the sort. They simply don't know what they can do, and unfortunately, neither do you.

Ultimately, it may prove impractical for you to reject every candidate who doesn't know how to manage cash, because you may end up with no one left you can hire. You can and should, however, run screaming from a candidate who cannot handle the absence of cash, because their position with you will be doomed before it even starts.

Fortunately, it can be surprisingly easy to figure this out. In general, asking someone why they left their previous jobs can be of limited usefulness, because people naturally tend to whitewash themselves, and with employers being reluctant to give negative evaluations of former employees, it can be tough to know what the truth really is. However, people are rarely reluctant to tell you that they left their last job because the company ran out of money. Most of the time they don't see this as a reflection on them, and will cheerfully disclose this information. You then need to discover exactly why they decided to leave – and if it was because they couldn't handle or didn't want to be bothered with managing money, you can almost guarantee that they won't work for you, either.

This can be a very painful realization for a cash-poor firm, especially one that's having trouble replacing a departing financial person over this very question. I remember one particularly uncomfortable situation myself, in which I and other key personnel interviewed a job candidate with impressive skills, a solid resume, and a nice personality to boot. Everyone else loved her, but I had to veto her application. Why? The reason she gave for leaving her current job was that there wasn't enough money, and she was tired of having to worry about covering payroll. Well, at that point it doesn't matter what her skills are, or how much experience she has, or how nice she is. Why waste our time hiring someone for a position that was exactly like the one she wanted to leave?

I've had a couple of jobs where the employer asked me in the course of my interview, "Oh, and you might get a collection call once in a while – are you okay with that?" And then I started work and discovered that "once in a while" meant "once an hour." This is not good vetting of potential candidates. Had I been a different type of employee, I might have bailed within the first week, leaving those companies without anyone to cut checks, run payroll, or even train a new employee. Don't allow yourself to get caught in such a precarious position. Be straightforward with your potential employees – to an extent. No, you never want to tell a potential new hire that you're on the verge of bankruptcy, because not only will they not want to come work for you, but people do talk and word does get around, which is not good for business. But you do want to be as frank and open with them as you would be with your vendors (refer to Volume 1 of this series, DEALING WITH VENDORS). Explain your current situation, how it came about, and what you've been doing to rectify it. Ask them if they feel comfortable talking to vendors, and what their skills are in budgeting and making cash flow projections. In good times, cash flow management might be a minor part of their job – now it's the most crucial part. And their ability to handle that may be what sets them apart from the hundred other candidates whose skill sets are all virtually the same.

Your candidate's persistence and tenacity, therefore, may become more important to you than technical skills when you're evaluating potential new employees. Of course you hope to get lucky and find someone who's terrific in every aspect of the position. But there is absolutely no point in hiring someone who can prepare beautiful financial statements if he locks himself in the bathroom every time a vendor calls looking for money. It won't last, and that is going to cost you.

I'VE GOT A NEW FINANCIAL PERSON – WHAT NOW?

As sad as you may be over the departure of your financial person, you should take comfort in the incredible parting gift that they've left you. Because having a new person in charge of your money will give you something you could never have obtained with your former employee – breathing room.

Being new is something everyone understands. Yes, there will be the occasional vendor who will attempt to use the fact of "newness" as a lever to pry extra money out of your company, but in my experience, vendors are pretty patient with new employees, as they should be. The change may prove to be a boon to them, too, after all. But even a superstar bookkeeper is not going to fully understand a company's financial operations on the first day, the first week, even the first month – not when they're still trying to figure out how the six-line phone system works. And it doesn't take a superstar to leverage the fact of being new into a tool that can effectively put a hold on those collection calls while your new person gets situated, giving you a rare opportunity to re-vamp and re-plan your financial strategy.

I also deal with this topic in detail in the DEALING WITH VENDORS and forthcoming CREATING A PLAN volumes of this series, but here's a quick guide on how a financial person can best take advantage of their newly-hired status as a means of improving your cash flow:

1) Have your boss and coworkers tell people you're new. If someone else happens to take a vendor call about money, they should say outright that there's a new person in the office and then put her on. The vendor's expectations will automatically

be lowered, and they'll be less likely to expect a quick answer to an unanswerable question (i.e., When am I going to get paid?).

2) Tell people you're new, too. My preferred response to vendors when they first contact me at a new job is to say, "I've only been here two days / two weeks / a short time and I don't quite have a handle on all of the A/P yet. Can I give you a call back in a couple of weeks?" I've never yet had someone say no. The trick is, then I actually do call them back, thus taking the first step in building a trust relationship with that vendor.

3) When in doubt, ask follow-up questions. If after a few weeks I'm still unable to work out a plan for paying a vendor – say, because such a plan is mathematically impossible in light of other company obligations – and they contact me again before I've contacted them, I will be prepared with follow-up questions. Maybe I'm missing some invoices, or some credit memos, or maybe my records don't match theirs – could they send me a new statement? This is also a good opportunity to feel somebody out as to whether they might be willing to consider an unofficial payment plan, or to subtly find out when they really *really* need to get paid. When you're brand new may be the only time you can safely ask this without sounding desperate.

4) Make it clear that you're making progress. "I've almost finished going through the A/P" or "I'm almost done with my budget for the next month" are good things to say – and hopefully, they're even true. Remember that confidence is the key to selling a cash flow plan to vendors, and here at the beginning is when you want to start establishing that as your dominant trait. You don't have to apologize for not being ready to talk to them yet, but you should sound as though you're getting close.

5) Blame the system. If you can avoid blaming your predecessor directly, do. Small businesses can exist in remarkably closed circles, and you don't want to badmouth somebody who may

be out there looking for another job if you don't have to. Instead, when vendors ask you questions like "Why is it taking me so long to get paid?" or "Is business really bad over there?" you can answer with vague but suggestive statements such as, "Honestly, the Accounts Payable… wasn't very well-managed. In fact, it's kind of a mess." This way you can avoid saying who was responsible for the mismanagement, imply that the problem is one of paperwork rather than cash flow, and give the impression that henceforth you'll be on top of it. In addition, you'll convey to the vendor that the problem you're dealing with is large and systemic and probably buy yourself a bit more time in the process.

6) Be ready to make an offer. If you've been letting weeks pass before you speak to a vendor – say, because you had several others that more urgently needed to be paid and you had to buy time before you could tackle this one – you need to be prepared for the inevitable "I need an answer now" call. Hopefully you will be able to sense when this is coming and you'll have a plan ready – or close enough to ready – to make a presentation. The absolute best way to answer that call, by the way? "Oh, I'm glad you called!" It bears the same implication as "I was just about to call you" but is far more believable and will dispel some of the vendor's frustration that they had to call you again.

7) Be firm but gentle. Even though you've made it clear by this point that you have a whole mess of A/P to deal with, be prepared for your vendor to be disappointed with your offer. It's okay at this point to be apologetic. "I know, I wish I could do more, but this is the best I can do for right now." It's also okay to project into the future – "Our busy season is coming up, and I'll be able to send you more then," or "In a couple of months I'll have a lot of the older stuff paid off and I should be able to send you more then." Again, you want to sound as though you're making progress – not only on a workable plan, but on actually catching up on the company debts.

8) Don't let other people try to do your job for you – even when they want to. Especially in the beginning, it can be tempting to let other people in the company take calls and handle inquiries, which, for a new person in a cash-poor environment, can rapidly become overwhelming. But this will give your vendors a bad impression and ultimately undermine their confidence in you. It's better to tell someone you don't have an answer for them yet than to avoid speaking to them altogether, and ultimately, it will be better for the company's cash flow if you put them off rather than permit someone else in the firm to make an uninformed decision on your behalf.

Although there will be vendors you will have no choice but to pay right away, all in all, your newness should be able to buy you a couple of months before you have to make major commitments to paying off some of the company's past due balances, precious months that are only granted once per position. Use them wisely, but more importantly, use them!

OTHER PERSONNEL MATTERS

TAKING THE DREADED COLLECTION CALL –
HOW YOUR STAFF SHOULD RESPOND

As I discuss in detail in the first volume of this series, DEALING WITH VENDORS, one of the worst things an Accounts Payable person can do is refuse to take or return phone calls from vendors. This avoidance technique that so many otherwise competent financial people employ only leads to trouble and frustration on the part of your creditors. However, there's no reason why your financial people should ever be forced to take a call for which they are not prepared – even if all they need to do to get prepared is to take a deep breath.

Now if your Controller has a dedicated phone line and Caller ID, he's less likely to get caught off-guard by a phone call he's not ready to take. But if your phone system has multiple numbers or lines, it's common for creditors to call the main office or the manager or even your retail store – whatever number they have handy. And unless your financial person is the fortunate type who is always cool and never flustered, you don't want your other staff members putting your Accounts Payable person in an uncomfortable situation, even if that's not their intention.

What your employees shouldn't say:

1) "She's right here; let me put her on." Unless you can see her and she's given you the nod, don't do it. A simple "Hold on, please, let me see if she's available," will work just as well.

2) "She just walked in; can you hold on a second?" Unless you were trying to blow off the caller and are now changing course because your financial person has given you the okay, this is

not a good idea, either. She's not settled in, her computer's not even on yet, and chances are pretty good she is not really prepared to take this call. As the A/P person, if you do get one of these first-thing-in-the-morning phone calls, it's perfectly acceptable to tell your caller, "Hey, I just got here, my computer's not even on yet, let me get settled in and I'll call you back in a bit."

3) "She's at lunch; I'll have her call you when she gets back." No, no, no! Your employee has essentially just told your vendor to expect a call back within an hour, maybe an hour and a half. Your financial person may have other things to do after lunch, may be too sleepy to talk coherently to a vendor, or may be in the middle of reconciling accounts and hasn't even looked at theirs yet. But now if she doesn't call this vendor back right away, they will assume that she's avoiding them and that will make them nervous – not at all the impression you want to give. Instead, your employee should say, "She's not in the office right now; can I take a message?" or "She's at lunch; would you like her voicemail?" Your employees should also never promise a callback first thing in the morning, and for the same reasons. Give your financial person some time to get through her morning routine and she'll be in a much better position to talk to an unhappy vendor.

If your employees have trouble grasping this concept or understanding why it's important, put it to them like this: pretend that the caller is your spouse's difficult mother-in-law / good-for-nothing younger brother / detested Aunt Sue. You're going to want to be polite to Aunt Sue – she gets pretty mean if you're not – but you sure as heck aren't simply going to shove the phone in your husband's face when she calls. Let him decide when he's ready to deal with her, and you'll both enjoy a much happier household.

GUARD AGAINST POTENTIAL DISASTERS

If there are people in your firm who would be incredibly difficult to replace if they were to leave on short notice, be sure to have safeguards in place against their sudden departure. More than one person in your company needs to know how to operate that expensive vacuum-packing machine. Someone else needs to know what the stupid 16-digit WiFi password is if your internet goes out and has to be rebooted. More than one person needs to have the safe combination or the key to the cabinet where the paychecks are stored.

Larger firms often draw up procedures manuals for various aspects of employee's jobs, and these can prove extremely useful in training (or reassuring) replacements. However, smaller businesses rarely have the time or personnel to embark on such enormous projects, or to keep such manuals updated as procedures change, and so they tend to go by the wayside. Thanks to modern technology, however, you can produce a "quickie" version of your internal procedures through the power of digital video.

I did this shortly before I left my last job – the one that was so difficult we had to hire eight people before we found one who could do it. It took me about 60 hours, but that was nothing compared to the many weeks I had spent training employees in person, and in any case it was well worth every second of the time I invested. I can't tell you how much more comfortable we all felt once those videos were made, because finally, here was a training program that the new person could look back on – over and over again, if need be – after I'd gone. Even more importantly, in a worst-case scenario those videos could be used to train a new person from scratch, thus protecting the company in future if their financial person left without warning.

I used a program called CamStudio, which is a free software product that allows you to capture video screen shots of your computer on a continuous basis, effectively letting you make a recording of whatever you're doing on your computer and allowing you to narrate with a headset to boot. I'm not going to recommend this product for everyone because my free download automatically included several other very annoying programs that I had to go in and uninstall right away before I forgot what they were, and people who aren't comfortable doing that kind of thing will find this even more irritating than I did. However, it was a serviceable program (and free) so I can't complain too much. The only significant flaw I found was that longer recordings – more than ten to fifteen minutes – tended to make the program freeze up, and I lost a fair amount of work that way before I figured this out. Once I split those longer tasks into multiple recordings, I had no more problems. This is one option – you may find other free or cheap products that work even better.

Anyway, I basically sat down and made separate recordings of each and every one of my tasks, and I mean everything, from daily bank account management and reconciliation to each of the forty-some journal entries required for the monthly close. I even made recordings explaining where I kept and stored various files, and how I organized the folders on my computer, because of course one of the toughest things about being a new employee is trying to figure out where the stuff you need is. I did these over several weeks in the course of my regular work in order to minimize the expense, and also to be sure I captured everything I did during the month. And then I backed these up onto two separate USB drives, and voila – a nearly-instant procedures manual that I didn't have to spend hundreds of hours writing and that was probably a lot easier to follow than a written manual would have been.

Thanks to the magic of the smartphone, you can easily make similar digital procedures libraries of your shop and field employees at work as well, which you may find incredibly useful both as reference tools and as low-cost aids in training new employees.

VOLUME 3: MANAGING ACCOUNTS RECEIVABLE AND PAYROLL

INTRODUCTION

In Volume 3 of the *Managing Cash When You Haven't Got Any* series, I discuss how best to manage your Accounts Receivable and Payroll when cash flow is a concern. I will tell you:

The importance of accurately predicting your inflows in creating a manageable cash flow plan.

Detailed examples on how to calculate how much money you'll have coming in and when you can reasonably expect it.

Setting monthly Accounts Receivable and cash projections and goals and how doing so can both create incentives for your employees and help you to predict how your month is going to go.

Suggestions for tweaking an Accounts Receivable schedule that always leaves you cash-poor.

The pros and cons of various methods for encouraging your customers to pay you early or on time – accepting credit card payments, offering cash discounts, etc.

How and why you should turn maintaining cash inflows into a cooperative company-wide endeavor.

Why you should empower as many people in your firm to collect payments as you safely can and how to do so without sacrificing security.

The "No, we're not desperate" plea for money and why you need to master it.

How properly setting payment expectations with your customers from the start will help to ensure that you get paid in full and on time.

How to approach collecting from private individuals versus collecting from businesses.

When to bring in the "big guns" in collections - and how using their ammunition sparingly can make it more effective.

How to make employees who are uncomfortable with the collections process more at ease when it comes to asking for money.

Lies I've heard collections people tell – which ones worked and which ones didn't.

Going beyond the telephone call – suggestions for taking the next step in collections.

How to select a payroll schedule that works best for your firm.

How changing your current payroll schedule may solve some of your company's cash flow problems – and possibly create others.

The differential cost of having more frequent or less frequent payrolls.

How payroll services are robbing you of control over your cash flow, and when it's time to take it back.

Tips for minimizing your worker's compensation expense and making sure you don't get hit with a giant bill when your policy ends.

Understanding payroll taxes – the comparatively small expense that can have a disproportionately large impact on your cash flow.

Why not paying your payroll taxes is a really bad idea – and what to do if you haven't.

How to deal with the IRS and other government agencies if you haven't fulfilled your payroll or other tax obligations.

THE IMPORTANCE OF HAVING PREDICTABLE INFLOWS

It seems obvious that having sufficient revenues is key to maintaining good cash flow. Clearly, making more sales and more profitable sales and acquiring new clients and more profitable clients is going to have an impact on your ability to manage your cash. But this book isn't about deriving ways for your business to make more money. Rather, we're proceeding here from the assumption that you're already doing everything in your power to generate income. What we want to discuss in this volume is how best to manage the money you do have coming in, and how to incorporate that income into a workable cash flow plan.

Having the ability to forecast your income stream with a reasonable amount of accuracy is the cornerstone of an effective cash management system. It's simply not possible to plot out payments for your expenses if you can't guess how much money you'll be getting during any given week, month, or sometimes even day. And as we have seen in the previous volumes of this series, making reliable and regular payments – even when they're many days late and many bucks short – is critical to maintaining your credit standing with your suppliers.

How, then, can you predict your inflows, and how far out should you be projecting? There are numerous ways you can approximate your income stream over the coming weeks and months, but there's no one-size-fits-all – every business will need to develop a customized methodology that takes into account its own special requirements. There are, however, some general approaches applicable to certain types of businesses that you might use as a launching pad to developing your own individual system. Here, therefore, are several sample approaches to get you started; as I discuss later, some of these may need to be used in combination to suit the needs of your particular business.

THE PROJECT-BASED FIRM

Inflows for a project-based firm are the simplest to plot out, but may also be subject to the greatest risk. If you're a contractor receiving progress payments, for example, then your payment schedule is likely going to match your projected work schedule, effectively tying your cash management plan to your operations. In fact, it can be quite helpful to make use of this fact when considering how to schedule phases of your operations. There's no incentive quite like cash paid on completion to encourage a company and its employees to get a job done.

If something goes wrong, however, and a payment is delayed because a particular phase of a project was not completed as scheduled, because a customer is unsatisfied and is withholding payment, or for some other reason, it can prove disastrous to your cash management plan, especially if you're a smaller operation with only one or two projects going at once. Your upcoming income projection can very quickly change from thousands to zero, which is why, as I will discuss in the forthcoming CREATING A PLAN volume of this series, it's vital that your cash plan be designed to easily accommodate last-minute changes and allow for quick refiguring so you can make last-minute adjustments as needed.

Because the consequences of last-minute changes can be so disastrous, it's particularly important for project-based firms to add contingencies into their projected payment schedules. For example, don't start plotting income into your plan for two months from now if you can't start a job until some product arrives in 8 to 12 weeks – or if you do, err on the side of caution and presume the job can't begin for at least three months.

It's also crucial to consider the practical implications of you getting paid, many of which are related to the design of the work-week itself. Finishing a business customer's project on a Friday afternoon does not mean that you're going to get a check in time to cover your Friday payroll. In fact, even if you drop off an invoice that day, chances are pretty good that no one will even look at it before Monday, and by the time the invoice is processed and the check printed, signed and mailed, you may be lucky to get it before the end of the following week – and this is assuming that the party that's paying you doesn't have its own cash flow issues. (See below for tips on how to guard against these possibilities).

So unless you're confident that your client is a very prompt pay, you need to factor in at least a week's delay between completion of a job phase and the date you expect to be paid, and probably even longer than that. It's better to tell your subcontractor upfront that it's going to take two weeks for them to get paid than to promise immediate payment and then have to backtrack because you didn't get paid, either. Also, always allow even more time for a project's final payment to reach you. Such a payment may require upper management approval before being issued, or the finalization of niggling details that can't be completed for whatever reason.

Let's look at an example. Suppose your firm performs complex computer software installations. Assume that an average installation takes four weeks, with payments due from the client as follows:

Due on start: $5,000
Due on completion of primary installation: $5,000
Due on completion of testing: $5,000
Due on completion of employee training: $5,000

Notice first of all that this schedule consists of four equal payments; if each of these tasks takes roughly one week, it will create an even income stream over a four-week time period. In a project-based environment, I personally prefer payment schedules of this design, in which weekly payments of similar amounts can be expected over the course of a project (for potential exceptions, see below). In general, such a schedule has a positive effect on a client's expectations and a corresponding positive effect on your cash flow. A client who is expecting to pay you once a week will be far more likely to make sure you get paid once a week – whereas a client who owes you two checks in the first week and then nothing for the next three weeks is not going to know what to expect. These are the clients who end up delaying your payment because they haven't transferred the money or it's not the time of the month when they pay bills or they've forgotten how much they were supposed to pay you. If your payment schedule is blatant, obvious and easy to follow, your payments are much less likely to be delayed for silly administrative reasons, and that can only benefit you.

Not everyone agrees with this methodology. Some project-based firms like to design payment schedules so that they get more money at points where they have to spend more – say, an uptick when tile or cabinetry is delivered and they have to pay for both the product and the installation. There is a certain logic to this, of course, and it can work well for firms who aren't too short on money. If you're very cash-poor, however, chances are pretty good you won't be forking that money over right away anyway, and how could you? A $20,000 payment isn't going to cover your subcontractor if your bills for the week total $30,000. No, that $20,000 is probably more likely to go towards paying your bills from three weeks ago, in which case you made things more confusing for your client for no reason because the net result is that no one got paid any faster. Even worse is the risk that can be involved, because what if your cabinets or tile don't get delivered on schedule? (And goodness knows that never happens!) Now you have this big pile of money that's completely uncollectible, leaving you hanging. A more even payment schedule would have allowed you to collect more of your money on completion of some other phase, thus ameliorating the consequences of your current payment delay.

A related – and often much nastier – problem is frontloading. It can be extraordinarily tempting when cash is short for project-based firms to frontload their payment schedules so that more money is received near the beginning of a project or even before it starts. I certainly concede that sometimes you have no choice but to do this, but try very hard to get out of the habit, as it creates an endless cycle of "feast and famine" that will ultimately undermine your cash flow plan and your ability to keep your jobs running smoothly.

Furthermore, excessive frontloading may even prompt distrust on the part of your client, which not only may cost you jobs, but also may incline those who do sign with you to cling to their money as long as they can. Clients know that something's not right when your payment schedule entails having them remit 50% of your payments when only 20% of the project is done, or when only 5% of the money is left for the 20% of work at the end. These are the clients who want to hold your checks all together, which not only threatens your cash flow but practically guarantees that your client is not going to be entirely happy with your performance, and there goes your repeat business as well as your recommendation. By contrast, giving you a check once a week for the same amount while the project is progressing looks very reasonable from a client's perspective and is unlikely to raise any red flags that can ultimately be damaging to your reputation.

If you find that your current schedule will not allow for even, regular payments, consider tweaking it. In the above situation, for example, if testing is typically completed only two days before employee training, and a week and a half after rough installation, then it might be better to have the payment due on "Commencement of testing" rather than "Completion of testing," particularly if a subcontractor who will expect to get paid on completion is involved, as this will give you time to collect before you have to pay up. Also, consider the practical aspects of your payment schedule from your client's perspective. Having your final payment due on completion of employee training may work fine if there are ten employees in a single office. But a firm with dozens of employees in multiple locations, or a few overworked employees whose available time is strictly limited, may be tougher to schedule for training in a timely fashion. Remember, just because *you* can theoretically complete training in a few days doesn't mean it will be possible on your client's end.

As I will detail in the forthcoming CREATING A PLAN volume of this series, I strongly recommend that project-based firms plot out their projected income on a week-by-week basis as soon as this information becomes available – even if this means entering the data some months in advance. The reason is twofold. One, because doing this before a project starts will make it easier for you to plan for the both the income *and* the associated expense at the same time. For example, if a particular payment to you is associated with a large material purchase for which you must pay cash, you can plug the income figure and the expense under the same or adjacent weeks, which will significantly enhance the accuracy of your cash management plan. Second, because your payment schedule is intimately tied to your work schedule, it will enable you to see if there are conflicts that will prevent you from completing the work according to plan. If you only have one software installer and he is scheduled for two jobs in the same week, you're unlikely to be able to complete both on schedule, which is going to mess up your projected cash inflows. Many project-based firms already track this type of scheduling information on a job board, Gantt chart, or similar device – what I'm recommending is that you add a financial component to this type of planning. This way you can see, at a glance, what the financial impact of changes in your job schedule will be.

THE SEASONAL BUSINESS

Seasonal businesses will have their own means of projecting their income for a given month, year, or quarter. There are all sorts of sophisticated formulas businesses use to arrive at these figures, but ultimately, even the most complex calculations will yield only estimates of varying degrees of accuracy. So don't fret if your small business doesn't have access to an expensive staff of accountants – you can probably do just as well working with some prior years' figures and a calculator in arriving at a best guess.

Here are some examples of simplified methods seasonal businesses might use to project income for a particular period:

1) Use the prior year's figure. Perhaps the simplest method of projection is to look at what your income was for the given month of the previous year and use that for your current year's estimate. If you took in $100,000 last March, then it might be reasonable to expect similar revenues this upcoming March. This presumption is bolstered if you also took in roughly $100,000 the year before that or the year before that, as multiple similar values would strongly suggest a consistent pattern in revenues.

2) Use the prior year's quarterly or annual figure. If your business' monthly revenues are not predictable enough to use prior year comparisons on a month-by-month basis, examine your revenues by year or by quarter instead. Perhaps your sales boost occurs in the summer, but sometimes it's in August and sometimes in July, if it depends on the weather. If your total quarterly revenues are roughly the same over multiple years, however, you can feel fairly comfortable projecting a similar level of income for the upcoming summer.

3) Examine the monthly, quarterly, or annual pattern. Many businesses don't maintain a set level of income from year to year – in fact, most hope to see their revenues steadily increase, while an unfortunate few see theirs decline. You can use this information in creating more accurate projections.

For example, if your summer revenues increased by 10% in both 2016 and 2017, you might feel comfortable projecting a similar increase in 2018. Be cautious when making such presumptions, however – especially when it comes to projected increases. Always ponder the source and size of the change before assuming that it's part of a pattern, and remember that you'll take profit margin into account when you plot your expenses; here your concern is straight revenue. So if your revenues increased by 20% the previous summer, but it was only because you added a salesperson whose salary ate up all the profits, then you have to assume that your revenues will decline to their previous levels if he or she has been let go. This doesn't mean you're any worse off financially, but it will affect your plan, so you need to make sure you account for it when plotting your income.

Suppose instead that your revenues increased by 20% the previous summer, but you now feel you've maxed out the amount of business your firm can generate in your community. You might feel comfortable using the elevated figure as your current year's projection, but you wouldn't want to assume another similar increase. Likewise, if your December revenues declined by 20% from one year to the next, that doesn't mean you should expect the same decline again the following year. Perhaps it was a poor holiday season, or perhaps the city was still completing construction on your business' street. Or maybe you raised your holiday prices as an experiment and, in fact, made higher profits than you did in previous years, even though you had less revenue. In such cases you will probably do better to assume that the pattern is an aberration and use an estimate closer to whatever your income level was before the alteration.

MONTH	2016	2017	AVERAGE	% CHANGE	REVENUE ESTIMATE
JANUARY	30,000	33,000	31,500	+10%	30,000
FEBRUARY	20,000	10,000	15,000	-50%	15,000
MARCH	30,000	30,000	30,000	0%	30,000
APRIL	40,000	50,000	45,000	+25%	45,000
MAY	50,000	50,000	50,000	0%	50,000
JUNE	70,000	60,000	65,000	-14%	65,000
JULY	90,000	80,000	85,000	-11%	85,000
AUGUST	80,000	90,000	85,000	+12%	85,000
SEPTEMBER	70,000	70,000	70,000	0%	70,000
OCTOBER	70,000	72,000	71,000	+3%	70,000
NOVEMBER	60,000	58,000	59,000	-3%	60,000
DECEMBER	50,000	50,000	50,000	0%	50,000
TOTALS	660,000	653,000	656,500	-1%	655,000

Example of revenue estimates for a seasonal business. Note that although there have been significant monthly fluctuations, and a decrease in annual revenues between 2016 and 2017, the overall revenue change is very small and probably insignificant for our calculations. March, May, September and December all had no change in revenues between the two years and it would therefore be reasonable to estimate the same amount of income for 2018. January, October, and November all had small and probably insignificant changes; in these cases I will usually choose the lower figure for my estimates. The revenue streams for June, July and August appear to be a part of a seasonal variation, suggesting that averaging the monthly figures might be the best approach for this period. Finally, although I've used the averages for February and April in making my estimates, I will want to delve deeper into why those two months had such large changes in revenue between the two years – perhaps this year I can even take steps to boost my sales in February and thus rectify whatever went wrong in 2017.

A large percentage change in either direction, also, should be grounds for caution. If, historically, your revenues have fluctuated by less than 5% from year to year and you have a sudden increase of 30%, consider the cause. Did you have an unusually large sale the previous year you can't expect to repeat? Did you lower your prices by 40% in an attempt to generate additional sales and have since raised them back to their original level?

The secondary advantage, incidentally, to performing this type of analysis is that it forces you to re-examine what your business did in previous years – what worked and what didn't. And the value in this process alone is well worth the time you'll put into it, even without regard to your cash flow.

THE RETAIL ESTABLISHMENT

Retail establishments perhaps enjoy the dubious distinction of having both the most and the least predictable income streams of any business. A retail firm's revenues can vary widely from month to month and year to year, but they are also so heavily influenced by conditions at the store location that the progression of ups and downs – if not necessarily their amounts – can often be easily tracked. Any retail firm knows if its business will decline when the local college kids go home for the summer, or if it will increase when they're on break. Most stores know to expect a spike in sales from before Thanksgiving until just after Christmas and a corresponding slump after New Year's. A local city beautification project may tank revenues while it's underway, and may also provide a boost when it's completed. The closure of a competing grocery store virtually guarantees an increase in business for nearby supermarkets, while the opening of a new one invariably drags business away.

The key for retail establishments when projecting income, therefore, is to take into account those factors that result from their physical location and to acknowledge that they are subject to local as well as larger economic forces. An independent bookstore will undoubtedly lose business to online retailers like Amazon and Barnes and Noble, yet its survival may be more greatly affected by a detrimental change in its town's parking policies or zoning laws. A recall on contaminated lettuce at the supermarket down the street may hit the local salad shop hard, even if its product derives from a different source.

In most cases, retail businesses can utilize the methods I've already discussed for projecting their income: looking at prior year figures, analyzing patterns, and recognizing seasonal variations. But in addition, they need to be even more keenly aware of outside events that may directly affect them and adjust their projections accordingly.

Retail establishments may also be more likely to have income schedules that follow a daily pattern – i.e., more money coming in on the weekends, or, conversely, during the regular workweek. If yours experiences these fluctuations, you want to pay particular attention to how the number of days in the month – and which days they are – will affect your income schedule. Your rent, insurance, etc., only get paid once a month, so if Thursday is your biggest day and there are five in the month you're projecting, then you can expect your income to be higher during that month. If this is the case, you may want to analyze your income figures on a day-by-day basis – that is, rather than looking at the prior year's income for a given month, look at how it broke down day by day. Then transfer those figures to the days of the week applicable to the current month and make any other adjustments necessary to arrive at your projection.

INTERDEPENDENT INDUSTRIES

Remember the automotive industry tanking a few years back? How about the real estate lending market? The repercussions of such large-scale economic events aren't only confined to the industries directly affected; they ripple into a wide variety of sectors that are dependent upon the strength of the related market. If automobiles aren't selling, a sunroof manufacturer can expect a downturn in business, as can a seller and installer of GPS units. Of course, this doesn't always happen in such predictable ways. During the recession many residential contractors saw revenues plummet, not because homeowners were uninterested in having work done, but because potential clients were unable to borrow against their home's equity to finance remodels and upgrades.

The reverse can also be true. When real estate prices go through the roof, many homeowners become MORE inclined to invest

$300,000 in fixing up their current home because it's financially more feasible to remodel than move. Likewise, car owners who choose to postpone purchases of new automobiles may decide to spend their money on that stereo upgrade they've wanted instead, or those new tires. Enhancements like these may become more appealing when drivers intend to keep their current vehicle for a longer-than-usual period.

There is usually no reasonable way for dependent industries to calculate exactly what effect these types of occurrences will ultimately have on their business – although thanks to the events of the past decade, many of us now know first-hand. My best advice here is to monitor the situation very closely, and adjust your projections as soon as it seems necessary. If the factory across from your diner goes out of business and your revenues drop by 30%, you can probably safely assume that this trend will continue and you'd better do your best to prepare for its effects on your income and cash flow. If the effects are positive, be conservative in adjusting your estimates. If that same factory re-opens several months later, don't automatically assume that your revenues will re-attain their former levels. The firm might have less business going forward, or its operations may have undergone widespread, cost-saving restructuring – and machines, useful as they are, don't break for lunch.

BREAKING IT DOWN – HOW TO DETERMINE YOUR FIRM'S CASH INFLOW SCHEDULE

The following discussion utilizes the terminology "cash-based business," which may require some explanation, as the phrase could have different meanings in other contexts. I refer here to businesses whose customers pay at the time of purchase, whether it be by cash, check or credit card. An Accounts Receivable-based business would be one whose customers – usually other businesses – mostly pay on account. The type of payment system a firm has in place will have a tremendous impact on its cash flow, as cash-based businesses collect their cash right away, whereas A/R-based businesses may have to wait weeks or even months after a sale before their payment comes through.

The difference this makes in projecting income is a highly significant one. Surprisingly, A/R-based projections can ultimately prove to be more accurate because of the time lapse involved; firms that carefully examine their historical data on how long it takes for them to get paid can usually derive some pretty good averages that will allow them to loosely predict when their cash will arrive. Cash-based businesses, by contrast, are more subject to the vagaries of the day-to-day – the joy when sales are higher than expected and the disappointment when the numbers come in under target. The cash-based business also has the opportunity, every day, to influence how much money goes into its bank account, while the A/R business is more dependent upon what happened in the weeks or months before now. A cash-based business benefits from a boost in sales right away; an A/R-based business may have to wait several weeks before enjoying an increase in funds. But the reverse is also true – an A/R-based business whose sales are lower than expected probably won't feel the effects on its projections until the following month, while in a cash-based business, the change will be both immediate and painful.

It's therefore important to recognize the limitations applicable to each type of system when you're making projections.

CASH-BASED BUSINESSES

If you're a cash-based business, you probably have a pretty good idea of when you make your money. Maybe your sales are highest over the weekend, or maybe on Tuesday evenings when you offer your family discount. Many businesses see a decline in income around the first of the month, when most people's rent is due – and those of you who remember when Social Security was always paid on the third might also recall a corresponding boost in business on that day and the next.

When you're struggling with cash, however, you can't afford to operate on the basis of your general impressions. Tuesday may be your busiest night – but if that's only because you sell a hundred cheap scoops of ice cream to Little Leaguers after their game, then it might not be the night you take in the most cash. Maybe your income is highest on that one day a month when you offer a discount to seniors – but if most of them pay you with personal checks that won't clear your bank for several days, then you need to account for that when planning your bill payments.

In other words, you probably already know which of your sales strategies produce the most business. But you might not know which ones generate the most – or the most quickly available – cash.

Skilled financial people may choose to break down their sales and cash figures in Excel, which will permit you to quickly make calculations and comparisons that will give you the information you need. But here's a quick-and-dirty way to do roughly the same analysis without having to work with Excel or make laborious calculations.

Take an ordinary wall or desk calendar and mark two figures on it every day. The first will be your sales for the day – your accounting or POS software probably generates this information in a daily summary report, and quite likely you're tracking it already. The second figure will be the amount of cash that became available on that day – that means actual cash deposits, credit card payments that hit your account, and check deposits that cleared your bank (if your bank puts a hold on your checks). You may find it useful to round the figures to the nearest hundred or thousand, as single and double digits can present a visual distraction and aren't usually relevant for this purpose.

At the end of the month, go through and look at these figures – just look at them. Having those numbers in a grid setup should make any patterns become rapidly apparent. For instance, you should quickly be able to see it if most of your sales come in on the weekend – and whether that makes Saturday, Sunday, Monday or Tuesday your biggest cash day. You'll be able to tell if your numbers are higher at the beginning or the end of the month, or whether you have more cash sales on Fridays when many people get paid, as opposed to credit card sales which may hit your account on other days of the week. All of these observations will prove indispensable to you in determining the ups and downs of your cash cycle, thus giving you a keener edge in creating your plan.

WHEN YOUR FIRM USES ACCOUNTS RECEIVABLE – HOW TO PREDICT WHAT YOU'LL COLLECT WHEN

Firms that utilize an Accounts Receivable system generally hope to be paid in accordance with their stated terms. That is, if their terms are Net 10th, they hope to be paid by the 10th, and if they're Net 30, they hope to be paid within 30 days (see Volume 1 of this series, DEALING WITH VENDORS, for a full explanation of terms). In practice, of course, this only happens a small part of the time, particularly if those firms' customers are companies like yours, for whom making such timely payments is only a pipe dream. There are things you can do to speed up the payment process (see SUCCESSFUL COLLECTIONS, below), but if you're in a cash-poor situation yourself, you do not want to be overly optimistic – at least not when you're creating your plan. Therefore the first step in figuring out how much you'll collect when is to determine how it has worked out historically (see AN ACCOUNTS RECEIVABLE EXAMPLE, below). Derive your estimates initially based on historical data and adjust them as needed – this will help to prevent you from being caught with your metaphorical pants down around your ankles, your empty wallet inside them.

The level of accuracy required in your estimate will increase the more dire your cash situation is. A firm with comparatively minor cash flow problems may have the luxury of enjoying a margin of error totaling thousands of dollars, while a desperately cash-poor firm may need to cut that margin to hundreds, or even less. I know I've been in situations where even $50 could make a difference, and others where $2,000 one way or another wasn't that big of a deal. Likewise with timing – you may need to count your pennies down to the day, or you may only need to ballpark how much you're going to get in a week. In general, arriving at more precise estimates is going to require more labor, so you can always trying ballparking your figures in the beginning and honing in for more detail if you think it will benefit you.

TRACK YOUR INFLOWS

As with cash-based businesses, I highly recommend that A/R-based businesses make a point of tracking both their daily sales and their daily cash flow. The quickie "calendar" method I describe above will work adequately for those who do not want to futz around with Excel. However, unlike with cash-based businesses, in which payment becomes available no more than a few days following a sale, if your firm runs on A/R, bear in mind that the time of collection is usually going to be far enough removed from the time of sale where one is unlikely to be directly traceable to the other without a great deal of paperwork. You therefore probably won't be able to see at a glance how one flows into the other, but as I discuss below, you should still be able, mathematically, to track it.

WHEN POSSIBLE, USE DIRECT TRACING

Under PROJECT-BASED FIRMS, above, I discussed how businesses who get paid upon completion of particular phases of a project should plot out their income on a timeline that matches their projected work schedule, but even non-project-based firms can benefit from this methodology. If your business is small enough to make it both feasible and cost-effective, you will want to plot out your projected cash inflows on a client-by-client, invoice-by-invoice, or statement-by-statement basis.

Suppose, for example, that your terms are Net 30, meaning that your invoices are due within 30 days. On Friday, the thirteenth of May you send out three invoices for $5,000 apiece. Based on your historical data, you are fairly confident that of your three customers, one will pay you in four weeks, one in five weeks, and one in six weeks. You could therefore plot out your projected income schedule as follows:

Week Ending June 10th: $5,000
Week Ending June 17th: $5,000
Week Ending June 24th: $5,000

Now maybe I don't know precisely on what day these three checks will arrive, but if I'm cutting my own A/P checks on Fridays, then all that really matters is that I'm pretty sure I'm going to have that money sometime that week, which is enough information to allow me to plan.

Now suppose that instead of my invoices being dated for the 13th, they're dated for Tuesday the 10th. In that case I'm probably not going to want to change my projected payment schedule because it's likely that I will still receive those payments at some point during those same weeks – in other words, they will still get rolled into that week's Accounts Payable run. If my invoices are dated for Monday the 16th instead, then I may want to push my collection schedule back a week, because I probably won't get my money until the week following – i.e., too late for the previous Friday's check run.

Now suppose that week-by-week planning isn't sufficient for some reason. Let's say I have to make an estimated tax payment on June 15th – if my money doesn't come in until the 17th, it might be too late. Then maybe I want to examine my five-week client's history more closely – do they really tend to pay me within five weeks, or is it within 32 or 33 days? Perhaps they're mailing their check out on the 30th day so I'm always receiving it a few days late (which, as I discuss in the first volume of this series, DEALING WITH VENDORS, is a strategy I myself recommend). If this is the case, then perhaps I will get their check on time, after all. But to be on the safe side, maybe I want to prioritize getting their invoice out early so I'll have a few days leeway in case they're a little later than usual.

Similarly, suppose that with my third client, six weeks is an average. In reality, they usually pay within 40 days, but occasionally that stretches out to 49. If I'm in a position where I don't want to count on that money unless I'm pretty darned sure I'm going to get it, then I may want to push their projected payment back to the week ending July 1st. If I really need to know whether I'm going to have it the previous week, then that might warrant a polite phone call to them around the 17th to check when their payment will be going out in the current month.

You can use the same methodology for other terms, too – in fact, sometimes it's easier. If your terms are Net 10th, for example, meaning that your invoices are due on the 10th of the following month, then you will probably find that most of your customers will tend to pay at roughly the same time each month – or at least within the same week. You can therefore plot their projected payments into your inflow schedule with a fair amount of precision – these five the week of the 10th, these ten the week of the 17th, and so on. Those of your customers who are unreliable can have their projected payments shoved back to the end of the month or even into the following month, as you won't want their unpredictability to affect your short-term planning.

Firms for whom the volume of business makes this method unreasonable – or whose customers' payment schedules are too volatile to effectively track – can nonetheless achieve similar results with a little more math.

WHEN YOUR MONEY IS DUE BY THE 10TH – OR THE 15TH OR 30TH, ETC.

If your receivables are due by a particular day of the month, then it should be fairly easy for you to calculate about how much money you can expect when. Consider the following example. Let's suppose that at the end of May, 2016, we have Accounts Receivable totaling $250,000, our invoices are due on the 10th, and that our actual collections schedule, broken down week by week, is as follows. (A tool like the table on Page 173 can help you keep track of this information; see ATTAINING YOUR GOAL, later.)

Week Ending June 3rd: $10,000 (these are likely unpaid bills from the previous month, April)
Week Ending June 10th: $40,000
Week Ending June 17th: $80,000

Week Ending June 24th: $80,000
Week Ending July 1st: $20,000
Total: $230,000

We can then use percentages to prepare a breakdown of how much money we received in each week of the month:

Week 1: 4%
Week 2: 16%
Week 3: 32%
Week 4: 32%
Week 5: 8%
Total: 92%

 The first thing we're likely to notice is that in spite of the fact that our invoices are due on the 10th, a fairly small percentage of our money actually arrives by the 10th – most of it comes in during the two weeks after. Following this influx is a rather long dry spell, stretching from the last week of one month through the first week of the next, in which very little cash is available. This pattern will have a huge effect on our ability to make payments during this period.
 The second thing we might notice is that our percentages and dollar amounts don't add up to $250,000, the total amount of our current A/R. This means we didn't get paid for about 8% of our previous month's Accounts Receivable, or $20,000. (In reality, some of the payments we did receive during the course of this month were probably not from May at all, but from April, as I discuss further below. For this purpose, however, we're mostly concerned with arriving at an average figure we expect to collect based on our total A/R.)
 The next noteworthy feature of this breakdown is that it has five weeks in it, whereas months really only contain four and a half. In practice I usually make this calculation on a four-week basis because I want my estimates to match the number of Fridays in a month, which is the day I like to cut checks – that way my projected income figures will coincide with my projected payment schedule. In this case, the final Friday (July 1st) was so close to the end of June that it made sense to include it. If I had been planning for the month of May, however, my breakdown might have gone more like this:

Week Ending May 6th: $20,000 (8%)
Week Ending May 13th: $40,000 (16%)
Week Ending May 20th: $100,000 (40%)
Week Ending May 27th: $70,000 (28%)
Total: $230,000 (92%)

This will approximate for me how much money I'm going to have available for each individual check run, of which there are now four. Again, the exact methodology I'm going to use is going to depend on how precise my estimates need to be. Perhaps I want to sum up my income over 5-day periods, so that there will be six to a month, and use that for planning. Perhaps I even want to calculate my percentages on a daily basis – although that may ultimately prove misleading unless my results are really, really consistent. In my experience, weekly works well and isn't overly burdensome in terms of calculations.

We aren't done yet, though! One month's worth of data may be instructive, but it's too small a sample size for me reasonably to rely on. I'm going to want to keep track of this not only for several months in a row, but probably also on an ongoing basis – this will make sure that I notice if my stats change. I'm then going to want to average out my collection percentages and see where they fall. For example, here's a sample breakdown over a four-month period:

Week 1: (6 + 8 + 8 + 6) / 4 = 7%
Week 2: (20 + 18 + 16 + 18) / 4 = 18%
Week 3: (40 + 36 + 38 + 38) / 4 = 38%
Week 4: (24 + 30 + 26 + 28) / 4 = 27%
Total: (90 + 92 + 86 + 90) / 4 = 90%

Note that not only have there been significant monthly variations when I calculate my income by week, but my average total percentage collected has dropped down to 90%. This is because I only got 86% in the third month, without a corresponding "make-up" increase in the following month. This is a statistically significant change, and I will probably want to go back and look at what happened if I don't remember off-hand. Did a customer go bankrupt? Was there a dispute? Did we issue a large credit or write off a balance? Whatever transpired here, I will want to determine whether it was an ordinary occurrence in the course of my business or an extraordinary event that's unlikely to happen again, as this will affect my long-term projections. As you assemble more data, these unusual events will have less of an impact, but in the meantime, it's important to be aware of noteworthy fluctuations, not only because of their effect on your cash flow, but because of what they can tell you about the state of your business.

So what now? It's surprisingly simple. Suppose we're in a different month all together, and our prior month's ending A/R balance was $300,000. Now we can predict the following inflows:

Week 1: $21,000 (7% of $300,000)
Week 2: $54,000 (18% of $300,000)
Week 3: $114,000 (38% of $300,000)
Week 4: $81,000 (27% of $300,000)
Total: $270,000 (90% of $300,000, with $30,000 left unpaid at the end of the month)

Okay, that's great, but what are we going to do about this huge unpaid balance? We'll get to that in a moment; but first let's finish talking about what this means mathematically.

For simplicity's sake, I've employed one figure here – a single percentage in relation to total A/R. For many firms, this will suffice, and if your total collections are roughly the same month after month as a percentage of your total A/R, you should be able to use this number satisfactorily. If your results are inconsistent, however, or your income varies widely enough where in some months your collections on past due balances form a significant portion of your total collections, then you may wish to get a little fancier.

Suppose, for example, that the breakdown of Accounts Receivable at the end of the $300,000 month above is as follows (you can generally access this information in your accounting software as an A/R Aging Report):

Current A/R: $220,000
1 –30: $50,000
31 – 60: $20,000
61 – 90: $5,000
Over 90: $5,000
Total: $300,000

On the last day of the month, my Aging is as follows. (Note that these figures exclude the current month's invoices, and that depending on how your accounting software works, some of the overdue balances may have changed columns during the course of the month.)

Current A/R: $10,000 (excluding the current month's invoices)
1 –30: $10,000
31 – 60: $5,000
61 – 90: $2,000
Over 90: $3,000
Total: $30,000

Now I can figure out how much I collected of each age of balance:

Current A/R: $210,000 ($220,000 - $10,000) or 95% of the beginning "current" balance
1 –30: $40,000 ($50,000 - $10,000) or 80% of the 1 to 30-day balance
31 – 60: $15,000 ($20,000 - $5,000) or 75% of the 31 to 60-day balance
61 – 90: $3,000 ($5,000 - $2,000) or 60% of the 61 to 90-day balance
Over 90: $2,000 ($5,000 - $3,000) or 40% of the Over 90 balance
Total: $270,000

If I keep track of this for a number of months, then eventually I will be able to put together some pretty good averages that I can use to more accurately estimate my potential collections. If my month-end A/R balance breaks down as follows:

Current A/R: $160,000
1 –30: $60,000
31 – 60: $40,000
61 – 90: $5,000
Over 90: $5,000
Total: $270,000

Then I can only reasonably expect to collect this much:

Current A/R: $153,000 (95%)
1 –30: $48,000 (80%)
31 – 60: $30,000 (75%)

61 – 90: $3,000 (60%)
Over 90: $2,000 (40%)
Total: $236,000 (87% of total)

As you can see, my net percentage of collections has dropped significantly, a difference that will become more pronounced the more aged balances you have on your books.

Furthermore, however your figures break down, I would caution you against relying too heavily on collecting on your older balances – the Over 60 and Over 90 columns in this example – unless your numbers are really consistent month after month, say, because you have customers who, like you, may be constantly behind, but not falling any further behind. Yes, your history may show that, on average, you eventually collect 12.5% of all balances that go over 120 days, and that can be informative when you're examining your overall return on receivables. But "eventually" is not a useful term for firms that need to know whether they'll be able to cover a check for $2,653 in four days if they only have $653 right now. If a balance is so aged that it forms a part of your "way past due" calculation, then it's simply inadvisable to depend on its remittance during any given time period. Instead, carefully examine each of your past due balances and try to determine when they might, in reality, actually be paid. If a particular client generally coughs up close to the 120-day mark, or at the end of each fiscal quarter, you can plug those values in as potential paydays under the relevant – and far-off – weeks. If you really have no idea when or if they might pay you, leave them off your predicted payment schedule all together. For your planning purposes, it's better to assume that the Easter Bunny isn't coming at all, than to count your chickens when they may in fact end up being nothing more than colorful rotten eggs.

ATTAINING YOUR "GOAL" – PLANNING TOOLS TO AID BOTH YOUR CASH FLOW AND YOUR OPERATIONS

I have found the following tool quite useful in performing the ongoing budgetary maintenance required in firms with cash flow issues. Like many such tools, it can easily be adapted as an "add-on" to other figures tracking you may already be doing, in this case, the setting of sales or collections goals.

I'm going to make a distinction here between these types of projection "goals" and the "goals" many firms set for their salespeople – the pipe-dream targets that are supposed to serve as an incentive but that no one really expects them to hit. No, the goals I'm referring to are more realistic because they represent what you actually *expect* to achieve rather than what you *hope* to achieve.

For instance, in the cash-based business example below under PUTTING IT ALL TOGETHER, we project income of $63,000 for June. Once we have this figure, we can set up a simple table to keep track of our progress:

June 1: Sold $3,000, Balance remaining $60,000
June 2: Sold $1,000, Balance remaining $59,000
June 3: Sold $2,000, Balance remaining $57,000

And so on. As the month goes on, the total sales and the remaining balance might tell us we need to adjust our projection. If we get to the middle of the month and we see this:

June 15: Sold $1,000, Balance remaining $35,000

Then we might begin to think it's unlikely that we're going to take in another $35,000 in the last 15 days of the month if we only took in $28,000 in the first 15 days. In fact, absent other information that suggests that our sales are about to go up, to be on the safe side, we should probably revise our cash flow projection to more like $56,000 ($28,000 times two), a decrease of $9,000. We won't be happy doing this, but we'll be a lot happier than we would be than if we wait until the end of the month to accept the fact that we're going to be short by $9,000.

You can use a similar setup to keep track of your outstanding A/R. Simply set columns – preferable in Excel or similar program – with your projected collections amount and then, in a separate column, subtract the amount you collect each day. Set the last column to keep a daily running total of how much A/R you have left to collect in the month, which will allow you to see if you're falling behind or even pulling ahead, and will cue you as to whether you might need to change your projection.

DATE	COLLECTION PROJECTION	AMOUNT COLLECTED	REMAINING BALANCE	% OF TOTAL
07/01/18	$200,000	$0	$200,000	0.0%
07/02/18	$200,000	$1,000	$199,000	0.5%
07/03/18	$199,000	$2,000	$197,000	1.0%
07/04/18	$197,000	$0	$197,000	0.0%
07/05/18	$197,000	$5,000	$192,000	2.5%
07/06/18	$192,000	$2,000	$190,000	1.0%
07/07/18	$190,000	$4,000	$186,000	2.0%
07/08/18	$186,000	$0	$186,000	0.0%
07/09/18	$186,000	$6,000	$180,000	3.0%
07/10/18	$180,000	$10,000	$170,000	5.0%
07/11/18	$170,000	$10,000	$160,000	5.0%
07/12/18	$160,000	$10,000	$150,000	5.0%
07/13/18	$150,000	$10,000	$140,000	5.0%
07/14/18	$140,000	$10,000	$130,000	5.0%
07/15/18	$130,000	$0	$130,000	0.0%
07/16/18	$130,000	$20,000	$110,000	10.0%
07/17/18	$110,000	$20,000	$90,000	10.0%
07/18/18	$90,000	$35,000	$55,000	17.5%
07/19/18	$55,000	$10,000	$45,000	5.0%
07/20/18	$45,000	$10,000	$35,000	5.0%
07/21/18	$35,000	$15,000	$20,000	7.5%
07/22/18	$20,000	$0	$20,000	0.0%
07/23/18	$20,000	$5,000	$15,000	2.5%
07/24/18	$15,000	$5,000	$10,000	2.5%
07/25/18	$10,000	$2,000	$8,000	1.0%
07/26/18	$8,000	$2,000	$6,000	1.0%
07/27/18	$6,000	$2,000	$4,000	1.0%
07/28/18	$4,000	$2,000	$2,000	1.0%
07/29/18	$2,000	$0	$2,000	0.0%
07/30/18	$2,000	$2,000	$0	1.0%
07/31/18	$2,000	$2,000	-$2,000	1.0%

Tracking your Accounts Receivable collections. In this case we came out $2,000 ahead of our projection – hence the negative $2,000 ending balance. Note also that there are "zeroes" on Sundays and holidays because there's no mail and banks are closed.

If you track this data for a few months, a table of this type can also serve the dual purpose of allowing you to easily determine what percentage of your A/R you can expect to collect in any given week of the month.

The second tool is not so reliable, and I have some reservations about recommending it, because its basis is so arbitrary; however, since I have found it useful, particularly in estimating an upcoming month's A/R, I'll share it with you and let you decide.

As I've mentioned, you want to plan pretty far ahead when you're working with cash flow. This is especially important with an Accounts Receivable-based business because your opportunities to affect your next month's income end with the previous month, not the current month. Therefore, if you want to stay on top of your A/P, you have to make assumptions about what's going to happen next month before the current month even begins. This tool gives you the opportunity to begin replacing those prior assumptions with semi-hard data in the middle of the current month.

It's a very simple calculation and easy to implement via formulas in Excel. All you're going to do is pro-rate the A/R you've accumulated in the month to date, and then multiply it out by the rest of the days in the month. So, for example, if your business is open every day, and by the 10th of June you've accumulated $60,000 in sales, that's $6,000 per day, which projects out to $180,000 for the month.

You see what I mean about this being arbitrary, because there's usually no basis for believing that if you had $6,000 in sales in the first 10 days of the month, that you'll have similar sales in the last 20 days of the month. In fact, I would be reluctant to rely heavily on figures like these until much later in the month, say, the 20th, when mathematically they are much more likely to reflect how your month is going. But if you do get to a number you feel comfortable with, you may be able to use it to get a jump on planning for the following month.

For example, if I've based my A/P payment schedule for July on the presumption that I was going to collect $190,000 in current A/R, and my new projection is only suggesting *total* sales of $180,000, then I'm going to be off – about $20,000 off if I only collect 95% of my current A/R. If this is happening, I can't wait until the end of the month, I need to know *now* so that I can make adjustments right away, and also alert management to the potential problem.

DATE	DAY OF MONTH	REMAINING GOAL	SALES	PROJECTED SALES
07/01/18	X	$200,000	$0	#VALUE!
07/02/18	1	$200,000	$2,000	$50,000
07/03/18	2	$198,000	$2,000	$50,000
07/04/18	X	$196,000	$0	#VALUE!
07/05/18	3	$196,000	$10,000	$116,667
07/06/18	4	$186,000	$10,000	$150,000
07/07/18	5	$176,000	$5,000	$145,000
07/08/18	X	$171,000	$0	#VALUE!
07/09/18	6	$171,000	$8,000	$154,167
07/10/18	7	$163,000	$8,000	$160,714
07/11/18	8	$155,000	$8,000	$165,625
07/12/18	9	$147,000	$10,000	$175,000
07/13/18	10	$137,000	$10,000	$182,500
07/14/18	11	$127,000	$4,000	$175,000
07/15/18	X	$123,000	$0	#VALUE!
07/16/18	12	$123,000	$6,000	$172,917
07/17/18	13	$117,000	$6,000	$171,154
07/18/18	14	$111,000	$6,000	$169,643
07/19/18	15	$105,000	$8,000	$171,667
07/20/18	16	$97,000	$8,000	$173,438
07/21/18	17	$89,000	$4,000	$169,118
07/22/18	X	$85,000	$0	#VALUE!
07/23/18	18	$85,000	$10,000	$173,611
07/24/18	19	$75,000	$10,000	$177,632
07/25/18	20	$65,000	$10,000	$181,250
07/26/18	21	$55,000	$8,000	$182,143
07/27/18	22	$47,000	$8,000	$182,955
07/28/18	23	$39,000	$4,000	$179,348
07/29/18	X	$35,000	$0	#VALUE!
07/30/18	24	$35,000	$12,000	$184,375
07/31/18	25	$23,000	$12,000	$189,000

Estimating projected sales by pro-ration, with Sundays and holidays excluded from the calculation because the business is closed. Note how the daily sales variations – especially early in the month – have a significant impact on the projected monthly sales. The total sales projections become more accurate towards the end of the month. By mid-month it already looks likely that I'm not going to meet my sales goal of $200,000 and I should adjust my cash flow plan accordingly.

In fact, the beauty of this tool, even with its flaws, is that it not only assists you in projecting your cash inflows, but it doubles as a report that can be useful for sales personnel and for management. While your accounting software will certainly track your monthly sales-to-date, it probably does not extrapolate those out into projections, and this simple and easy-to-maintain spreadsheet gives you a quick way to present that data. Even more importantly, as the accounting person, this gives me the opportunity to make changes *before* I'm stuck with a massive cash shortage. Maybe the checks I send out in the last two weeks of this month are going to need to be smaller than I expected, or maybe I have to postpone a payment to a vendor until I see what happens in the rest of the month. Making this quick calculation in advance may in fact save me from making serious errors in my payment schedule, errors from which it may take me months to recover. Even better, I now also have the opportunity to intervene in operations if the situation demands it. What if there are expenses next month that can't be put off? What if I absolutely must pay off the line of credit or make a large tax payment and there isn't much wiggle room in my payment schedule? Then it behooves me to take my concerns directly to management. Management can then take steps to alleviate the problem before it occurs. Perhaps the big sales push that was planned for next month needs to start early. Perhaps it's time to get aggressive with collecting on our customer's old past-due balances, or to negotiate a settlement over an invoice dispute. Even if there's nothing that can be done, key personnel should be forewarned that next month is going to be a bad month – which might mean no unnecessary expenses, postponing large inventory purchases, cutting labor hours, etc.

Now, of course, if I have a means of figuring out what my actual sales are going to be – say because of work that's booked or scheduled – that's going to be far more precise and will give me the information I need without resorting to this somewhat arbitrary method of estimation. But if I have no way of tracking that – or no *cost-effective* way of tracking it – then prorating and extrapolating my projected A/R can be quite useful, particularly as my firm approaches the end of the month.

So when it comes to this tool, use it if you think it may help you, but use it with caution, because it can also mislead you.

PUTTING IT ALL TOGETHER

Now that we're familiar with all of the pieces that go into predicting an income stream, let's put it all together. Let's begin with a retail business operating on a cash (as opposed to an Accounts Receivable) basis, and suppose that it's April of 2018 and that we're currently planning for the month of June.

Since my business is in a summer vacation destination and is seasonally affected, I'm going to begin by looking at my prior year sales figures for the month of June.

2017: $60,000
2016: $50,000

From these two figures, it looks like my business is trending an increase of about 20%, but this is probably too big an increase and too small a data set for me to rely on, so let me take a look at some earlier figures as well:

2015: $55,000
2014: $50,000

Hmm. Well, I still seem to be showing an increase, but not a perfectly steady one. Let's see how I'm doing for the first quarter so far:

2018 (through March): $200,000
2017 (through March): $190,000
2016 (through March): $180,000

This is more promising. Now I'm showing an upward trend over a three-year period, although it's only about 5%, and not 20%. Since I probably want to err on the conservative side, let's figure an increase of 5% over 2017, or $63,000 for the month of June.

If my income arrives in a relatively even stream, I can estimate my daily revenues by simply dividing $63,000 by 30 days, which comes out to $2,100 a day. I can then use this figure in determining how much cash I can reasonably expect to have available on individual days. If my income stream is highly unpredictable, I will probably want to use the same figure because while I can't really guess how much I'll take in on individual days, I can be fairly confident in my average.

Now suppose instead that prior analysis has shown me that 50% of my income comes in on Friday, Saturday, and Sunday. Half of that is cash which is immediately available; the other half credit card payments which, because of my processor's submission schedule, aren't available until Tuesday morning. The other 50% of my money comes in evenly over Monday through Thursday, so that each day generates 12.5% of my weekly income. In reality, therefore, Tuesday, while not my biggest sales day, is actually my biggest cash day because I will receive 50% of my weekend income via credit cards, as well as half of Tuesday's income in the form of cash payments.

What conclusion can I draw from this? Well, if my weekly payday is on Friday, then I probably want to plan to send A/P checks out no sooner than Monday so I can be sure I made what I expected to make over the weekend and still be able to cover my payroll. Most likely I will not even want to cut checks before Monday so I know exactly how much I have available.

BUT WAIT – WHAT IF MY MONTH HAS FIVE WEEKENDS?

It happens – four times a year, to be precise – which can create planning and additional cash flow difficulties, especially for those with weekly or biweekly payroll.

In the preceding example, the cash-basis company will probably make out all right because although five Fridays in a month means an additional payroll, this firm makes more of its money over the weekend. And, in fact, if this is our pattern, then we ought to go back and check the calendar for the previous June to see if day-of-the-week timing was actually the source of our increase in income. If last year contained five weekends and this year does not, then we may wish to reduce our income estimate further, or even calculate it on a day-of-the-week basis.

For example, let's suppose again that we took in $60,000 last June, or an average of $2,000 a day. If last year we had five sets of Fridays, Saturdays, and Sundays, on which we made $2,500 apiece, plus another 15 non-weekend days in which we made only $1,500 apiece, then clearly this would affect our estimate considerably. If my current year's month only has four weekends or twelve days at $2,500 apiece, totaling $30,000, and 18 days at $1,500 apiece, totaling $27,000, then my projected total might only be $57,000, a decrease over the previous year.

Therefore, if your company's sales vary widely based on the day of the week, then this is definitely an analysis you want to perform, as accurate projections require more than a surface understanding of what these figures mean. When in doubt, assume the lesser amount – if more money comes in, I'm sure you'll find a use for it somehow!

AN ACCOUNTS RECEIVABLE EXAMPLE

Now let's suppose that we anticipate the same level of income – $63,000 – but we're a wholesaler whose clients are other businesses. Here we're most likely to be operating under an Accounts Receivable system, and this may have a huge effect on our cash flow.

So first of all, let's assume the following.

1) We collect 90% of our current month's A/R before the end of the following month.

2) We collect 5% of our current month's A/R by the end of the month after that.

3) 5% of our A/R goes beyond 60 days, making the timing of collections unreliable.

So, out of the $63,000 I'm anticipating earning in June, I can reasonably expect to collect about 90%, or $57,000 rounded, in July. Now if my income in May was $80,000, then I may also have 5% or

$4,000 in leftover A/R that I can reasonably expect to collect in July as well, making my total about $61,000. I can double-check this by looking at my outstanding A/R from the end of May – if it's $8,000, then it seems likely that $4,000 will come in during the course of the month.

Suppose now that my client invoices are due on the 15th and I've previously determined the following breakdown of what comes in when:

Days 1 – 5: 10%
Days 6 – 10: 15%
Days 11 – 15: 15%
Days 16 – 20: 25%
Days 21 – 25: 25%
Days 26 – 30 (31): 10%

Now I'm looking at about $6,000 in income the first five days of the month, $30,000 between the 16th and 25th, and so on. Clearly I will do well to schedule my bulkiest A/P payments in the latter half of the month, especially if I have pesky large payments like rent due on the first of the month and won't be able to pay much else.

In practice, I would be unlikely to use a five-day breakdown, however; although it divides the month up quite neatly, it doesn't jive very well with my weekly payroll and A/P schedule. In this case, I would probably arrange my breakdown more like this and recalculate my income on a roughly weekly basis:

Days 1 – 8: 15%
Days 9 – 16: 25%
Days 17 – 23: 45%
Days 24 – 30: 15%

Using figures rounded to the nearest five hundred, I'm figuring on collecting about $9,500 in the first week, $16,000 in the second week, $28,000 in the third week, and the final $9,500 during the last week of the month. I can compensate for any minor timing discrepancies by holding A/P checks for a day or two if I need to do so.

You can clearly see how much easier performing this analysis makes it to plan. I quite literally have almost three times as much cash coming in during Week 3 as I do in Weeks 1 or 4, and although I can't schedule everything for that week because I would run out of money, I do want to time my payments accordingly when I can. It's extremely helpful when vendors call to be able to tell them to expect payment by the 23rd – especially when you know, mathematically, that you can deliver.

ONCE YOU'VE DETERMINED YOUR INFLOW PATTERN

The detailed information you've assembled regarding your inflows will form an integral part of your ultimate cash flow plan, and we will discuss further how to plot your income into your cash flow schedule in the forthcoming CREATING A PLAN volume of this series. But you can clearly see how knowing your pattern can have an immediate and positive effect on the financial decisions you make concerning your cash flow. For instance, if you are able to determine that Wednesday is your lowest-cash day of the week, and your payroll taxes come out on Wednesdays besides, then you may not want to schedule additional Accounts Payable payments for Wednesdays unless you really must do so. But while it's important to think about the effect of your collection schedule on your cash flow, you should also be careful to consider whether, in light of this data, making changes to your operations or financial policies might benefit your company as well.

For example, if Wednesday is your bad cash flow day and you are a cash-based rather than Accounts Receivable-based business, then you may wish to consider whether offering a discount on Wednesdays could provide a boost to your mid-week slump. If you're an Accounts Receivable-based business and your cash flow always tanks around the first of the month when you're trying to come up with your rent, consider offering a prompt-payment discount for customers who pay by the first. If you're concerned about how much this might cost you, don't worry – you can always reverse this policy if it proves to be too expensive. And when you're constantly desperate for cash, it can be nice to have a new thing to try, even if it ultimately doesn't work out.

SHOULD YOU ACCEPT CREDIT CARDS?

If your business sells its service or product directly to individual consumers, then accepting credit cards for payment is standard practice nowadays and very tough to avoid. While there are firms who can get by without them and the fees they entail, most businesses will need to offer credit card acceptance or suffer loss of sales accordingly.

It's important to consider the nature of your business, however. Businesses selling high-cost products or services for which check payments have long been the norm may find that offering credit cards as a method of payment does nothing more than pad their customers' rewards accounts while the firm pays the expense.

Take a car dealership, for example. Most people are unlikely to finance a vehicle purchase by putting it on a credit card when low-interest-rate auto loans are so readily available. It's far more likely that someone who does wish to use a credit card has the cash to pay for their vehicle in full and only wants to use the card to rack up their miles. Will your dealership lose the sale if you don't accept credit cards as payment, or will that customer, if they're happy with their deal, simply agree to pay by check instead?

This may depend not only on your policy, but on the policy of the firm down the street. If they're accepting credit cards, then it is entirely possible that you'll need to as well if you want to compete. But be very careful to consider the cost before you make such a leap. If your credit card processor charges 2% and you make a $10,000 used vehicle sale, it's only costing you $200, which doesn't sound so outrageous. But remember that once you start offering card payments, you're going to get people who will make them when otherwise they would have been happy to pay you by cash or by check. Yes, maybe you made a $10,000 sale you wouldn't have made without taking credit cards – but you may also have spent some serious money processing cards for other sales you would have made anyway, and your profit margin will suffer accordingly.

Residential contractors provide another excellent example. It's been my experience that clients do sometimes want to make payments via credit card, even for jobs in the hundreds of thousands of dollars. Now you know that someone who can afford to charge a job of that size has plenty of cash available, and they will also often tell you outright that they're only doing it for the miles. Will you lose their project if you don't accept credit card payments? It's highly unlikely. Selecting a contractor for a large project like that requires lengthy and careful consideration, and decisions are often based as much on intangibles such as whether the clients like the crew members as on price. In such a case, there's really no point in you forfeiting literally thousands of dollars in fees so you can finance someone's VISA rewards.

The story may be different for a smaller or handyman-type contractor. On-call plumbers, electricians, etc., may not only win more business by accepting credit card payments, as their services often fall into the category of urgent repairs, but they may also experience less risk than they would by taking personal checks, which will certainly help to defray the cost of credit card processing.

What about those who perform both large and small jobs? Unless you have specific evidence to the contrary, or the ratio of large to small jobs is really low, I would argue against it. If you accept credit cards in the hopes of winning more small jobs, and the price you pay is having your clients with larger jobs also pay you by credit card, then you're unlikely to come out ahead.

And in general, this is also true for businesses that provide products or services to other businesses. Yes, you absolutely will have customers who will pay you more promptly if you accept credit card payments. You may even have some who won't pay you at all if they can't charge their remittance. But if you let one firm do it, you're probably going to be letting all of them do it, and that can very rapidly rack up your processing fees to dangerous levels. In my experience, many firms that have always paid promptly by check are delighted to start using their AMEX instead once they know you'll accept it – at your expense, of course.

Don't want to spend the money, but hate to surrender completely the option of getting those quick payments? Consider an alternate solution. Rather than accepting credit cards across the board, offer the option only to those customers who are having difficulty making their payments. Clarify that it's a "one-time deal" or an "experiment we're trying" and then you won't have to commit to taking those payments forever. In the meantime, you'll have a source of emergency funding you can turn to during those times when paying 2% on sales is worth having the cash in hand.

WHERE DO I FIND THE BEST DEAL ON CREDIT CARD PROCESSING?

Unfortunately, there is no quick answer to this question, as it may vary considerably from business to business, and no real way to know without analyzing the expense in-depth, as we shall see below.

I will tell you this, however; *beware* of companies that seem to offer the lowest base rate, especially if it's substantially lower than what your current bank charges. Yes, their 1.3% may seem like quite a bit less than the 1.6% you're currently paying, but these companies' dirty little secret is often that the base rate isn't even half of the story of what they'll be charging you. Not only may there be monthly and per-transaction fees that will drive up your rate as a percentage, but most often the *rate itself* will change based on the type of card being processed. So yes, you may only pay 1.3% to process a basic credit card that doesn't offer rewards – but that rate may jump to 1.8% for a VISA offering a cash back reward.

So how can you know what you'll really be paying? Ask for a detailed breakdown from the proposed processor. Then take their numbers and examine them, side by side, with what you're paying your current (or other proposed processor) on a line-by-line basis by type of card. This information should be on your current statement, although chances are pretty good the line items won't match exactly, so feel free to make your best guess as to what's comparable.

If you have recent data, use it. This is the best way to know what types of cards your business actually processes and what your expense is therefore likely to be if you make a switch. I also recommend analyzing at least two to three months of statements so you get a good average – it's tedious work, but not too bad once you get in the swing.

Then set up a chart like this, in Excel or on your lined yellow pad if you prefer, and do some serious comparison shopping. I'm only using three line items here as an example, but be prepared – there may be two dozen or more on your proposal or monthly statement. (Also, note that these are sample numbers only and are not intended to reflect what you might actually pay for processing certain types of credit cards):

Type of Card: Basic
Monthly Charges: $5,000
Current Percentage: 1.5%
Current Monthly Fees: $75
New Percentage: 1.3%
New Fees: $65

Type of Card: Rewards Visa
Monthly Charges: $10,000
Current Percentage: 1.7%
Current Monthly Fees: $170
New Percentage: 1.8%
New Fees: $180

Type of Card: Rewards Mastercard
Monthly Charges: $15,000
Current Percentage: 1.7%
Current Monthly Fees: $255
New Percentage: 1.9%
New Fees: $285

Totals
Monthly Charges: $30,000
Current Monthly Fees: $500
New Fees: $530
Difference: $30

TYPE OF CARD	BASIC	REWARDS VISA	REWARDS MASTERCARD	TOTALS
MONTHLY CHARGES	$5,000	$10,000	$15,000	$30,000
CURRENT %	1.5%	1.7%	1.7%	1.67%
CURRENT FEES	$75	$170	$255	$500
PROPOSED %	1.3%	1.8%	1.9%	1.77%
PROPOSED FEES	$65	$180	$285	$530
DIFFERENCE	-$10	+$10	+$30	+$30

Comparing credit card fees for different processors. Note that in this example, although the base rate of the proposed processor is lower, its rate for the cards the company actually processes most are higher and will cost us more.

If there are also per-transaction fees involved, then naturally you will want to include those in your analysis. Simply take the number of your current transactions (this should also be on your statement), multiply by any per-transaction fee and then compare that to the competitor's fee per item. Add those fees to the percentage fees you've already calculated and you'll have a much better idea of which processor is going to save you the most money.

Note, too, that there is absolutely no way I could have made an informed decision on this at a glance – the figures really had to be analyzed mathematically, line by line, for me to be able to figure out which deal is better for my company, which isn't necessarily the same as the deal that's better for the firm down the street.

Incidentally, this type of analysis can also prove useful when you're looking at banks. If you're a very small business paying a flat fee per month, it may not matter, but for larger firms running hundreds of checks and near-daily deposits, those per-transaction fees can add up quickly, and only by looking hard at what your company actually does can you hope to figure out which of a handful of deals will work best for your firm. You can use the exact same methodology – examine your statement and make a list of your bank's charges and how many of them you actually accrue in a month for each type of transaction. Then multiply those same numbers of transactions by any competitor's per-transaction charge and compare the grand totals. Figure in any caveats and potential overage fees if you go over a certain number of transactions, and you should be able to pinpoint pretty precisely how much you'll save by making a switch, or by choosing to stay where you are.

BRINGING IT IN – HOW TO GET CASH IN YOUR HANDS AS QUICKLY AS POSSIBLE

In the next few chapters, I discuss specific strategies for increasing the amounts you can collect from your customers and decreasing the amount of time it takes to collect from them. But first, let's take a look at some general strategies for handling cash that's so, so close to being within your grasp.

SEND YOUR INVOICES OUT RIGHT AWAY

It may sound obvious, but I confess I've frequently been astonished by how often companies fail to do this. I remember starting at one firm where the office personnel were debating over where to keep the "To Be Invoiced" pile. I was so confused – why did they have a pile, and what were they keeping it for?

Of course, sometimes it can't be helped. Maybe the person who does the invoicing only works one day a week, or maybe the billing can't be done until the payroll data comes in or invoices from subcontractors are received. But even these are surmountable problems, and if you're really struggling to keep your accounts in the black, you want to find creative means of solving them. I've sent invoices from home, trained other people to prepare them while I was away, and even printed them in advance just in case a project was finished before my next scheduled day at the office. You can always call your suppliers and subcontractors for invoice copies if you need them to complete your billing, and demanding time data promptly from your employees will even help you – and your bank account – to prepare early for your next payroll.

If it really is impossible within the confines of your system to issue an invoice right away – within one day after a job / sale / phase of a project is completed, and your accounting software allows it, then pre-date your invoice to the date the job was completed, *not* the date you're creating the invoice. DO NOT, <u>DO NOT</u> DELAY SENDING AN INVOICE FOR A WHOLE WEEK AND THEN LET THE DATE OF IT DEFAULT TO THE CURRENT DAY! Most firms decide what to pay based on the age of the invoice, and if you do not pre-date it back to the day it should have been done, you are practically guaranteeing that your payment will go out a week later than it otherwise might have.

SEND MONTHLY STATEMENTS

While larger firms with lots of A/R generally issue monthly statements as a normal part of their month-end routine, sometimes this can seem like a waste of time and postage for companies whose customers might only owe for a few invoices. However, even in those situations, I've found sending monthly statements to be well worth the effort. While it's true that some of them do simply get shredded or filed away or ignored, many of your customers will reconcile them against their own accounts, which gives them an opportunity to request invoices they might not have received right away. You might be grinding your teeth waiting for a customer to cough up your payment, and then find out four weeks later that the original invoice went to the wrong mailing address / email address / person / department. Your monthly statement can resolve many of these issues before they start, and they can also prove useful to you in catching errors such as duplicate invoices and incorrect dollar amounts.

Personally, I prefer to print statements and mail them, even when billing is usually done via email. If you haven't been paid for an invoice, then there's always a chance that something has gone wrong with the intended recipient's email address, or maintenance of your account has been transferred to another department, or the Controller at your client's office is unaware that his company owes you a big chunk of money because his Accounts Payable clerk is a flake and hasn't bothered to input your invoices yet. A mailed statement gives you a second chance to reach someone else – and you can always also send one via email to your usual contact if you'd like to do so. Finally, I find printing helpful because it allows me to pull out those statements that need special review – ones that look as though they might contain errors, or which concern accounts I want to draw to my boss' attention. It gives me a neat, clean, once-a-month way to ask, "Has this dispute been resolved yet?" or "What are we going to do about this past due balance?"

For those of you using Quickbooks, I strongly recommend employing the "Open Item" format, which details all of the invoices that are still open, including any that may have been partially paid, and with their original balance. The "Transaction Statement" will only list activity on the account for the specified period, while "Balance Forward" will only show the total dollar amount the customer owes – not very informative. I also highly recommend dating your statements for the last day of the month, and sending them out as soon as possible after month's end – preferably as soon as all of the prior month's billing is done. While some more sophisticated accounting and point-of-sale programs won't allow you to enter transactions in a previous month once the new month begins, if you're using Quickbooks or similar software, you should be able to create an invoice on the 1st that's dated the 30th, and that will permit you to include those final invoices on your monthly statements. Finally, make sending statements a matter of routine whenever a customer has an open balance – not only when they're past due. That way your customer will interpret the statement more as a matter of accounting procedure than as a thinly-veiled attempt to collect.

EMPOWER AS MANY PEOPLE AS YOU CAN TO COLLECT

In cash-based businesses, particularly retail establishments, it's clearly necessary, for security reasons, to place strict limitations on the number of people in your company who are authorized to handle customer cash. But for firms whose income flows mostly as check payments through an Accounts Receivable system, and where check theft or fraud would be easy to trace, it behooves you to empower employees to collect on your behalf.

If you want to keep your cash flow running smoothly, then nearly everything you do for your A/R should be the *exact opposite* of what you do for your A/P. You want only one person nominally in charge of your A/P; by contrast, *everyone* should be responsible for your A/R. In A/P you never want to let your vendors pick up a check; in A/R – if you can do so cost-effectively – you most definitely want to pick up your checks, preferably with your bank deposit slip clenched in your fist.

Of course, you don't want to seem desperate, but don't let your fear of looking like you need the money prevent you from getting it. If your clients are mainly other local businesses, there isn't much risk that you'll be their only supplier who shows up on their doorstep with your hat in your hand. In fact, it's quite common for businesses to pick up checks in person, and unless you know you operate in an environment where this "just isn't done," you shouldn't let it embarrass you because there's usually no stigma attached to it. In addition, the beauty of check payments is that unless there's serious concern about potential loss or fraud, most of the time you don't have to assign this task to persons of high responsibility within your company. You can entrust almost any one of your employees with the job of collecting the payment – which may save you time and money *and* might also offer opportunities for you to nudge your debtors into remitting their payments.

For example, suppose your delivery guy needs to drop off product with one of your clients. Or your salesperson is stopping by to check in with the manager. Or your counterperson happens to drive by their office every morning on her way to work and would be happy to drop by and pick up a check. These are all neat and clean and not at all desperate-sounding ways for you to request payment without seeming pushy or rude.

You can say to the other firm's A/P person, "Oh, Jose is going down there this morning – if our check is ready, he can stop by the office and pick it up." Or "Do you think it might be ready by this afternoon? Marsha has an appointment with your store manager – I can have her pick up the check while she's there, that way you won't have to mail it." See how nice you are there? You're saving them the cost of a stamp! Or even "I'd really like to be able to post this before the end of the month – do you mind if I send someone out there to get it?" thereby suggesting that you have some mysterious accounting-type reason for getting the payment onto your books before the month ends – not because you need the money, oh no!

I will say that I personally prefer not to send anyone – either employees or management – out of their way to retrieve check payments unless it truly needs to be done. It costs time, it costs money, and it costs lost productivity because that person can't be doing his job while he's driving around fetching checks. But in certain circumstances a pickup is clearly in order if the other firm will allow it; for instance, if you can make the pickup convenient because you will have an employee on site. Perhaps you've often had trouble getting money out of this particular client in the past, or perhaps the checks that they "mail" mysteriously always take a week and a half to arrive at your office. If you have a large client whose checks are correspondingly large, then you simply may not want to chance their check getting lost in the mail so that you have to wait for them to issue a stop payment and then a replacement. And, of course, if you simply need the money badly enough where it's worth sending even your CEO and his dog out to fetch it. But do bear in mind that inefficient and costly procedures like these ultimately undermine your cash position and lower your company's profitability. As your cash flow improves, therefore, one of your goals should be to get to the point where you can confidently say to your clients, "Oh, that's all right, you can just mail it."

WHEN YOU ABSOLUTELY, POSITIVELY HAVE TO HAVE THE MONEY

This happens, right? The money needs to be in your bank *today*. This can be especially important if it's the end of the workweek and you're not going to be able to get a new check if there's an error, so you'd better make darned sure that there's been no error. In this case, don't wait for the employee who's picking up your check to get back to the office; have him or her call you to confirm that they got the check. Most of the time it will be sealed in an envelope, so your employee won't know how much it's for or if it's correct. In fact, many firms consider it tacky to examine a check upon pickup, so employees should be instructed not to open envelopes in the front office.

If it's in the nature of your business to keep payments private, then by all means, do so. However, if there's no privacy issue, and you really, really need to be sure that check is right before your employee leaves the premises, have her open it in her car and either send you a picture or read every line of it aloud to you over the phone. This is *especially* true if it's a personal, hand-written check, because there isn't much that's more frustrating than experiencing the relief of knowing you have the money, only then to experience the despair of discovering that the check has been post-dated or made out for the wrong amount right before your client goes out of town for three weeks.

Therefore, you should have your employee check both the numerical amount and the handwritten amount – don't forget, the handwritten amount is the *legal* amount, so it takes precedence – and either way, you don't want a discrepancy between the two because there is always a chance that your bank will reject it. Confirm the date and signature, too – you want to be sure that check is ready to be deposited before your employee leaves that office or home.

What you do next will depend on how badly you need the money. You may need the employee to bring the check to your office immediately, or, if they've stopped off on their way home, you might let them hold it until they come to work the next day. In a small enough company, or with selected staff members, you might even feel comfortable allowing your employee to take the check to your nearest bank branch and deposit it directly so that it goes in right away. If you do so, however, be sure to remind them to ask the teller to make a photocopy of the check before they deposit it so you have one for your records – banks are generally happy to do this.

WHAT IF YOUR CLIENT IS AN INDIVIDUAL AND NOT A BUSINESS?

If you're dealing with a person and not a company, a dollar's worth of prevention will be worth a thousand dollars' worth of collection efforts later. Because if you think it's difficult getting businesses to pay up, getting money out of regular people can be even worse.

Now if you're a retail business, or automotive repair shop, or something of that nature, you probably don't have much trouble with collections because people usually can't leave your store or shop with their merchandise without paying you first. But if your company does, say, website design or residential construction, then you are likely going to be routinely put in the position of having to collect progress payments.

The special problem here is that unlike businesses, individuals simply don't understand that you really, really need the money, and you need it *now*. They want to put your bill on the pile of other bills they pay mid-month; they want to mail you a check when they get around to it; they have no idea what every day's delay in your payment does to your heart rate and blood pressure and number of pills left in your bottle of anxiety medication. And of course, you can't tell them, right? A business you can pressure for payment; a business understands how the money thing works. But you can't very well give your individual clients the impression that you're about to go bankrupt without having them worry that you might not be able to finish their project. You don't even want to try to make them understand that yes, it really does make a difference whether you pick their check up today or get it in the mail at the end of the week, because unfortunately for you, it does.

So how do you avoid this problem? The best way is to make your payment terms startlingly clear at the beginning of your project. Alert your clients verbally – and, if you use a contract, also in writing – that your payments are due upon receipt of invoice. If you can't wait for the mail, tell them that you will pick up checks in person; that you prefer them not to be mailed. Most of the time, you shouldn't need to explain why, but if you do, you can say that you don't trust the mail, or you're concerned about identity theft, or you've had issues before – you don't have to say it's because you don't want to wait. And then make sure they're prepared for you to collect your check in advance. Offer to email or fax invoices or credit card authorizations the day before a scheduled meeting so that they have a chance to review your bill and cut you a check to pick up when you see them. If you will have employees on site able to accept payments, tell them they can give their check directly to so-and-so.

Your on-site employees, too, need to be prepared to collect a check if one isn't offered. Not all of your employees are going to be comfortable with this – collections probably isn't their job, after all – so my advice is to make it as easy as possible for them. Notify your client ahead of time that your employee "Bob" will pick up a check from them tomorrow for whatever phase of the project has been (or is going to be) completed. Email works great for this if you don't want to do it via phone call, but be sure to send it at least 24 hours in advance, because even now, not everyone reads their email continually. Ask them to leave their payment on the kitchen table or other suitable location where your employee can find it if they won't be at home. If your management team lays the groundwork for ensuring that the client is prepared to make payment, then your employee needn't be put in the awkward position of having to ask, "Um, could you pay us, please?" Instead, if a check hasn't been offered, Bob can simply say, "My Project Manager said you have a check I'm supposed to pick up." Much easier on everyone concerned, and much more likely to achieve the desired result.

BRING IN THE BIG GUNS

No matter what the personnel structure of your company is, or how many employees you have in your accounting department, there ought to be someone in your firm who can intervene if the person in charge of your Accounts Receivable is unable to collect the money that's owed you. This doesn't necessarily have to be your A/R person's supervisor, or your Store Manager or CEO, as long as it's someone with sufficient pull in your company to make your debtor say, "Oh, crap – I guess we'd better pay them."

The person you utilize as your "big gun" will vary depending on the nature of your firm and your owners and employees. It may be a task you assign to the owner or upper management, which works well if your client has a vested interest in continuing to do business with your firm. It may be a salesperson or Project Manager – someone who has the power to determine whether work gets done for the company that hasn't paid you, or for the company that has. It may even be a job for your second accounting person if he or she is not normally in charge of collections – the important point is, it needs to be "someone else." Having a different person from your firm approach a customer for money is roughly the equivalent of asking to speak to someone's supervisor – except in this case, you're bringing out the supervisor, which should show that you really mean business.

I would caution you, however, to use this ammunition sparingly. If your A/R person calls in your big gun too often, then three things will happen: 1) No one will bother to ever respond to the A/R person alone, 2) You will lose the surprise value of the attack and thereby reduce its efficacy, and 3) You will be taking time away from that person's regular job. When they get that contact from your alternate collections weapon, you want your clients to feel the impact of it; you want them to feel as though they're in trouble – and hopefully incline them to stay out of trouble the following month.

DON'T BE AFRAID TO REACH OUT IN CASE OF EMERGENCY – BUT DON'T CRY WOLF, EITHER

If you have a serious, serious cash shortage – we're talking one that threatens the continued existence of your business in the short-term – and you have business clients who haven't paid you, don't be afraid to ask for their help. If you reserve this approach for dire emergencies, you may be surprised by how often your customers will cough up some cash when you really need it, and that can be an invaluable means of snatching your fat out of the fire.

What sorts of situations warrant this approach? Here are some examples:

1) "We have a tax payment due and it's a lot bigger than I expected." Everyone hates taxes. Everyone has sympathy for people who have to pay taxes, and most businesses have been in the position of struggling to make their tax payments. This is a great excuse for needing cash fast without reflecting poorly on your company planning.

2) "We have a large unanticipated expense that we can't cover quickly." Examples might be a building repair or emergency replacement of technological items.

3) "Money we were expecting didn't come through." Perhaps your biggest client has just declared bankruptcy, or your bank has cancelled your line of credit. The important point is that the shortfall isn't your fault.

Notice that in each of these examples, the cash crunch was sudden and unexpected, and this is key to successful use of the "emergency" strategy. If you're that short on cash without there being a good reason why, then your clients will presume that either 1) Your business is in trouble or 2) You're poor at managing money. These are not the impressions you want to give to your clients.

This is also why it's so important to be careful not to cry wolf every time you're short on money. Quite likely every week for you is a cash emergency, but that's not going to get you any leverage with your customers, and letting on that you're that desperate isn't going to do much for your firm's reputation, either. Save the cries for help for when you absolutely must have it and your positive response rate will be much higher.

If you do need to reach out to your clients for emergency money, remember to follow these two rules:

1) Be prepared to negotiate. If someone says they can't pay their full balance, ask them for less. "Could you possibly pay just this one invoice then? It would help us out a lot." And if they still insist they can't pay you yet, ask for a follow-up if anything changes. "Okay, well, if something should happen before the end of the week and you can send us a check after all, would you please call and let me know? I'd really appreciate it." This will give them a few days to mull over your situation and maybe see if they can't squeeze out a payment for you.

2) Thank them – profusely. I know it sounds counter-intuitive to express gratitude to someone for paying you money that they owed you, anyway, but this is no time to get logical. Make sure they know how much you appreciate them making an effort to specially cut you a check and get it out quickly and they'll be more inclined to help you the next time. Plus, it will make them feel good if you sound grateful and happy, and who doesn't want that?

SUCCESSFUL COLLECTIONS – DON'T BE A ONE-TRICK PONY

When you're short on cash, there are few things more frustrating than knowing you've earned the money, now if only that #%&#&@ customer would just pay you! If your firm uses any type of Accounts Receivable – even if you're only handing out invoices marked Due on Receipt – you know that successfully managing collections is an integral part of maintaining your cash flow. Yet many owners and employees alike are so uncomfortable with the collections process that they're often relegated merely to gnashing their teeth in frustration when clients don't pay them – while oftentimes the client simply hasn't gotten around to breaking out their checkbook.

So whether you work with individuals or with other businesses, detailed below are some essential strategies you can use to leverage some sorely-needed money out of your clients – and hopefully also encourage them to pay you more promptly in future. But first, let's take a look at some of the more commonly employed collections personas – these should sound very familiar to anyone who has been late with payments themselves – and the pros and cons of assuming them when dealing with your own clients.

THE THREATENER

"If this account isn't paid by the end of the week, I'm sending it to a collection agency!"

The Threatener has already pulled out all the stops – there's no compromise, no negotiation, no arguing with them. They've already made up their mind that you're a deadbeat, and the only way they can hope to get any money from you is by beating you into submission with threats and unpleasantness. This can work for a one-off customer, but for those with whom you have – or would like to have – an ongoing business relationship, it's a bad strategy. Nobody likes being threatened, and unless you are so fed up with this customer that you don't even care how badly you piss them off, refrain from threatening them with formal collections or other legal action.

THE JERK

"I'm not hanging up until you tell me when this account is going to get paid!"

The Jerk screams, shouts, slams down the phone, calls three times a day, makes a nuisance of himself with entire departments and drives Accounts Payable personnel to tears with his viciousness. The biggest potential upside of The Jerk persona is that if you're good enough at it, people will get so sick of having to talk to you that they might just pay you to get you to shut up. Of course, the flip side is that if you're too big a jerk, no one will actually want to help you get paid, and over the long run, that can be a much more insurmountable problem.

THE PROFESSIONAL

"Oh, well, you see, my commission is based on how much I collect before the end of the month, so if you could just pay us by next week…"

Some firms don't even do their own collections – instead they hire people out to bring in the money. I knew an A/R person once who, although she was an ordinary employee, posed as one of these people in order to persuade customers to cough up checks so that she could meet her target or quota for the month.

I personally would not recommend a strategy based on lying or impersonation because, moral implications aside, it would be incredibly embarrassing if you got caught. But it is interesting to note that this strategy did often succeed, and as I discuss under SET DEADLINES, below, having a construct in place that makes it so that you need a check or at least an answer by a fixed deadline can be very helpful in getting your clients to hurry your payment along.

THE MOUSE

"Um, so, do you think maybe you could pay us… um, sometime soon?"

Perhaps the most common of the collections personas, The Mouse is the accounting person who got stuck doing collections because it's part of their job, while in reality, they're either entirely unsuited for this aspect of the position or they've simply never been trained how to do it. They hate making collection calls and it shows in the timidity with which they approach their debtors, if they dare to approach them at all.

It's quite likely that those of you with small firms have a Mouse occupying your Accounts Receivable chair, and most likely this is because that chair also seats your Accounts Payable person, Payroll person, and Bookkeeper all rolled into one. It's simply impractical for you to employ someone whose specialty is collections when there's only room in your office – and budget – for one or maybe two administrative employees, and even more impractical to try to convert your Mouse into a Threatener, Jerk, or Professional collector. By making the job more manageable, however, you can turn your Mouse into something even better – an Alley Cat, let's call it, a creature who is smart, savvy, and resourceful, an animal that can fend for itself. The Alley Cat doesn't have to claw its way around town every day to make sure it gets fed; rather, it knows when a well-placed caress might just earn it a nice fresh bowl of milk.

MAKE YOUR INQUIRIES ABOUT PAYMENT STATUS

"Hello, I'm calling to inquire about payment status?"

I personally love this phraseology. Many A/R people will say bluntly "When can we expect payment?" or "Your payment was due last week – when are you going to pay us?" But these are tough questions for many people to ask, mostly because they reek of, well, collections. But inquiring about payment status – even though it basically means the same thing – is so much more elegant and so much easier to say that even a non-A/R person won't blush to speak it.

The phrase simply carries much better connotations. It's not aggressive or accusatory. It isn't desperate. It hardly even sounds as though you're asking for money – rather, you're inquiring about *when* that money might come along. It gives exactly the impression that you want to give – that you expect to be paid promptly or at least to be notified when payment will be forthcoming. And even if you don't get the answer you were hoping for – the check's already on its way – you just might get the next best thing, an answer to your inquiry. And as we know, good cash flow management is as much about planning as it is about cash.

The other advantages of the payment status phrase? First, you can use it, quite comfortably, far earlier than you might if you were taking a more aggressive approach. You probably wouldn't want to hassle somebody when their payment is only a day late, but calling them merely to inquire about when they will be sending it out seems quite reasonable. Second, because it's easy to say, both employees and owners are far more likely actually to say it. And if it seems as though your A/R person is just never getting around to making those collection calls, consider the possibility that he or she is simply uncomfortable having to ask your clients for money. The beauty of inquiring about payment status is that they're not asking for money, they're asking for answers, and that's much easier for many people to handle.

Inquiring about payment status works better for the other firm's A/P person, too. They don't have to get defensive because your payment hasn't gone out, and they don't have to start ignoring your phone calls – instead, they can volunteer what you asked for, information. And knowing when you'll get your payment can be almost as useful from a planning perspective as actually getting it.

WHEN YOU CAN'T PRESS FOR MONEY, PRESS FOR AN ANSWER

Even if your business is in serious trouble, you likely want to avoid sounding as though you're desperate for money unless you're at a point where you have no choice but to beg, and that should be reserved for the direst emergencies. It's not good for business or your client relationships, and in the long run will cause you more trouble than it will cure. So using phrases such as "I have to have it by tomorrow" or "How soon can you get it to me?" and similar "hard sell" tactics may not work to your best advantage. Try initiating conversations like these instead:

You: Hello, I'm calling to inquire about payment status?
Them: Your check hasn't gone out yet.
You: Ok, well, can you tell me when it might be ready?
Them: It's on the boss' desk, awaiting signature. I don't know when it will be going out exactly.
You: Do you think it might be by the end of the week?
Them: Well, he usually signs checks on Fridays, so, I don't know – probably Monday or Tuesday by the time you get it.
You: Ok, great! That's what I needed to know. Thank you so much!
The key to this conversation: Asking when the check might be ready. Without being accusatory, this implies that you're waiting on the Accounts Payable person to cut your check – a fact that she will be quick to deny. Rather, she'll want to assure you that her part of the job is done; that checks are only awaiting the boss' signature. The information that she then gives regarding the company's procedures – the fact that the boss signs checks on Fridays, along with the implication that they're mailed promptly once they get signed – suggests that her estimate of a check by Monday or Tuesday is probably reliable.

You: Hello, I'm calling to inquire about payment status?
Them: I cut the check, it's on the manager's desk, but I have no idea when it might go out.
You: Oh, I see. So she just needs to sign it, but you don't know when that will be?
Them: Right.
You: Ok, well, could you do me a favor? Call and let me know when it goes out? And then if I haven't heard back from you by the end of the week, I'll give you a call to check up on it.
Them: Will do.
The key to this conversation: Recognizing that the Accounts Payable person in this company has almost no control over when payments are made. He cuts the checks and gives them to the manager, who probably then decides what will go out on a day-by-day or week-by-week basis. What this tells you is that there's probably little point in pestering the A/P person for payment – he's already cut your check,

after all – because the real decision-making power lies with the manager. If payment continues to be delayed and you haven't been able to get any answers, you'll want to ask politely to speak to the manager while making it clear that you recognize that the delay is not the A/P person's fault.

You: Hello, I'm calling to inquire about payment status.
Them: Um, yeah – I'll try to get that out to you as soon as I can. (Translate – I don't know how to say I'm going to be really, really late.)
You: Any idea when that might be?
Them: Um, I don't know…
You: Well, are we talking next week? Or maybe not until the week after that?
Them (with sigh of relief): Yeah. Yeah, probably not until the week after that.
You (pregnant pause): Well, I guess I can work with that as long as I know that it's coming. How about if I check back with you next week and you can give me an update?
Them: Sure, no problem. And if I can get it to you any sooner I will.
You: Thank you so much – I appreciate that!
The key to this conversation: Giving implied permission for payment to be late in exchange for an accurate estimate of when it might actually be made. The Accounts Payable person here was unwilling to admit that there was no chance that payment would be made in the following week. Because she didn't know what to say, she said nothing – and nothing is more useless to you than no information. By suggesting that it might be another two weeks before she makes payment, you've given her the opportunity to admit that your payment will be delayed, and also extracted an implied promise of delivery the week after that. Now she knows in advance when she needs to pay you, and if she knows you're going to check back the following week, she's much more likely to make sure your check will be ready.

You: Hello, I'm calling to inquire about payment status?
Them: Um, she's not in right now.
You: Oh. Well, is there someone else who can help me? I just need to find out when a check will go out.
The key to this conversation: Being casual and non-threatening. Firms that use the "She's not in right now" tactic tend to do so over

and over, ad infinitum. It's hard to get anywhere with them when they repeatedly ignore your emails, voicemails, and phone messages, and you can spend weeks bobbing up and down on this merry-go-round before you finally stumble off, too dizzy to continue – which is exactly what they are hoping. If your first and second calls are ignored, don't even bother getting in line for the next ride; move to the kiddie coaster instead and ask to talk to someone else. If they say there is no one else, then ask, "Well, is there maybe a manager or a supervisor I can speak to? I really need an answer on this today." But always remember to be polite, at least in the early stages of uncollectability. Getting angry and demanding to speak to a supervisor right away will often prompt the person to whom you're talking to shield the responsible parties on their end, and this is exactly what you don't want. You want to be able to get through to someone who has the authority to deal with your payment, and screaming at a receptionist is rarely going to help you accomplish this goal.

Those of you who read the first volume in this series, DEALING WITH VENDORS, will recognize that some of the Accounts Payable people we're coming into contact with here are doing the exact same things I told you *not* to do as an A/P person. Making vague, empty promises, refusing to take phone calls, not having a plan. Your goal here should be to nudge them into better, more manageable, and ultimately, more useful behavior – persuade them into making half-promises, or scheduling a payment, even if it's a few weeks out. You don't necessarily have to get someone to commit to cutting a check, but you do need to convince them at least to commit to making the next step – following up with their supervisor, or calling you back in a few days with an answer, or letting you know when the check has been signed. And if you're unable to obtain even that minor level of commitment, then you might as well move that payment out of your current cash flow plan because you probably won't be getting it anytime soon.

SET DEADLINES

Perhaps the greatest bane of the collections system is the manner in which it tends to sprawl endlessly between you and your debtor. You call and call, and they put you off and put you off some more, until eventually it becomes like a routine, with the two of you having the same conversation week after week and you still not getting paid.

Break out of this rut by setting a deadline. Remember, this doesn't have to be a date by which you need to get paid; it can be a date by which you need a positive answer.

"Can you let me know before the end of the week? I have to report to my supervisor first thing on Monday."

"It would be really helpful if we could get this cleaned up before the 30th. My boss is going to be pretty unhappy if this balance runs over into next month."

These are good things to say (and policies to have) because they both create a deadline and also place the responsibility for the demand – in absentia – on someone else. This can work for the owner as well.

"I can let you slide as long as we can get paid by the 15th – I have to pay my taxes by then."

"Could you possibly let me know by tomorrow? We have to prepare a statement for our bank for our line of credit, and we're trying to minimize our aged receivables."

Again, I don't recommend making things up just to get paid – but you certainly do want to take advantage of opportunities like these when they present themselves. These are believable scenarios, they create sympathy for owners and employees, and most importantly, they make your Accounts Receivable contacts want to help you plan and even get paid.

FOLLOW A PATTERN

In Volume 1 of this series, DEALING WITH VENDORS, I detailed the importance of establishing patterns with your vendors. Even if you're short or late with your payments, you can avoid a large number of nasty collection calls simply by adhering to a pattern of payment that will make your creditors not want to be bothered making those calls. Why should they, when they already know what you're going to do?

The same holds true when it comes to collections, except in reverse. Now you want your collection efforts to be so predictable that your customers will go out of their way to avoid getting phone calls from you – and if you're lucky, that will mean sending your payment before you can call.

BUT DON'T WASTE YOUR TIME – OR THEIRS

There's nothing wrong with pursuing an aggressive collections strategy, but if you have a client who consistently pays you on the 30th of the month when their bill is due on the 15th, you may want to question whether it's worth the aggravation to the both of you to continue calling them on the 16th. Chances are that, just like you, they're following that payment pattern for a good reason, and trying to get them to pay you sooner will merely be beating your already aching head against an unmoving brick wall.

If you do decide to lighten up, however, make sure they know it. You don't want to give the impression that you're backing off because they've finally worn you down – rather, you want to establish that you're doing so out of professional courtesy. Here's an example of how such a conversation might go:

You: I've noticed that you normally pay us at the end of month rather than on the 15th, when your bill is due – is there a reason for that?
Them: Most of our money comes in the third week of the month, so it's a lot easier for me to pay you then.
You: So you think you'll be able to continue making those payments before the 30th then?
Them: Yes, I expect to be able to do so.
You: Okay, well, here's what I'll do. I'm going to make a notation on your account, and I'll ask my boss to let you slide just a couple of weeks on payment each month. If he says okay, then I won't have to bug you with these phone calls anymore. It should be fine as long as we keep getting your checks before the end of the month so your balance doesn't show up in our monthly aging reports.

Them: That would be great – thank you! I'll make sure your check goes out by the last week of the month.

You've accomplished several positives here. One, you've lightened your workload by eliminating a task that wasn't doing anything for you, anyway. Two, you've improved your relationship with the other firm's A/P person, which is always a help. And three, you've essentially extracted a promise from that person to pay you by the 30th every month, which both helps you to plan and is quite reassuring. Up until now, you had no guarantee that this was going to continue to happen. Now that you've made a special exception for this firm in allowing them to delay making payment, you can be fairly confident that their A/P person will make a special effort to keep her end of the bargain – which places you in a much more secure financial position.

KNOW YOUR ENEMY

While it's true that in many small firms one person is in charge of making the payments, it's equally true that that person is usually not the ultimate decision-maker when it comes to managing money. Rather, that role is often occupied by the man or woman signing the checks. So most of the time, there's little to gain for you in being antagonistic to your A/P contact at another firm – all you will accomplish is to get on bad terms with the person who cuts your checks, which is rarely a good thing. Yes, sometimes you do need to get upset when calling your contact in order to ensure that he or she will convey your displeasure to the people in charge. But even when this becomes necessary, don't blame your contact if he's not to blame. Instead, give that person an incentive to act as your advocate with the person who's really in charge by being civil, polite, and understanding, but firm. Even if that A/P person isn't in charge of making payment decisions, he may be consulted about whom to pay, and you want to make sure that your firm is at the top of his list.

"I know it isn't your fault that they haven't released our payment, but anything you can do to get it going would be greatly appreciated."

"I know this isn't your decision, but if you can put in a good word for me with your boss, I'd really appreciate it."

"Well, thanks for cutting our check, anyway. I'll keep my fingers crossed that they'll send it out soon!"

GOING BEYOND THE TELEPHONE CALL – WHEN TALKING DOESN'T WORK, PUT IT IN WRITING

Many small firms do collections via telephone call and telephone call alone – mostly because it's comparatively easy to pick up the phone. The problem with sticking to this system in a business-to-business environment – and most of you who employ Accounts Receivable are dealing with other firms – is that it's far too easy for you to be given the runaround through a gamut of employees, none of whom has an answer for you or is authorized to make a payment commitment. Most A/R collections people will therefore call five or ten times before they finally give up in frustration – which is exactly what your debtor is hoping will happen. The open invoice then sits on the creditor company's books until the decision is made to write it off with no further effort being made to collect the debt.

This may work fine for companies where cash isn't a problem, especially because at some point the cost of trying to collect on a small invoice may well exceed the outstanding debt. It may also become necessary in situations where there's a nasty dispute and the other firm simply refuses to pay all together, or if the other firm declares bankruptcy and your debt merely joins the pile with all of the others. But more often than not, companies that aren't paying their bills aren't paying for the same reason you aren't paying yours – they simply don't have enough money to pay everybody, which means that somebody has to get stiffed. Therefore, your job as a collector is to make sure that you aren't that somebody.

Making those telephone calls is the first step. By verbally touching base, repeatedly if necessary, you're making the point that you aren't willing to merely write off this debt and forget it. By persisting in making contact, you're sending the signal that you are not going to give up in frustration and stop calling. And believe me, your A/P contacts *are* telling their supervisors when you keep calling. In fact, this is often the question Controllers ask their subordinates before they cut checks – who called looking for money this week? And while many financial people follow the dubious practice of only paying firms when they really need to stay in their good graces, others will prioritize payments to those whose wheels squeak loudest and most often. There's a reason why collections tend to be done in a barrage – because unending onslaughts are more likely to crack open the vault.

Therefore, if your firm is not at the top of your debtor's to-be-paid list, it may behoove you to find ways to ensure that the priority of your payment climbs above some of the others who are competing for the very same funds. It's at this point that you may want to consider setting the phone down and sending a letter.

THE POLITE REQUEST

Many firms begin their correspondence collections by sending a statement, often stamped "Past Due" in bright red letters and with a highlight over the outstanding balance. Your accounting software may allow you to set statements on past due accounts to automatically print out with a notation of your choice, such as "Please contact us to make payment arrangements." I personally prefer a handwritten notation to the effect of "Please contact me ASAP with payment status!" along with my name and number. (My handwriting is difficult enough to decipher where I can virtually guarantee that someone is going to have to stare at it a moment to figure out what it says, which ensures that my message will get across.)

These are good first steps. Unfortunately, depending upon their company organization, the people in charge of making payment decisions at the debtor firms may never even see these reminder statements. They may not even make it out of the mail room, or they may get filed away (or even shredded) by the receiving A/P department without anyone even bothering to read them. Even a well-organized firm will likely balance the statement to their own records and then studiously ignore your polite request – after all, they already knew they were past due, so what do they care if you sent them a statement?

Another month or two goes by and you still haven't received payment – or even the promise of payment – and this is when you might up the ante by sending a letter.

THE NOT-SO-POLITE REQUEST

If you're dealing with a firm with many unpaid bills, then your letter may simply end up in heap with all of the others and be promptly forgotten. However, unlike utilities and other massive firms, which employ formal collection agencies to pursue aged debts, it's quite rare for small companies in the ordinary course of business to send letters asking for payment. In fact, most simply continue to keep sending statements, often with larger and larger red letters and unhappy faces drawn on them, which eventually become so routine that, like your phone calls, they too get ignored and dumped in the two-foot-tall "TBD" pile.

Sending a letter, therefore, has two immediate effects: 1) It makes your correspondence (and your debt) stand out from all of the others and 2) It shows that you take the debt seriously enough to be bothered with writing and sending a letter.

In practice, of course, you don't really have time to hand-craft these letters, but thanks to the wonders of the modern age, you can very easily draw up some boilerplate correspondence which will allow you to generate letters to various firms without having to do much more than change the heading and the address. Here I am going to show you what, in my opinion, are the essential elements of such a letter so you can customize one to suit your company's style. I have made my example as generic as possible to permit you to merely spit out a copy and send it as is; see my notes below for suggestions on potential customizations if you're inclined to put in the time.

Dear So-and-So (1),

Enclosed please find your firm's most recent statement (2). As you will note, your account is seriously past due (3). We have made repeated calls to your office and have been unsuccessful in obtaining any information on when we can expect payment (4). We must insist that you contact us immediately to provide payment status (5).

If you are unable to remit full payment due to a shortage of funds (6), we will be happy to consider a payment plan arrangement which will allow you to get caught up on your outstanding debt over time and keep your account in good order. (7) Please contact us right away to discuss your options.

Sincerely,
So-and-So (8)

1) I suggest addressing this to either a financial supervisor or owner – preferably the owner if you know that he or she regularly works on site. As the party ultimately responsible for the company's debts, the owner is most likely to be concerned by the implications of this letter. In addition, it's quite possible that the owner is unaware just how past due your account is. Finally, in firms with more than one financial or administrative person, letters addressed to the A/P department or even the Controller may be opened and processed by an underling, who may file away your collection letter automatically based on standing instructions. But few employees will dare to throw away a letter addressed directly to the owner of the company, which will help to ensure that it gets seen by the right eyes.

2) You could change this to "for the month of June" etc. I strongly recommend always enclosing a statement so that recipients can immediately check your figures against their own should they wish to do so. The statement will also instantly clarify the amount that's past due and by how much so that you don't have to bother detailing this in your letter.

3) You could use this line to state exactly how much is past due and how old the debt is, which may be useful if the amount is large or very old. "As you can see, you now have an outstanding balance exceeding $5,000, most of which is more than 180 days past due. This is unacceptable by any industry standard."

4) Here you could say to whom you spoke, and what they gave you for an answer (if any).

5) You could also make this "to make payment arrangements," but as I described above, I personally prefer the language "provide payment status." The point is that you want them to contact you, and they're more likely to do that if you don't insist on an immediate payment that they probably can't make.

6) This line is here because it cuts to the quick, and right to the heart of the matter. Essentially, you're telling the other firm that you know they're not paying you because they don't have any money, and the only way for them to effectively protest that is by sending your payment. And some will actually do that in order to save face, because otherwise they would have to admit that they can't afford to remit the measly $500 that they owe you. Well, you can't afford to be shorted $500, either, so they'd better cough up!

7) I'm referring here to an informal payment plan arrangement, but I have seen larger debts successfully converted into legal Notes Payable with terms like any other loan. I suggest making both options available to your reforming deadbeats.

8) The letter should be signed by a person with substantial authority – upper management or ownership rather than strictly financial personnel. Again, this will send the signal that dealing with this debt has been elevated beyond your finance department and into the highest echelons of your firm.

THE THREATENING LETTER

If you haven't received a response to your not-so-polite request after say, 30 to 60 days (the appropriate time frame is up to your best judgment), you may want to follow up with a threatening letter. The threatening letter, while it still leaves open the possibility of rapprochement, is really only intended to be sent to those customers with whom you have no intention of ever pursuing a business relationship again. Therefore it would generally be inappropriate for firms with whom you've continued to do business but who have refused to pay one old invoice for whatever reason, such as a paperwork error or unresolved dispute. At this point, you should have nothing left to lose with this client and can throw everything into one last-ditch effort to get them to pay you.

Dear So-and-So (1),

We still have not received a response from you regarding our previous correspondence, or any of our many telephone calls. (2) As you can see from the enclosed statement, your account is now ridiculously past due (3) and your failure even to contact us regarding this matter makes us question whether you have any intention of ever paying this debt. (4) While we don't wish to tarnish our relationship with you as a customer, we have no choice but to suspend your account until your outstanding invoices have been paid in full. (5)

We expect a response within seven (7) days of the date of this letter, and full payment within thirty (30) days. (6) If you fail once again to contact us to make payment arrangements, we will not hesitate to take legal action in pursuit of this debt. (7) We hope that you will not force us to take such a step, so please, we ask you one last time to take care of it promptly.

Sincerely,
So-and-So (8)

1) The threatening letter should be addressed to the owner or CEO. If you don't know who this is, call and find out. If they don't want to tell you, feel free to explain exactly why you need to know and to sound very ominous while you're doing it.

2) You might also say "our letter of such-and-such date."

3) If calling the account "ridiculously past due" is too over-the-top for your taste, feel free to say "seriously past due" instead. I like "ridiculously past due," however. It conveys that the

debt is so old as to border on ludicrous that they've let it go for so long.

4) If this sounds like an accusation, it's because it's intended to.

5) By this point you may have already suspended or frozen the customer's account – if they've even dared to try to use it – in which case you can say "permanently close your account." I personally prefer to leave the implication that the account may be salvageable, even though by this point it probably isn't.

6) These are pretty generous terms, but I prefer to give the customer adequate time to respond – my goal here, after all, is to get paid, and if I demand payment within 3 days I'm unlikely to get it at all. You can shorten this time frame, though, if you prefer a harsher approach.

7) You and I both know that you can't afford to "take legal action," although turning the debt over to a collection agency that works on commissions might be an option if the debt is substantial and you feel comfortable taking that step. The point is to make them wonder if you'll really go so far, and whether the idea of that makes them uncomfortable enough to decide to cough up your payment.

8) The threatening letter needs to be signed by your owner or CEO.

MANAGING PAYROLL

For many firms, payroll is the largest ongoing expense and may often cause the most worry when cash flow is an issue. It's one thing not to pay a supplier because you don't have the money – but few firms can get away with withholding paychecks from their employees. Not only can such a move have legal ramifications, it can wreak havoc with a company's relationship with its personnel, and understandably so, because, after all, a paycheck is typically an employee's sole source of support. Unlike a business, an employee cannot ramp up collection efforts with his or her other debtors, delay payment to a supplier when cash is low, or simply land a new job that will cover the shortfall in the short-term. Employers therefore have a greater responsibility to ensure that even if other financial matters have to go by the wayside, that payroll is met and in a timely fashion.

When we come to the forthcoming CREATING A PLAN volume of this series, therefore, making payroll will nearly always be the top priority for a company's cash – indeed, it will be the one obligation that cannot be moved from one week to the next, or reduced in amount, or repaid in installments if the firm is unable to raise the full amount due. In fact, planning is comparatively easy when it comes to payroll precisely because our options are few.

Our goals, therefore, when it comes to managing our payroll will be:

1) To be able to calculate precisely how much will be due, and

2) To minimize its effects on our cash flow, either by reducing any associated expenses, such as worker's compensation, or by shifting the timing of outflows to maximum advantage.

ESTIMATING PAYROLL

In most small firms, payroll tends to be pretty consistent. The net amount of the checks will be roughly the same week after week, perhaps a bit more when it's busy, a little less when it's not. Firms that follow this pattern will generally be safe in using an average that they can plug in to their cash flow plan many weeks in advance, and will only need to make adjustments seasonally or when there has been a change in staff or pay rates.

But of course, the level of persistence will depend on the nature of the business and the compensation structure of its employees. A company with a staff of full-timers is more likely to have consistent net payroll amounts, even when business activity varies, while one that engages part-time employees as needed will tend to have payrolls that more directly parallel up- and down-swings in business. As I discuss in the MANAGING PERSONNEL volume of this series, this is because employees who were hired to work full-time tend to stay on the clock for their full forty hours, whether they need to or not.

Whichever path your company follows, you can use this information to estimate your upcoming payrolls with a fair amount of accuracy. I recommend taking the following steps:

1) Look at your average net payroll over the previous several weeks or months. By net payroll I mean the total actual amount of your paychecks, and not the gross amount that's recorded on your books. The reason I like to use the net rather than the gross is because the difference between the two is payroll taxes, which, for small businesses, are generally due days or even weeks after the applicable payday. In my experience, payroll taxes can amount to as much as a third of the gross payroll, so, for a cash-strapped firm, separating payrolls into the amounts actually paid out on paychecks and those paid out in taxes can make a significant difference in cash flow and planning. This may not be true if you use a service (see HOW SERVICES ARE ROBBING YOU OF CONTROL OVER YOUR CASH FLOW AND WHEN TO TAKE IT BACK, below).

2) Are your net payroll and payroll tax amounts fairly consistent? If so, you can plug this figure into your long-term cash flow plan and be done with it; however, don't forget to update your estimated figures with the actual numbers for each pay period as soon as you have them. Also, if you gain or lose an employee, raise or cut pay, or receive a change in tax withholding request from an employee – which will alter the net amount of his or her paycheck – you'll want to update your previous estimates as well.

3) If your payroll amounts are inconsistent, then start by pulling out any employees whose pay is fixed. These would include any salaried employees as well as those who, practically speaking, may as well be because they almost always work the same number of hours no matter what goes on with your business. Examples might include your company owner, your administrative person, a floor supervisor, or an outside salesperson. Tally up the typical net payroll for these personnel, as well as the payroll taxes associated with them, and set those two figures aside. This will be your "fixed" payroll amount going forward and will not need to be recalculated unless there's a change such as those I discuss under #2, above.

4) Calculate the variable amount of your payroll. This would be money you pay to employees who work on an as-needed basis or whose pay is inconsistent from week to week. There are numerous methods you might use to do this, depending upon how your business functions, but all will revolve around uncovering the relationship between how much you pay those variable employees and how much business your firm does. For example, if your payroll increases as your revenues increase, you might estimate your variable payroll as a percentage of your revenues. If your payroll only increases in relation to total hours scheduled or worked, you might come up with an average pay rate for the applicable employees and arrive at your estimate that way. This could be a good solution for a construction or other project-based firm, for which the work done in any given week might not immediately affect

revenues. Or, if your payroll varies seasonally, you could look at your total payroll by month or by quarter, subtract out the amount you figured for your fixed-rate employees, above, and make adjustments to the balance as necessary. Don't drive yourself nuts with this, though, trying to get it just right month by month or week by week. Any figure you derive is going to be an average, and while that will work great for long-term planning, it won't necessarily reflect what's going to happen in any given pay period.

5) Add your fixed and variable payrolls. If your payroll has enough variability to require this type of tracking, I recommend splitting these into separate line items in your cash flow plan to make them easier to modify and to track.

6) Don't forget to account for special circumstances. If you pay your salesperson a bonus once a month, remember to include it in your calculations. If a given month has three or five payrolls rather than two or four, add in the extra as well.

7) Figure your payroll taxes. Because of the complexity of the calculation for income tax withholding, which, unlike FICA (Social Security and Medicare), is not a fairly straightforward percentage, there's no simple way to do this without actually running payroll that won't drive you insane. My recommendation is to let your accounting software do it for you, and then base your estimates on your typical payments. If your software doesn't give you the amount of the employer's share of FICA until you actually pay it, remember that it matches the employee-contributed amounts, or you can ballpark it at 7.65% of your payroll.

8) Do your payroll. The most foolproof method of making sure you have an accurate estimate is to actually cut paychecks and calculate your payroll tax payments. And if cash is a problem, I highly recommend doing this as soon as is humanly possible. If you have guys in the field, make it a rule that they have to submit their timesheets first thing on Monday morning – or even end of day Friday – if they want to get paid. If a

supervisor has to approve timecards before you can cut paychecks, make sure she knows how important it is that your financial person gets those right away. Don't put it off if you can help it – if your payday is Friday and you don't know how much payroll is going to be until Thursday, that is going to seriously hamper your planning and may harm your cash position.

AN EXAMPLE

Let's suppose we have the following employees, with the following net payrolls (for simplicity's sakes, we'll disregard payroll taxes for the moment):

Manager – $1000
Supervisor – $1000
Salesperson – $500 salary plus weekly commissions averaging $500 when shop is operating at full capacity
Installers – 5 at an average of $800 per week when full-time

So the first thing I'm going to do here is figure out that, under normal circumstances, my weekly payroll is going to be $7,000 – $1,000 each for my Manager, Supervisor, and Salesperson, plus another $4,000 for my five installers. How will this change if my workload isn't full-time?

Well, even if I have no sales at all, my fixed payroll is still going to be $2,500 – $1,000 each for the Manager and Supervisor, because they get paid no matter what, plus $500 for my salesperson, who will still have to show up to work even though he isn't getting any commissions, while the regular installers will (theoretically) stay home. In fact, even if I have no work scheduled, I'm probably still going to need to keep one guy on hand, just in case something comes in, so realistically, my fixed payroll is probably more like $3300 if I include one installer.

But of course, it's unlikely I won't have any sales at all – let's hope – so how would I estimate partial payroll if sales are down?

In this scenario, I now have two choices. If I have historical job

MANAGING CASH WHEN YOU HAVEN'T GOT ANY

costing or productivity data at my disposal, then I should be able to determine how many hours my guys will need to work to produce the amount of revenue I'm expecting with relative ease. For example, if I already know that, on average, one guy working one hour at $20/hour produces $100 in revenue, then if I have $1,000 worth of work scheduled, I can easily determine that that's going to cost me ten hours of labor, or $200. If I haven't gotten advanced enough in my accounting yet to have this data on hand, I can still ballpark it by looking at my historical changes in revenue, and relating that to the hours worked by my guys. For instance, if I had $100,000 in sales each month over three months, and my installers worked an average of 1000 hours per month, then I can simply divide to get my revenue generated per hour of $100. Suppose I review my shop records on productivity and they show the following:

200 hours of labor (all 5 installers working full-time, cost $4,000)= $20,000 of revenue
160 hours of labor (cost $3,200) = $16,000 of revenue
120 hours of labor (cost $2,400)= $12,000 of revenue
80 hours of labor (cost $1,600)= $8,000 of revenue
40 hours of labor (cost $800)= $4,000 of revenue

No shop is going to be this consistent across the spectrum, of course - in fact, what you'll typically find is that the cost of labor versus revenue is more like a curve than a straight line – but presuming that these numbers are accurate, I'm now in a good position to estimate my payroll even before I've gotten my timecards in. If I took in $12,000, the payroll for my installers should be about $2,400, or 60 percent of my full-time payroll of $4,000. (In this example, another way of looking at this would be that each hour of labor generates $100 of revenue. Since my installation labor costs $20 an hour, my labor cost will be twenty percent of my revenue.) Quite likely my salesperson's commissions will follow a similar pattern, making his total pay for the week $800, or $500 salary plus $300 commission, but I can also estimate his commissions as a percentage of revenues if that provides a good approximation of how he gets paid. And, of course, for longer-term planning, I can make a whole range of similar calculations. If I expect $16,000 in revenues during a given period, then I can estimate my variable payroll at $3,200. By contrast, if I'm looking at $4,000 in revenues, I know I'm going barely going to have enough to cover my fixed-rate employees at $2,500, plus my one installer at $800, plus my salesperson at $600, or $3900 total.

Knowledge of this type often proves tremendously useful, not only for cash flow planning, but for operational analysis as well. For example, quite likely such an examination would show that the less work there is, the less my company earns per hour of labor, because workers – not necessarily through any fault of their own – tend to be less productive when the workload is light. My data for a given month or quarter might show that my earnings per hours worked were lower when I hired temporary employees last summer, or that my revenues versus payroll were highest before my firm's Christmas vacation. As with many aspects of cash flow planning, it's often simple enough to make your reports dual-purpose by tweaking data you're already collecting to include a cash flow angle, which will both reduce your paperwork burden and ultimately make it more enjoyable.

ACCOUNTING FOR OWNER'S DRAWS

If your company is a corporation, then your owner will most likely be paid a fixed salary as a part of your normal payroll, and you can safely include him or her in your general payroll estimates. If you're a sole proprietorship, however, you may need to adopt a modified approach in accounting for owner's draws.

If the owner receives a fixed amount each week or month, then you can effectively treat this like any other fixed expense for cash planning purposes. If the owner's income varies in accordance with the company's income – for example, if the amount of the draw is a percentage of profits or revenues – then you'll want to work that calculation into your cash flow plan. You can easily do this in Excel by using a formula that figures the appropriate percentage of your projected revenue. If, however, your owner is pulling out money based on how much is available – or, as is even more common, based on his or her current personal needs – then the calculations become more complex and even more urgent to get just right.

Sole proprietors in particular may have complex and sometimes massive cash needs. Not only must they juggle their family's cash and their business cash, but they have to meet large cash expenses at regular intervals, such as their quarterly estimated income tax payments, which can easily run into the tens of thousands of dollars, even for a company that doesn't seem to be making much money. In addition, many sole proprietors find themselves getting deeply into debt in the early years of their businesses, often financing operations through personal loans and home mortgage refinances – debts that may continue to eat up their available cash long after their companies have become profitable. Indeed, as we will discuss in detail in my forthcoming CREATING A PLAN volume, servicing debt is one of the main reasons otherwise profitable companies are constantly forced to scramble for cash. And finally, as we discussed in Volume 2 of this series, MANAGING PERSONNEL, the owner of the company, however brilliant he or she may be in other aspects of running a business, is not necessarily adept at managing cash, and that may apply to their personal finances as well as their business affairs.

What frequently happens, therefore, is that the owner, recognizing that there isn't enough cash for him or her to draw a sufficiently high fixed amount every week, simply pulls money out when he or she needs it. And while a thousand dollars a week might not be a big deal, what happens when the mortgage payment on the home they've refinanced six times is due? What happens when they need twenty grand as a payment on their kid's college tuition? Strictly speaking, these are not company expenses – they will never show up on the firm's P & L. Yet they are required cash outflows nonetheless, and they can rapidly derail a company's finances – without proper planning.

There are numerous ways of managing this. In the bulk of the sole proprietorships in which I've been involved, I've ended up managing the owner's personal finances as well as the company's, sometimes entirely, and sometimes only to an extent. In a desperately cash-poor environment, total control can be the most effective way of ensuring that the needs of the owner are accounted for in the company's cash flow planning. I know when his car payment is due, I know how much he's spent on his credit card in the last month, I know how much he wants to spend on his wife's birthday gift. The downside is, I may also become privy to a ton of very private information – does my boss really want me to see the fee for her monthly subscription to "Adult XXX?" Letting your financial person manage your personal finances means you have to be willing to lay yourself pretty bare, and that's a step you should take *only* if you really feel you would benefit from letting someone else manage your monthly bills, and if you're really confident in the competence of the person occupying that chair. On the plus side, those who do feel comfortable in that scenario may be delighted to pass on the responsibility for routine bill-paying to someone else, as it's one more unwelcome pile of ugly vegetables they can dump off their own plate.

Nonetheless, when discussions involving managing an owner's personal finances come up, I normally present them with alternate options. First, I point out that it's going to cost them additional money, because I'm paid hourly, and then I give them an estimate of probably six to eight hours a month, depending on their needs. Second, I mention the inevitable violation of their personal privacy. Except in the most egregious circumstances, I'm pretty careful not to berate an owner for spending a big chunk of personal money that I then have to try to repay out of the company's coffers, but it can still be pretty irritating having your bookkeeper know that you wrote a check there wasn't enough money to cover or that you took your fourteen closest friends out to dinner last night. Finally, I suggest possibilities involving partial control, in which I manage, for example, his personal credit card, while he manages his bank account, or vice versa. I suggest alternate pay structures, say, in which he receives a weekly check of x dollars for his personal use, while I attend to the more formal bill-paying on his behalf. These modified options preserve a certain amount of the owner's privacy while still ensuring that I'm able to stay on top of his personal bills. And for owners who are particularly negligent about attending to their personal bills – ones who are always racking up late fees and credit card interest – the potential savings can even outweigh the additional costs of accounting.

No matter what option you choose, and even if you don't want to involve your financial person in your personal finances at all, *it is absolutely vital* that you keep him or her abreast of upcoming major expenses, like your estimated tax payments, or your kid's college tuition. If you have any hope of being able to pull that money out of your firm's account, you need to begin preparing not weeks, but months in advance. The amount you will need in excess of your normal draw should be plotted into your cash flow plan like any other expense, and the earlier, the better.

PLANNING FOR PAYROLL AND OWNER'S DRAWS: SOME EXAMPLES

Here are some examples of different scenarios involving fixed and variable payroll amounts coupled with various versions of owner's draws. Taking again the full-time shop scenario we employed earlier and a fixed owner's draw, our effective payroll plus draw estimates might look something like this:

	WEEK 1	WEEK 2	WEEK 3	WEEK 4
REVENUES	$20,000	$20,000	$20,000	$20,000
MANAGER	$1,000	$1,000	$1,000	$1,000
SUPERVISOR	$1,000	$1,000	$1,000	$1,000
SALES - FIXED	$500	$500	$500	$500
SALES – COMMISSION	$500	$500	$500	$500
INSTALLERS	$4,000	$4,000	$4,000	$4,000
OWNER'S DRAW	$2,000	$2,000	$2,000	$2,000
TOTALS	$9,000	$9,000	$9,000	$9,000
CASH AFTER PAYROLL	$11,000	$11,000	$11,000	$11,000

Now suppose my scenario is less than full-time. Once I include my owner's draws as if they're a fixed payroll amount, my ability to cover the expense drops drastically as my revenues decline.

	WEEK 1	WEEK 2	WEEK 3	WEEK 4
REVENUES	$20,000	$16,000	$12,000	$8,000
MANAGER	$1,000	$1,000	$1,000	$1,000
SUPERVISOR	$1,000	$1,000	$1,000	$1,000
SALES - FIXED	$500	$500	$500	$500
SALES – COMMISSION	$500	$400	$300	$200
INSTALLERS	$4,000	$3,200	$2,400	$1,600
OWNER'S DRAW	$2,000	$2,000	$2,000	$2,000
TOTALS	$9,000	$8,100	$7,200	$6,300
CASH AFTER PAYROLL	$11,000	$7,900	$4,800	$1,700

I could ameliorate this problem with an alternate pay structure. Let's suppose instead that I pay my owner 10% of our weekly revenues. Not only will this provide better matching of our incoming and outgoing cash, but it will provide the owner with a further incentive to increase the company's revenues:

	WEEK 1	WEEK 2	WEEK 3	WEEK 4
REVENUES	$20,000	$16,000	$12,000	$8,000
MANAGER	$1,000	$1,000	$1,000	$1,000
SUPERVISOR	$1,000	$1,000	$1,000	$1,000
SALES - FIXED	$500	$500	$500	$500
SALES – COMMISSION	$500	$400	$300	$200
INSTALLERS	$4,000	$3,200	$2,400	$1,600
OWNER'S DRAW	$2,000	$1,600	$1,200	$800
TOTALS	$9,000	$7,700	$6,400	$5,100
CASH AFTER PAYROLL	$11,000	$8,300	$5,600	$2,900

By contrast, the problem becomes more difficult to manage if I'm paying the owner on an as-needed basis. While doing so will help to ensure that I'm only paying out those monies when they're really needed, this can also create wild variations in my outflows:

	WEEK 1	WEEK 2	WEEK 3	WEEK 4
REVENUES	$20,000	$20,000	$20,000	$20,000
MANAGER	$1,000	$1,000	$1,000	$1,000
SUPERVISOR	$1,000	$1,000	$1,000	$1,000
SALES - FIXED	$500	$500	$500	$500
SALES – COMMISSION	$500	$500	$500	$500
INSTALLERS	$4,000	$4,000	$4,000	$4,000
OWNER'S DRAW	$1,000	$5,000	$1,000	$3,000
TOTALS	$8,000	$12,000	$8,000	$10,000
CASH AFTER PAYROLL	$12,000	$8,000	$12,000	$10,000

	WEEK 1	WEEK 2	WEEK 3	WEEK 4
REVENUES	$20,000	$16,000	$12,000	$8,000
MANAGER	$1,000	$1,000	$1,000	$1,000
SUPERVISOR	$1,000	$1,000	$1,000	$1,000
SALES - FIXED	$500	$500	$500	$500
SALES – COMMISSION	$500	$400	$300	$200
INSTALLERS	$4,000	$3,200	$2,400	$1,600
OWNER'S DRAW	$1,000	$5,000	$1,000	$3,000
TOTALS	$8,000	$11,100	$6,200	$7,300
CASH AFTER PAYROLL	$12,000	$4,900	$5,800	$700

Compensating an owner on an as-needed basis. In this scenario you would want to treat the varying amounts of owner's draws like overhead expenses, and schedule them into your plan as far in advance as you could. Although a draw is technically not an expense, for cash flow planning purposes, you will want to pretend that it is.

In practice, if I'm paying the owner "as needed" on a regular basis, I generally wouldn't include her draws in the payroll portion of my cash flow spreadsheet. Rather I would plot out her personal expenses along a timeline in much the same way I would plot the company's – and with the same awareness of what's absolutely critical to pay and what we can let slide if circumstances are dire. The owner may be willing to sacrifice a vacation in order to pay her suppliers, but missing a mortgage payment is not an acceptable option. Having a solid plan in place will also permit the owner to see in advance what might – or might not – be possible in light of both her personal and company finances.

There's no "right way" to compensate a sole proprietor, not even from a cash flow perspective. While it's certainly simplest if you just pay out a fixed amount each week or month – and may be easier to plan for – there is something to be said for adopting an "as-needed" strategy when the cash situation is particularly dire. I've even had success with melding the two alternatives, in which I regularly pay a fixed amount into a secondary account on the owner's behalf, and then use those funds as I need them to cover her personal bills. Since your financial person can't spend your money on clothes or weekends away with his girlfriend, he may be more adept at setting aside funds for those major upcoming expenses than the person to whom the money belongs.

HOW OUTSIDE SERVICES ARE ROBBING YOU OF CONTROL OVER YOUR CASH FLOW, AND WHEN TO TAKE IT BACK

These days there are a plethora of services available to small businesses and entrepreneurs for handling financial matters. Full-service remote payroll and bill payment providers abound, and these can prove a godsend for businesspeople who don't keep a financial person on staff or who don't want to take chances with their payroll tax payments, returns, and so on. However, not only can these services cost a substantial amount of money – they often take a percentage of the total payroll – but in a highly significant fashion, they can rob you of control over your cash.

Here's how. Take a payroll service, for example. If you're using a cheaper option like Quickbooks Basic Payroll, then you're essentially running payroll yourself, printing your own checks, scheduling your own tax payments, etc. – it's very hands on, and the pricing reflects that. However, if you move into one of the fancier services like ADP, then you're basically plugging in the pay rates and hours and they're doing everything else. But what is it really costing you to be taken care of?

From a cash flow perspective, the most horrifying aspect of most of these services is that they pull the money for your payroll – *and* payroll taxes – out of your company's bank account *on payday*. This can be an enormous problem, especially in the beginning of the year when most of your payroll is subject to unemployment taxes, which most of us only need to pay once a quarter. Yes, having that money on deposit with your payroll service provider will certainly ensure that both your payroll and your payroll taxes do get paid, because you can't spend money you haven't got. On the other hand, you can't spend money you haven't got – and having your hard-won cash sitting uselessly in some payroll provider's bank account for days, weeks or even months until they fork over your payroll taxes can prove rather irksome when you can't afford the inventory you need to produce income.

In the DEALING WITH VENDORS volume of this series, I discussed the continuing power of check float, and the principle here is the same. Suppose my payday is on Friday. If I'm what's known as a semi-weekly schedule depositor for payroll taxes, then my tax withholding and FICA need to be paid the following Wednesday. For most small businesses, unemployment taxes – which the Federal and California state governments charge on the first $7,000 of wages per employee – are due once a quarter. If I run payroll myself, then I will issue checks on Friday, most of which won't clear my bank until Tuesday or Wednesday. I'll schedule my payroll tax payments for Wednesday, so that those won't come out of my account until Wednesday or Thursday. And I'll hold off on paying the unemployment until it's actually due at the end of the quarter. In other words, not only did I save a substantial amount of money by not using a service, but I bought myself a fair amount of extra time with my cash on hand as well.

If you really need to use a service, then by all means, use a service. But if you have a competent financial person at your disposal, then seriously consider whether a less expensive option that won't hold your cash hostage might work better for you. Personally, although I haven't used it in a couple of years now and can't speak to its current content, I always highly favored Quickbooks Assisted Payroll, which for less than $400 a year runs all your payroll calculations, automatically figures your payroll taxes, and pre-fills the information on your payroll tax returns. Yes, there is more manual labor, but it's really quite simple once you know what you're doing, and, in my opinion, often less burdensome than doing the data entry, status updates, and journal entries required with some more full-service providers.

Here's a real-world example of the cost savings I've achieved by making this kind of switch. One company I worked for had semi-monthly payroll for twenty-five employees, which was costing them about $400 a month through their payroll provider. Under the Quickbooks system to which I switched us over, we paid $300 a year ($25 a month), plus the cost of checks and check envelopes, plus an additional twenty minutes of my labor for each pay period to pay the payroll taxes and assemble checks manually. In addition, once a quarter I spent half an hour printing and submitting the payroll tax forms, and about an hour once a year printing W-2s – which, incidentally, the employees loved because I would have them done on January 2nd rather than January 31st. In sum, running payroll myself only cost about an hour's additional labor a month, bringing our total payroll cost down from $400 a month to less than $100 and giving us back the control over our cash that we desired.

Now you do need to have someone who's comfortable working with that type of system, and it can be intimidating for a newbie, especially if you're nervous about things like payroll taxes. However, particularly when Quickbooks is involved, it's more intimidating in principle than difficult in practice. I've successfully trained non-financial people who had never touched accounting software to run payroll when I was going to be out of town, and as long as the system is set up properly, it's pretty easy to maintain and to operate. Other inexpensive services undoubtedly work just as well and may be worth looking into if this is an area of concern for you. Before you make a decision, though, be sure to check rates with your local Costco – members get a discount on Quickbooks Payroll and a variety of other merchant services.

Whatever payroll system you're using, I recommend opting out of direct deposit as long as cash flow is an issue. Not only do some payroll providers charge a fee for direct deposit, but opting in means that the money will get pulled out of your account on payday, causing you to lose several potentially precious days of float on your physical paychecks. If employees ask for it, simply tell them that it's not available at this time.

HOW OFTEN SHOULD I RUN PAYROLL?

If you're using a payroll service, its fee structure may determine the answer to this question. If you're charged a base fee per payroll, then having weekly payroll versus biweekly or semi-monthly may prove too expensive for you, whereas if your base fee is monthly, more frequent payrolls may be a feasible option.

If you're running payroll in-house, other considerations come into play, many of which have to do with your cash flow. Generally speaking, the more often you run payroll, the better it will be for your cash flow because not only will you even out your outflows, you'll also consistently have more checks in float. And as I discuss in Volume 1 of this series, DEALING WITH VENDORS, in general it's much easier for a company to cover multiple small expenses than a few large ones, even when the total outlay is the same.

However, this approach can be contraindicated in a wide variety of circumstances that may apply to your company, so it is definitely not a situation in which one size fits all. Suppose, for example, that your A/R schedule is such that most of your money comes in between the 20th and the 30th, and that you're running semi-monthly payroll on the 5th and 20th of the month. This would not be a good payroll schedule, because your payroll is always happening when you're cash-poor – last month's cash has mostly run out by the 5th, and this month's cash has barely begun to trickle in by the 20th. In this case, redistributing those outflows over four weeks – or even just changing the pay dates – would likely prove beneficial. But if instead most of your money comes in between the 1st and the 15th, then making a move to weekly payroll might not be a good option because you'd have one to two payrolls at the end of the month that might be tough to cover. On the other hand, if you're a retail establishment and your biggest bill – your rent! – is due on the 1st, then having a massive semi-monthly payroll due just four days later on the 5th might prove impractical and a smaller weekly payroll option would sound more appealing.

While a major advantage of running more payrolls is that each one is smaller and more manageable from a cash flow perspective, there are a number of practical complications that must be considered. Additional payrolls cost more in checks and envelopes, they require more approvals and signatures, and they may depend upon a single person to process them, which can be an issue if your bookkeeper wants to take a week off and there's no one to cover. But as I will detail in the forthcoming CREATING A CASH PLAN volume of this series, especially for labor-intensive firms with large payrolls, spreading this flow of cash over four weeks instead of two can be a terrific boon for cash flow management. In addition, there may be an added bonus for firms whose billing cycle revolves around payroll completion, as more frequent processing may give you the opportunity to do more frequent billing.

In any case, selecting the payroll schedule that works best for your firm is a highly individualized process that will depend on the particulars of your situation, all of which must be carefully evaluated before any decision is taken.

THE SNEAKIER SIDE OF PAYROLL – PAYROLL TAXES AND WORKER'S COMP

WHAT HAPPENS IF I DON'T PAY MY PAYROLL TAXES?

Of all of the cash flow decisions business owners are required to make, one of the most tempting and potentially also the most damaging is the decision not to remit payroll taxes, otherwise known as "trust fund" taxes. As you probably know, an employer is required to withhold taxes from its employees' paychecks – income taxes in accordance with their Federal Form W-4 and equivalent state form, as well as Social Security, Medicare, and state Disability programs (Federal Unemployment or FUTA is wholly employer-paid). Employers then match their employees' FICA (Social Security and Medicare) contributions and deposit these according to their assigned tax deposit schedule, which for most of you reading this is likely either monthly, meaning your deposit is due by the 15th of the following month, or semi-weekly, meaning that your tax deposit is due within several days of your company payday.

These are called "trust fund" taxes for good cause – because you, as the employer, are taking that money out of your employees' paychecks with the implicit agreement that you will then turn over those funds to the government. In other words, if you fail to remit those taxes as promised, you have effectively stolen money both from the government and from your employees!

As you might imagine, the penalties applicable for such violations can be high – as high as 75% of the unpaid taxes if the failure to remit is deemed to be fraud. Even worse, the liability doesn't end with your company – an officer who is determined to have been responsible for taxes going unpaid can be held *personally liable* for the unremitted taxes,

230

penalties, and interest. In other words, if you signed checks for your suppliers instead of paying your payroll taxes, you willfully refused to pay your trust fund taxes and can be held financially accountable, even if your firm is a corporation. And no, in case you're wondering, unpaid payroll taxes do not go away in bankruptcy. These taxes are simply not optional, and neither you nor your firm can afford to refuse to pay them. When planning your cash flow, therefore, treat them with the seriousness with which you'd treat your payroll, as another expense you can't delay or postpone.

(On a related note, failure to remit your employees' 401(k) contributions can have similar really awful consequences and may even disqualify your retirement plan entirely. All of your employee contributions can be invalidated and thus become taxable, getting you into a world of trouble all over the place. Worse yet, unlike with payroll taxes, where your employees likely won't know that you haven't paid them, employees are sure to notice from their statements that their contributions have not been paid into their accounts, which will make them – understandably – very angry. Trust me, you do not want to go there.)

UH, OH… WHAT IF ALREADY DID?

If you've already missed some tax payments, or even a whole bunch of tax payments, don't panic. As stiff as those penalties can be, you will often find that the IRS will be willing to waive them if it's your first offense and you demonstrate a sincere desire to catch up on your past obligations and keep current with your future ones. In fact, in spite of its rather onerous reputation, in my experience, the IRS can be surprisingly easy to work with – all it takes is respect, professionalism, and a hefty dose of patience for paperwork.

The IRS is the perhaps the most overworked agency in the Federal government, and it may take a while – months, even – before they contact you regarding your unpaid payroll taxes. Once they do, however, be sure to respond to the written notice they send you within the allotted time frame, usually 30 days. Read the notice carefully to examine your options, but don't be surprised if you still don't understand them. If it's your first time dealing with something like this, then quite likely you're going to want to call the IRS anyway, where a real person will be able to answer your questions – once you get one on the phone.

If your debt is comparatively small – as of this writing the cutoff is $25,000 – you will usually qualify for an Online Installment Agreement, where you will fill out some simplified paperwork, tell the IRS how much you can pay towards your back taxes each month, and likely receive automatic approval if your offer is satisfactory. (Although I don't know if this is officially true, an IRS agent once told me that the IRS will generally accept an offer that will get the debt paid off within two to five years, so you might want to consider this when calculating how much you can pay.) If you owe more than $25,000 and you want an Installment Agreement, you'll have to complete and submit many pages of paperwork, including detailed information on all of your debts, assets, income and expenses, and you may even receive a visit from a local IRS agent who will want to ensure your compliance.

You can also make an Offer in Compromise, which is a settlement for a portion of the unpaid balance, which the IRS may accept if it deems it unlikely it will ever be able to collect the entire back balance from you. You may be able to get a better deal on an Offer in Compromise by offering a lump sum payment rather than an installment arrangement. However, for companies without any cash, this is less likely to be a feasible option, and in spite of what those ads on TV might tell you, getting the IRS to waive your tax debt for "pennies on the dollar" is not as simple as it may seem – as you'll see when you go to fill out the many pages of paperwork required to request one.

Incidentally, the same general guidelines apply if you owe income taxes, and similar options may also be available if you owe payroll or other taxes to your state as well. But no matter who you owe money to, or how you feel about the tax system in general, don't fall into this common trap – taking your financial frustrations out on an agent.

NEVER YELL AT AN IRS AGENT

Seriously, I know it's tempting for a lot of people, and I've heard several give in to the temptation, but trust me – don't do it. I don't care how annoyed or frustrated you get, how long you've been on hold on the phone, or how many different representatives you've had to speak to without getting any answers, DO NOT GET UPSET WITH THE AGENT. Your venting accomplishes *nothing* and can only make your situation worse.

It's no fun having a tax problem, but dealing with other people's tax problems all day is no picnic, either. The work of IRS agents and representatives is responsible for the funding of most government programs, yet they are some of the most despised people in the whole country. They spend their days dealing with angry citizens who have gotten bills and notices they don't understand, trying to distill thousands of pages of tax law into a few sentences that might possibly be comprehensible to the average taxpayer even though most of it isn't even comprehensible to Congress, which wrote the laws in the first place. Although the IRS' job is to generate revenue, its budget has been repeatedly slashed over the past decade, leaving its staff with workloads they will likely never escape from underneath. They can't even come close to answering all of the phone calls that they receive, and then they have taxpayers blaming staffers because they were placed on a lengthy hold in the middle of tax season. But it isn't staffers' fault that the IRS doesn't have enough money to support its operations. They're the victims, not the perpetrators.

So when you speak to someone at the IRS, either by phone or in person, try to remember that they're not the enemy. They sincerely want to help you resolve your tax problems, even if they have limited resources with which to do it. So don't be ticked off that you were on hold for an hour – be glad that you got through at all.

If you find yourself simply unable to control your temper when speaking to the IRS or other government agency – or if what they tell you all sounds like gobbledy-gook – consider appointing a representative. You can file a limited-purpose Power of Attorney form (Form 2848, available on IRS.gov) that will allow another party to talk with IRS on your behalf about your tax issues without granting any other powers (i.e., they can't touch your money), and it doesn't have to be your $200 an hour CPA. If you have an employee who is more financially or paperwork-savvy than you are, or if you're trying to arrange an Installment Agreement and need to make repeated contacts with IRS without breaking the bank, it may behoove you to allow that person to handle IRS conversations while you listen in. Give that job to someone for whom it's a job and not a personal problem, and you may find that they're able to handle it more calmly and successfully than you can.

WORKER'S COMPENSATION – TRICKS SOMEONE SHOULD HAVE TAUGHT YOU BUT DIDN'T

My knowledge of how worker's compensation insurance works is based almost entirely on California state rules and regulations – which are subject to change – and may also differ from policies and procedures in other states. Therefore you should be careful to do your research before relying on any of the following advice, as some of these items may not apply to you.

That being said, over the years I have learned a number of tips and tricks that can be very helpful in managing both worker's compensation expense and the vagaries in cash flow associated with paying the wrong estimates or being substantially "over" on audit.

MINIMIZING YOUR RATES

We've probably all sought ways in which to get our employees covered under Worker's Compensation laws for the least amount of money, and insurers themselves are often happy to provide you with information on how to keep your rate down, such as by offering "light duty" as part of a return-to-work program for injured employees. Here, however, are a few tricks I've learned over the years that aren't so apparent in the language of those many-pages-long policies.

1) Clerical employees must only do clerical work. While I won't try to attach numbers to it, because these are always in flux, this can be a very big deal – for example, I once worked for a company whose "Clerical" rate was literally an eighth of their "Retail Store" rate. However, although the retail employees spent nearly as much time on their computers as the clerical employees, in most situations, an employee performing both functions will be billed out at the higher rate, even if the majority of their work is clerical. If you have the ability to segregate the work functions of such employees – say, by

giving your dual-function employee's "store" duties to someone else, and thus removing one employee from the retail function all together – consider doing so, as it may save you substantial sums of money. One exception to this are "Outside Sales" people. Their WC rate is generally almost as low as the clerical rate, and they are permitted to perform clerical functions as part of their duties.

2) Take the bags off your Project Managers. If you're in construction and your Project Managers do mostly administrative work – sales, estimating, planning, and supervision – and then occasionally help out in the field, you may be losing an opportunity to save bundles of money. A worker who performs *any* field duties will have *all* of his or her wages billed as carpentry or concrete or whatever, even if he or she spends 90% of his or her time doing clerical work in the office. If this is the case and your personnel situation permits it, consider prohibiting those people from performing field work. I was once able to reclassify such an employee from Carpentry to Outside Sales and literally saved my company $10,000 a year.

3) Be aware of upticks in rates. Construction and other jobs that have different levels of employees – apprentices versus journeymen, for example – often have different worker's comp rates as well. These are based not on education or actual skill level, but on how much you pay your employees, as it's presumed that more qualified and experienced people will earn more money. Since higher-level folks are presumed to be less likely to be injured, their insurance rates can be substantially lower, with sometimes unexpected effects. I once saw a situation in which the WC rate for an apprentice carpenter making less than $26 an hour was literally three times the rate for a journeyman carpenter making $26 or more. In fact, in this circumstance there was no point in *ever* paying a guy between $21 and $26 an hour because the additional worker's compensation expense made the apprentice's total cost per hour more than a journeyman's! So be aware of any cutoffs like these that may apply in your

industry. It may seem counterintuitive to pay a less qualified person more money than you think they deserve, but I guarantee you'll feel much better about giving the money to your employee than to your worker's comp carrier.

MANAGING THE AUDIT

Worker's compensation audits happen every year, and whether yours is via correspondence or in person, there are certain steps you can take to make it go more smoothly.

1) Have a space set up in which the auditor can work. An open desk or a table and comfortable chair is fine. If your office has severe space limitations, ask someone to clear out for the duration, which can be several hours. The auditor will generally need room for a laptop and your pile of paperwork, and if you can provide them with a certain amount of peace and quiet, so much the better. Easy access to an electrical outlet is also helpful, as they are frequently on the road all day and won't necessarily have a fresh computer battery, and it's polite to offer them water or coffee if it's available. You may wish to position them close to your payroll or other financial person – whoever is going to be in charge of answering questions if they come up – although if you're really confident that your paperwork is in order, you can even give them their own private space and then simply check in after an hour or so to see if they have any questions.

2) Have your paperwork in order. Make sure, before your policy even begins, that you will have available the information that your auditor will want to see. If your time cards are not designed the way your worker's comp carrier wants them, change your time cards so that they're in compliance. Make sure your accounting software is set up to break out the overtime, on which you only pay insurance at the straight time rate. Auditors will generally be checking the payroll amounts reported on your policy against the amount reported on your

payroll tax returns (here in California, they generally use the state returns, but often ask for the federal as well). Make sure you have those returns available so that they can easily match them to your workers comp reports. Also, prepare a list of all the employees who worked for you during the previous year with their pay rate, their worker's comp classification, how much money they earned during the period in question, and a short description of their job duties. In my experience, you'll want to list several tasks in the job description for your clerical employees – since the rate is so low, they're unlikely to accept "Clerical" alone as a duty. Instead you can put in items like data entry, bookkeeping, answering phones, filing, etc. – whatever your person actually does.

The auditor will generally send you a list of records they want to see when they call to schedule your audit. You won't necessarily need to present everything on the list – for example, I have never once been asked for Daily Sales Journals, although these are always on the list, and a good thing, too, because those would be a pain to provide – but you should be prepared to generate additional reports on the fly if needed. You should therefore make sure that your financial or administrative person is going to be available for the duration of the audit, as the auditor may be annoyed if she has to wait for your employee to return from an errand before she can ask a pertinent question and move on to her next job.

3) Pre-audit your paperwork. Nothing – and I mean, nothing – will make your worker's comp audit go more smoothly than if you've already checked your numbers, and it's pretty easy to do when you understand what your auditor is doing. The main thrust of the audit is going to be verifying the payroll of each individual employee on either a month-by-month or quarterly basis against your internal payroll records and against your payroll tax returns. In other words, if your payroll records show that you paid an employee $10,000 in a particular quarter, then your quarterly payroll tax returns should show the same figure, as should any mid-term reports you submitted to your worker's comp carrier. If your figures don't match, figure out why ahead of time and be prepared to explain that

to the auditor as soon as he or she gets settled. Not only will the auditor be thrilled that you're so well-prepared, he or she will be less likely to have to request additional documentation or go poking around looking for further errors.

CHOOSING A PAYMENT PLAN

Since worker's compensation was deregulated some years ago, there has been a virtual explosion in the number of companies offering WC insurance. Gone are the days when we had to report our payroll monthly to State Fund and pay the applicable premium or lose our coverage – nowadays many carriers offer cash-friendlier alternatives, including monthly payment plans of equal amounts based on your estimates of your upcoming annual payroll, and no mid-term reporting even if those numbers change. But while these improvements may protect us from the big outflows required in those off-months when payroll was high because of the third biweekly or fifth weekly payroll, they have presented us with other problems, because when it comes to our cash, we're doing a great deal more guesswork.

The main advantage of submitting your paperwork and paying your premium monthly is that you're never running behind – unless you've made an error, you're going to pay what you owe for a given month soon after month-end, and not accumulate a large balance that you will have to remit upon audit. Since the more recent installment-type plans rely on estimates, however, there's a far greater risk that we will either 1) Overestimate our coming year's payroll and fork over more cash in advance than we need to, or 2) Underestimate our payroll and owe thousands of dollars at our policy's end.

Now if your worker's comp carrier operates on an installment basis and you're short on cash, it can be very tempting to fudge your estimate of your next annual payroll in order to lower your current deposit and monthly installments. Try very hard to resist this temptation, because as we very well know, it's a lot easier to come up with $500 a month than with $6,000 all at once, and losing your worker's compensation insurance is the kind of event that can kill your business permanently.

I strongly suggest being conservative, however. Don't automatically assume that your payroll next year is going to be the same as it was this year, or that it will increase by 10% because this was your pattern in the previous year. Take the list you prepared under MANAGING THE AUDIT, above, with all of your employees for the past year and how much they were paid, and go through it, line by line. If someone received a pay raise, you'll want to up your estimate of their pay for the coming year; if another employee has cut their hours, you may want to reduce it. If you've eliminated employees and/or their positions, take them off the list; if you've added some, don't forget to include them. When you've finished, you'll have a very solid estimate of what you reasonably expect your payroll by classification to be, which you can then submit to your carrier for the upcoming policy year.

Be mindful, too, of different carriers and their deposit and/or installment requirements. If the rate and terms of coverage are the same, you might prefer a company with a smaller upfront deposit and ten installments to one with a larger deposit or nine bigger installments.

If your carrier or agent does not do this for you, you may also want to check your progress mid-year. Look at your payroll by employee thus far for the current policy period and compare it to your projections. If the prorated amounts are more than you expected, you may end up owing money on audit; if less, you may get a refund. If the numbers are significant, you'll want to be forewarned when planning your cash flow.

MEET LORI SCHAFER

Are you a small business owner? Do you wonder why you aren't making more money – or if you're making money at all? Are your financial statements incomprehensible to you, or do you question their accuracy? How do you know if you're charging the right amount for your product or service? Do you know how much selling and producing your product really costs you?

Do you feel as if your business is succeeding, **yet you never seem to have enough cash?** Does your Income Statement show a profit, but your debts keep increasing? **Are you racking up late fees and being overwhelmed by calls from suppliers who haven't been paid?** Are you wondering where your cash is going?

You're not alone. Many American small business owners are asking themselves these very questions, and they don't know who to turn to for answers. Their CPAs don't know very much about the day-to-day operations of their businesses because they only handle their tax returns. Their bookkeepers may be able to prepare their financial statements, but they can't explain what they mean. And in a time when many businesses are short on cash, **no one in your company seems to be able to figure out how to allocate the funds that are available where they're needed most.**

Not all businesses will succeed. Some are built on models that are simply not sustainable, or on models that, in today's economy, are no longer sustainable. **But for others, the problem is not a bad business, but bad financial management.**

This is where I come in. **I'm an Enrolled Agent with a Masters in Taxation** and more than thirty units of formal coursework in accounting. I have the education to become a CPA if I had any interest in that. But I don't want to be that person that you see once a year when you do your taxes and it's already too late to do any planning. I don't want to be involved with accounting for large corporations with full accounting staffs at their disposal. I like working with small businesses, where my skills can really make a difference to the owners and the individuals who work there, where I can fill the gap between a standard bookkeeper and a certified accountant. And as a Full Charge Bookkeeper with more than ten years' experience, **I have the practical, hands-on experience with running the financial operations of a small business that most CPAs lack**.

I'm no longer a full-time bookkeeper, and my tax work isn't year-round. **The rest of the time I'm an author of fiction and non-fiction memoir**. But I do still occasionally offer consulting services to selected clients in need of my particular skills.

The first of my specialties is financial statement analysis, with an eye to the needs of small business. I will examine your financials and determine what they indicate about the health of your company and its recent financial trends. I can tell you whether you're correctly pricing or costing your jobs, whether your gross margin and overhead are sufficient and stable, and **what you need to take in to cover not just your expenses, but also your payments on any debts.** I can even tell you if your accounting methods and procedures are sufficient to supply the information you need to even make such an analysis, which I've found is a frequent source of difficulty for a small business.

But perhaps my most unique – and certainly most appreciated – skill is **my ability to manage cash flow for companies without enough cash.** I'm not the person you consult about where to invest your excess funds – I'm the person you consult when your credit card payments are late and your hundred-dollar phone bill hasn't been paid. **Managing cash isn't easy, and it isn't something they teach you in school.** Often in small businesses, the owner or the bookkeeper is put in charge of who to pay when – but neither one of them may be very good at making decisions like these. I can't promise that my methods will save your business if you're seriously in trouble, and in the interest of privacy, I won't offer specific examples here of companies I've assisted or how exactly I helped them. But I have succeeded in keeping companies alive that were in dire danger of failing, and I have succeeded in transforming companies that were desperately cash-poor into companies that pay virtually all of their bills on time. **It's the same amount of cash, only managed much better.**

If these are the issues with which your company is struggling, **send me an email at lorischafer(at)outlook(dot)com** briefly explaining your situation. I reside in the San Francisco Bay Area (East Bay), and although I generally work from home, anyway, I prefer local clients so that I can make recommendations in person and consult physical records if needed. However, I will also work remotely with out-of-town clients if the nature of your business permits adequate access to the required information.

In the meantime, feel free to **visit my author website at lorilschafer.com**. My award-winning memoir, *On Hearing of My Mother's Death Six Years After It Happened: A Daughter's Memoir of Mental Illness*, was released in November 2014, and my forthcoming book *It's the Iron: How My Iron Deficiency Anemia was Misdiagnosed as Arthritis, and Why Your Depression, Fibromyalgia, and Chronic Pain and Fatigue Might Be Low Iron, Too* will be the first book to uncover a major public health issue that affects many millions.

And be sure to subscribe to my newsletter at **http://eepurl.com/bDHufD**, because I am in the process of making a product available that will make managing your cash much easier – a series of books entitled *Managing Cash When You Haven't Got Any: Practical Cash Flow Strategies for Small Business*. These books detail exactly how I've become successful at managing cash, and how you can do it successfully, too.

www.ingramcontent.com/pod-product-compliance
Lightning Source LLC
Chambersburg PA
CBHW071641200326
41519CB00012BA/2357